IDAHO

The Heroic Journey

Cityscape, Boise

IDAHO

The Heroic Journey

KATHERINE AIKEN

KEVIN R. MARSH

LAURA WOODWORTH-NEY

This book is the official centennial publication of the Idaho State Historical Society. Cherbo Publishing Group gratefully acknowledges the society's important contribution to *Idaho: The Heroic Journey.*

 cherbo publishing group, inc.

president	JACK C. CHERBO
executive vice president	ELAINE HOFFMAN
editorial director	CHRISTINA M. BEAUSANG
managing feature editor	MARGARET L. MARTIN
senior feature editor	TINA RUBIN
contributing editor	ERICA RHEINSCHILD
senior profiles editor	J. KELLEY YOUNGER
profiles editors	BENJAMIN PROST
	LIZA YETENEKIAN SMITH
associate editor	SYLVIA EMRICH-TOMA
proofreaders	ELIZABETH FENNER
	REBECCA SAUER
profiles writers	LINDA CHASE
	SYLVIA EMRICH-TOMA
	KATHLEEN GILBERT
	TERRI E. JONISCH
	BETH MATTSON-TEIG
	RODD MONTS
	LIZA YETENEKIAN SMITH
	STAN ZIEMBA
creative director	PERI A. HOLGUIN
senior designer	THEODORE E. YEAGER
profiles designer	NELSON CAMPOS
photo editor	WALTER MLADINA
contributing photo editor	DAVID ZANZINGER
digital color specialist	ART VASQUEZ
sales administrator	JOAN K. BAKER
client services supervisor	PATRICIA DE LEONARD
senior client services coordinator	LESLIE E. SHAW
client services coordinator	KENYA HICKS
administrative assistants	JUDY ROBITSCHEK
	BILL WAY
publication director	BART B. BARICA

Cherbo Publishing Group, Inc.
Encino, California 91316
© 2006 by Cherbo Publishing Group, Inc.
All rights reserved. Published 2006

Printed in Canada
By Friesens

Subsidiary Production Office
Santa Rosa, CA, USA
888.340.6049

Library of Congress Cataloging-in-Publication data
Aiken, Katherine, and Kevin R. Marsh and Laura Woodworth-Ney.
A pictorial guide highlighting 19th-through-21st-century Idaho.
Library of Congress Control Number: 2006929716
ISBN 978-1-882933-73-0

Visit the CPG Web site at www.cherbopub.com.

The information in this publication is the most recent available, has been carefully researched to ensure accuracy, and has been reviewed by the sponsor. Cherbo Publishing Group, Inc. cannot and does not guarantee either the correctness of all information furnished it or the complete absence of errors, including omissions.

Dedication

This book is for our children, grown in Idaho.

Acknowledgments

This work affectionately rests on the shoulders of countless men and women who have recorded, taught, and interpreted the history of Idaho. They have left a rich legacy in which to pursue our studies. We also want to recognize those mentors from whom we have learned so much: LeRoy Ashby, Judy Austin, Peter Boag, Ron Hatzenbuehler, Paul Hirt, Carlos Schwantes, Todd Shallat, David Stratton, and Orlan Svingen. And to our spouses and families, thank you for your support.

—Katherine Aiken, Kevin R. Marsh, and Laura Woodworth-Ney

Stanley Lake, Sawtooth National Recreation Area

TABLE OF CONTENTS

Shoshone-Bannock men in traditional regalia

Nez Perce boy

Skiers, Sun Valley

COMPANIES & ORGANIZATIONS PROFILED

The following organizations have made a valuable commitment to the quality of this publication. The Idaho State Historical Society gratefully acknowledges their participation in *Idaho: The Heroic Journey.*

Governor Frank Steunenberg statue, Idaho Capitol building, Boise

Fourth of July parade, Sandpoint

BUSINESS VISIONARIES

The following companies and organizations are recognized as innovators in their fields and have played a prominent role in this publication, as they have in communities throughout Idaho.

Albertson College of Idaho
2112 Cleveland Boulevard, Caldwell, ID 83605
Contact: Bob Hoover, Ph.D., President
Phone: 208-459-5011 / Fax: 208-459-5175
E-mail: admissions@albertson.edu
Web site: www.albertson.edu
"Idaho's Liberal Arts College"

Albertsons
250 East Parkcenter Boulevard, Boise, ID 83706
Contact: Teresa Alexander, Manager, Community Affairs
Phone: 208-395-6200
Web site: www.albertsons.com

AMI Semiconductor, Inc.
2300 Buckskin Road, Pocatello, ID 83201
Contact: Christine King, President and CEO
Phone: 208-233-4690 / Fax: 208-239-7012
E-mail: kelli_schwab@amis.com
Web site: www.amis.com
"Silicon Solutions for the Real World"

Boise State University
1910 University Drive, Boise, ID 83725
Contact: Dr. Robert W. Kustra, President
Phone: 208-426-1000 / Fax: 208-426-3779
E-mail: bsuinfo@boisestate.edu
Web site: www.boisestate.edu
"Beyond the Blue"

D. L. Evans Bank
397 North Overland Avenue, Burley, ID 83318
John V. Evans Sr., President
Phone: 208-678-9186 / Fax: 208-678-9093
E-mail: jevanssr@dlevans.com
Web site: www.dlevans.com
"Idaho's Hometown Community Bank for 100 Years"

Franklin Building Supply
11700 Franklin Road, Boise, ID 83709
Contact: Dick Lierz, CEO and President
Phone: 208-322-4567 / Fax: 208-322-4476
Web site: www.franklinbuildingsupply.com
"Service Is Our Specialty"

Group One
913 West River Street, Suite 300, Boise, ID 83702
Contact: Sally Howard, Broker
Phone: 208-287-5000 / Fax: 208-338-9215
E-mail: showard@group-one.com
Web site: www.group-one.com
"A Sign of Excellence"

Home Federal Bank
500 12th Avenue South, Nampa, ID 83651
Daniel L. Stevens, Chairman, CEO
Phone: 208-468-5189 / Fax: 208-468-5001
E-mail: invest@myhomefed.com
Web site: www.myhomefed.com
"Home Federal Bank. With Us, It's Personal.SM"

Idaho State University
921 South 8th Avenue, Pocatello, ID 83209
Contact: Libby Howe, Director of University Relations
Phone: 208-282-3620 / Fax: 208-282-4982
E-mail: howelibb@isu.edu
Web site: www.isu.edu

Mercy Medical Center
1512 12th Avenue Road, Nampa, ID 83686
Contact: Marketing and Public Relations
Phone: 208-463-5000 / Fax: 208-463-5876
Web site: www.mercynampa.org
"Spirit of Innovation . . . a Legacy of Care"

Micron Technology, Inc.
8000 South Federal Way, Boise, ID 83706
Phone: 208-368-4000
Web site: www.micron.com

Northwest Nazarene University
623 Holly Street, Nampa, ID 83686
Phone: 208-467-8531; (toll-free) 877-NNU-4-YOU
(877-668-4968) / Fax: 208-467-8775
E-mail: info@nnu.edu
Web site: www.nnu.edu
"Great Minds. Great Hearts. Great Futures."

Regence BlueShield of Idaho
1211 West Myrtle Street, Suite 110, Boise, ID 83702
Contact: Georganne Benjamin, Assistant Director,
Strategic Communications
Phone: 208-395-7723 / Fax: 208-395-7709
E-mail: georganne.benjamin@regence.com
Web site: www.id.regence.com
"Take Charge"

Saint Alphonsus
ADVANCED HEALING BEGINS HERE

Saint Alphonsus Regional Medical Center
1055 North Curtis Road, Boise, ID 83706
Phone: 208-367-2121
E-mail: inquiries@sarmc.org
Web site: www.saintalphonsus.org
"Healing Body, Mind, & Spirit"

St. Luke's Health System
420 West Idaho, Boise, ID 83702
Phone: 208-381-1200
Web site: www.stlukesonline.org
"Improving the Health of People in Our Region"

Continued on next page

Continued from page xv

United Heritage

707 East United Heritage Court, Meridian, ID 83642
Contact: Rob McCarvel, Senior Vice President, Marketing
Phone: 208-493-6100 / Fax: 800-240-9734
E-mail: heritage@unitedheritage.com
Web site: www.unitedheritage.com
"For the Life You Deserve.®"

Varsity Contractors, Inc.

315 South Fifth Avenue, Pocatello, ID 83201
Contact: Don Aslett, Chairman of the Board
Phone: 208-232-8598 / Fax: 208-232-6068
E-mail: daslett@varsitycontractors.com
Web site: www.varsitycontractors.com
"Peace of Mind and Repeatable Success!"

University of Idaho

University of Idaho
P.O. Box 44264, Moscow, ID 83844-4264
Phone: 1-888-884-3246
E-mail: askjoe@uidaho.edu
Web site: www.uidaho.edu
"Top Quality. Top Students. The Top Choice."

Washington Group International

Washington Group International, Inc.
720 Park Boulevard, Boise, ID 83712
Contact: Laurie Spiegelberg, Vice President–Communications
Phone: 208-386-5000 / Fax: 208-386-5668
E-mail: laurie.spiegelberg@wgint.com
Web site: www.wgint.com
"Integrated Engineering, Construction, and Management Solutions"

Bruneau Dunes State Park

Bike trail, Pocatello

Lolo Pass, U.S. Highway 12

FOREWORD

The production of this book has occurred in conjunction with the centennial commemoration of the 1907 creation of the Idaho State Historical Society as an agency of state government. Just as this publication acknowledges the importance of our heritage in the context of the state's culture today, Idaho's elected officials acknowledged the importance of preserving our state's history a century ago with the transformation of the Historical Society of Idaho Pioneers (established in 1881) into a state agency with the express intent of ensuring the heritage of Idaho would be documented.

In its look at our past, this book reveals how Idaho became a western crossroads, both geographically and historically. It shows that our state is part of at least three distinct geographic regions—the Plateau, Great Basin, and Rocky Mountain West—and notes that, at one time, the Idaho territory sat between and was influenced by two international boundaries—British Canada and Northern Mexico.

The region has long been a crossroads for diverse peoples, from native groups to Oregon Trail travelers, from explorers to present-day tourists. Using the concept of Idaho as a crossroads, the authors of this book have been able to present the impact and experiences of many different individuals and diverse groups who lived in the region, passed through it, immigrated to it, or migrated to it. The crossroads theme explores the interaction of people with the landscape and highlights the environment as a factor in our state's history.

Appropriately, the publication also acknowledges business, industry, and education as important contributors to the heritage of our state. As the reader will discover, many of the elements that make Idaho unique have been influenced by a variety of factors, all combining, over more than a century, to create a special place well worth preserving.

Tony Edmondson
Chairman of the Board of Trustees
Idaho State Historical Society

Steve Guerber
Executive Director
Idaho State Historical Society

IDAHO TIMELINE

Selected Highlights from More than Two Centuries of Social, Cultural, and Historic Events

Lewis and Clark fending off bears, painted by Alfred Russell, circa 1904

1790 Sacajawea is born in present-day Idaho. She will become a legend for her inestimable value as an interpreter and trader during the Lewis and Clark expedition.

1805 On their way to the Pacific Northwest, Captains Meriwether Lewis and William Clark descend Lemhi Pass into what will become present-day Idaho and then spend six weeks with the region's friendly Nez Perce Indians.

1863 Congress creates Idaho Territory, with Lewiston as the capital. The U.S. government begins forcing Indians onto reservations.

1864 Idaho Territory is reorganized with Boise as its capital. A public school system is established.

1867 Gutzon Borglum is born in Bear Lake County. He will become a sculptor, best known for carving the faces of four U.S. presidents on Mount Rushmore in South Dakota.

Poster advertising steamboats to Idaho's gold mines, 1863

1874 Silver City achieves communications milestones for the state when the first daily newspaper, the *Owyhee Daily Avalanche*, is printed and the first telegraphed message is received.

1874 The first railroad service reaches Idaho when the Utah Northern comes to Franklin.

1877 Chief Joseph and the Nez Perce Indians surrender to the U.S. Army after battling over lands that are then opened to white settlement.

1882 Idaho's first telephone service begins in Hailey; its first electric light goes on at the Philadelphia smelter in Ketchum.

1884 Prospectors stampede when one of the world's richest deposits of silver and lead is discovered in the Coeur d'Alenes. The next year, Noah Kellogg unearths America's largest underground mine, the Bunker Hill and Sullivan.

1810 Fort Henry, the first American fur-trading post west of the Rockies, is built by Andrew Henry of the Missouri Fur Company; it is abandoned the next year after an extremely harsh winter.

1818 Donald Mackenzie is the first to lead an expedition of trappers up the Snake River. A year later he coordinates a trappers' rendezvous that becomes an annual event.

1824 The Salmon River and its rugged backcountry are explored in separate expeditions led by Alexander Ross and Jedediah Smith.

1836 Presbyterian missionary Henry Harmon Spalding establishes a mission near Lapwai, bringing Christianity to the Nez Perce Indians. He will be credited with Idaho's first potato crop, school, and printed book.

Henry Harmon Spalding

1843 Hundreds of wagons follow the Oregon Trail across the southern part of Idaho in the first great wave of westward migration. This portion of the trail takes pioneers across deserts, mountains, and treacherous river crossings.

1846 Along with Coeur d'Alene Indians, Jesuits build the Mission of the Sacred Heart in Cataldo.

1855 Fort Lemhi is established by Mormon missionaries.

1860 Franklin, named after Mormon apostle Franklin Richards, becomes Idaho's first town when 13 families settle there.

1860–63 Mining discoveries at Pierce, Florence, the Boise Basin, and Silver City turn these areas into boomtowns as thousands of fortune seekers flock to the Gem State for silver and gold.

1862 The state's first newspaper, the *Golden Age*, begins weekly publication in Lewiston to serve miners in the region.

University of Idaho students, 1899

1885 Ezra Pound, who will become a poet and major force in 20th-century literature, is born in Hailey.

1889 The Territorial Legislature establishes the University of Idaho in Moscow.

1890 Idaho is admitted to the Union as the 43rd state, with a population of 88,548.

1890 The Great Northern Railway line is completed through northern Idaho.

1894 Under the federal Carey Act, more than two million acres of land in Idaho qualify for reclamation and irrigation.

1899 Members of the Western Federation of Miners in the Coeur d'Alene district blow up the office and concentrating mill of the Bunker Hill and Sullivan mine; martial law is declared.

Aftermath of the explosion at the Bunker Hill and Sullivan mine, 1899

1901

1901 The Academy of Idaho opens in Pocatello; it will become Idaho State University.

1906 The Potlatch Lumber Company opens the largest white-pine sawmill in the United States and builds a town to house its workers and their families.

1908 President Theodore Roosevelt's forest conservation policy leads to the formation of Idaho's national forests, which comprise half the state.

1910 Devastating forest fires destroy one-sixth of the state's forests. The fires claim a total of three million acres and 86 lives in Idaho and Montana.

1920 Fourteen-year-old Rigby resident Philo T. Farnsworth conceives of a vacuum-tube television. Five years later he fully develops the idea, and electronic television becomes a reality.

Philo T. Farnsworth holding television components, 1935

1975

1939 Joe Albertson opens a small grocery store in Boise. He will develop a supermarket chain that for a time is the second-largest in the United States, with 2,500 stores in 37 states.

1939 Outdoorsman and author Ernest Hemingway comes to Sun Valley to work on his novel *For Whom the Bell Tolls*. After living in Europe, in 1960 he will move to Ketchum, where he dies the next year and is buried.

J. R. Simplot

1941 Idaho is known nationwide for its excellent baking potatoes and high grading standards. J. R. Simplot becomes the largest single shipper of the state's potatoes, operating 33 packing warehouses.

1949 The National Reactor Testing Station opens near Idaho Falls. In two years, its scientific research will enable the generation of electricity from nuclear energy for the first time in history.

1952 Gracie Pfost, of Nampa, becomes the first Idaho woman elected to Congress; she also will be the longest tenured, serving until 1962.

1953 KIDO-TV signs on in Boise on July 6, becoming Idaho's first television station. TV inventor and former Idaho resident Philo Farnsworth is on hand for the occasion.

1921 Lana Turner, whose films and television roles will earn her a star on the Hollywood Walk of Fame, is born in Wallace as Julia Jean Turner.

1922 KFAU Radio, "the voice of Idaho," begins broadcasting from Boise High School under the direction of Harry E. Redeker.

1924 Craters of the Moon, a volcanic formation that includes a 62-mile crack in the earth's crust, becomes a national monument.

Lana Turner

1926 The first airmail service in the Columbia Basin stops in Boise after taking off from Pasco, Washington, on its way to Elko, Nevada.

1932 Boise Junior College is founded in the capital; it will grow to become Boise State University, the largest institution of higher education in the state.

1934 Large-scale gold and silver mining developments take place in central and northern Idaho; the state leads the nation in silver production.

1936 Union Pacific Railroad chairman W. Averell Harriman establishes Sun Valley as a ski resort and orchestrates the invention of the world's first chairlift.

Ernest Hemingway at Sun Valley, 1939

Materials Testing Reactor, National Reactor Testing Station near Idaho Falls, 1954

1955 When 12 nuclear-powered light bulbs burn for two hours, Arco becomes the first city in the world to be lighted by atomic energy.

1962 The Lewis and Clark Highway (U.S. 12) is completed, following the wild and scenic Lochsa River from Lolo, Montana, to Lewiston.

1965 Nez Perce National Historical Park, headquartered in Spalding, is established to preserve and document the Nez Perce (Nimíipuu) culture through 38 sites in four states.

1975 The Port of Lewiston opens as the final stop on the Columbia/ Snake River transportation highway leading to the Pacific.

IDAHO TIMELINE

1977 Governor Cecil D. Andrus leaves his post to become Secretary of the Interior under president Jimmy Carter.

1980 Congress passes the Central Idaho Wilderness Act creating the 2.3 million-acre River of No Return Wilderness, the largest such area in the lower 48 states. Senator Frank Church will have his name added in 1983.

1984 Payette native and power hitter Harmon Killebrew, who played for the Washington Senators, Minnesota Twins, and Kansas City Royals, is inducted into the National Baseball Hall of Fame.

1984 The Boise Division of the Hewlett Packard Company revolutionizes the printer industry with the LaserJet, a low-priced entry that dominates the market.

Harmon Killebrew playing for the Minnesota Twins, 1964

Robot that can detect radioactive material in pipes, Idaho National Laboratory, 2001

2000 According to the U.S. Census, Meridian has the state's highest home ownership rate, at 84.3 percent.

2002 Idaho ranks third among all states in its percent of exports coming from high-tech firms.

2005 The U.S. Patent & Trademark Office ranks Idaho first in the number of patents per capita, many of which come from Hewlett-Packard, Micron Technology, and the Idaho National Laboratory.

Linda Copple Trout

1992 Linda Copple Trout is the first woman to serve on the Idaho Supreme Court when she is appointed by Governor Cecil Andrus.

1995 Picabo Street, a Triumph native, is the first American skier to win the World Cup downhill series. She will win it again in 1996, capture an Olympic gold medal in 1998, and be inducted into the National Ski Hall of Fame in 2005.

Gold medal winner Picabo Street at the 1998 Winter Olympics in Nagano, Japan

1997 Treetop Technologies is founded in Boise. Seven years later, *Inc.* magazine will rank it as the fastest-growing private company in Idaho and the 18th-fastest-growing private IT services firm in the nation.

1999 Ninety-seven percent of Idaho schools have access to the Internet.

2000 Science and technology account for 30 percent of the state's economy ($11 billion).

2005 The Milken Institute ranks Idaho as having the nation's fifth-lowest cost of doing business (16 percent below the national average), based on tax structure and costs of wages, electricity, and industrial and office space.

HazMat Cam

2005 The HazMat Cam, a wireless video camera developed by the Idaho National Laboratory (INL) for use by first responders, is named to *R&D* magazine's annual list of top 100 technologies globally. An INL technology has made the list 10 years in a row.

2005 Boise ranks first on *Forbes* magazine's list of best metros for business and careers and second on *Inc.*'s list of the top U.S. cities for doing business. The rankings factor in job growth, costs of doing business, quality of life, and more.

2006 Idaho governor Dirk Kempthorne becomes Secretary of the Interior in place of Gale Norton, who resigns.

2006 Idaho passes a two-year moratorium on coal-fired power plants to study their impact after a California company proposes to build one—the state's first—near the Snake River in Jerome County.

FAVORITE MOMENTS
IN IDAHO HISTORY

JIM RISCH
Governor of Idaho, 2006–

Over the last 30 years, Idaho has changed dramatically. When I entered the state senate in 1974, money from taxes came primarily from three industries: agriculture, timber, and mining. Today, although agriculture is very important, it is very small compared to other industries. Mining and timber are also very small today.

Our state has gone from an economy based primarily on natural resources to one that is cosmopolitan, diversified, and modern. Population and businesses have gravitated to the metro areas (Ada, Canyon, Kootenai, Bonneville, and Twin Falls counties), a breathtaking change that has resulted in prosperity becoming more centralized. This explosive shift began in the mid to late 1980s and has increased rapidly—and starkly—from the 1990s to today.

The change is directly due to private enterprise expanding in and to Idaho, and indirectly to the state government's highly business-friendly policies.

Although Idahoans are experiencing "in-migration"—they are becoming geographically centralized—and their occupations have changed, they themselves have retained their traditional values. Idaho's people make the state as vital today as it was 30, 50, or 100 years ago.

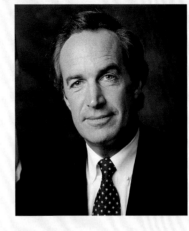

DIRK KEMPTHORNE
Governor of Idaho, 1999–2006
U.S. Secretary of the Interior, 2006–

One of the most significant moments in Idaho's history was a relatively recent one. I have never been prouder to be an Idahoan than when our state underwent the single largest mobilization of National Guard troops in its history.

In November 2004, the 116th Brigade Combat Team was deployed to Kirkuk, Iraq. With unsurpassed valor, these men, women, sons, daughters, mothers, fathers, husbands, and wives gave the gift of self-determination and democracy to an ancient land—the Cradle of Civilization and the birthplace of law—which had been riddled by generations of lawless tyranny and oppression.

As these marvelous citizen-soldiers oversaw two historic elections and opened the way for freedom in the Middle East, they redefined the image of the American soldier in the eyes of the people of Iraq and they set a new standard of excellence for those Americans who came after them. Upon the completion of their tour of duty the Iraqi leadership of Kirkuk literally shed tears as they bid goodbye to these noble ambassadors of liberty.

While the flames of terrorism and insurgency blazed, these soldiers endured as the crucible of our nation's values. Our American ideals, which shine like a beacon for the entire world, were held high in the grasp of the Idaho National Guard.

They, along with all of our soldiers, airmen, sailors, and marines—both active and reserve—are heroes, and history will honor them as such.

PHILIP E. BATT
Governor of Idaho, 1995–99

My chosen item may not be the most glamorous occurrence in Idaho's recent history; however, our way of life has been changed dramatically by the introduction of irrigation water to the Treasure Valley.

Irrigated land was limited to that in close proximity to the Boise River until construction began on the New York Canal in the 1890s. This was followed by a series of events including the building of the Diversion Dam, construction of Arrowrock, Payette, and other dams, creation of Deer Flat reservoir (Lake Lowell), and a frantic rush of homesteaders (my grandfather and father included).

Our beautiful, productive valley and our magnificent capital city would never have reached their potential without this bountiful resource and the forward thinking of the people, both in and out of government, who brought the water to us.

JOHN V. EVANS, SR.
Governor of Idaho, 1977–87

My special recollections include being invited to the White House by President Jimmy Carter, who was honoring Pope John Paul II during his first visit to the United States. We had the honor of hearing the Pope speak and meeting him personally at a reception later in the White House.

One of the major successes we achieved in finding a way to stimulate Idaho's economy was the creation of the Department of Commerce to attract businesses and industry to the state. We were able to promote Idaho tourism through the Idaho Travel Council and the 2 percent Hotel Motel Tax that funded tourism publicity.

CECIL D. ANDRUS
Governor of Idaho, 1971–77 and 1982–94
U.S. Secretary of the Interior 1977–81

I have always been struck by the story of the generosity of the members of the Nez Perce Tribe, who first encountered the Lewis and Clark expedition on the Weippe Prairie in the fall of 1805. The Corps of Discovery had struggled through an early snowstorm in the Bitterroot Mountains, and when they encountered the Native Americans, the members of the corps were desperately tired and hungry.

Even though the explorers were well armed by the standards of today and would well have been seen as a major threat to the tribe, they were welcomed, fed, nursed back to health, and given directions. Stephen Ambrose, in his widely respected book on the journey, commented that, had the Nez Perce been different people, they might have done away with the expedition, taken its weapons, and become the best-armed tribe west of the Mississippi River.

I have often wondered whether, if this early encounter had become a model for our nation's relationships with the Native Americans rather than the exception, our history might have been different and better. While we now commemorate the expedition as "opening the West" and celebrate the courage of Meriwether Lewis, William Clark, and the members of the expedition, the events on the Weippe Prairie more than 200 years ago are properly seen by the Nez Perce as the beginning of the deterioration of their control over and outright loss of their historic lands. It is a chapter of American history worth remembering and analyzing for the lessons it contains . . . and it happened right here in Idaho.

PART ONE

THE PATH TO PROGRESS

Unfolding Visions

The grandeur of the Sawtooth National Recreation Area's snow-capped mountains and lush meadows has inspired generations of writers, artists, and humanitarians. A road curves through the two extremes, evoking the spirit of Idahoans themselves. Sometimes challenging formidable odds, sometimes enjoying the richness of life in the Great Outdoors, Idahoans have carved a history marked by passion and will.

Beginnings

Legendary Idaho writer Vardis Fisher (1895–1968) proclaimed that Idaho is a state "parceled from many." This is true in terms of geography, people, and perspectives. As one of the last of the continental areas to become a state, Idaho was literally what was left over after other state boundaries had been drawn.

Several Indian tribes inhabited the area at the time of first direct Euro-American contact, the Meriwether Lewis and William Clark Corps of Discovery expedition. The Nez Perce (Nimíipuu), Kalispel, Kutenai, and Coeur d'Alene (Schitsu'umsh) lived in the north; the Shoshone, Bannock, and Paiute in the south. The Lewis and Clark expedition journals recount a remarkable journey of almost 8,000 miles. Idaho's Indians, however, still struggle to interpret the impact this journey has had on their societies and cultures. By all accounts, without the assistance of Idaho tribal peoples, Lewis, Clark, and the 31 other members of their party would not have survived to travel to the Pacific Coast.

The fur trade brought entrepreneurs to Idaho, rugged trappers and traders who could supply the men's hat-making industry with the thousands of beaver pelts it needed. These men were indeed the stuff of legends. The actual operation of the fur trade, however, depended upon large corporations such as Britain's Hudson's Bay Company and often pitted Americans against their English competitors. Idaho was frequently the location of their intense rivalry. Boston businessman Nathaniel Wyeth founded Fort Hall (north of present-day Pocatello) for American traders in 1834, the same year that the Hudson's Bay Company established Fort Boise (at the mouth of the Boise River) for British traders. Wyeth could not compete with the British operation and sold his post to the company in 1837.

As the fur trade introduced commercial goods, such as liquor, to Idaho's native people, Christian missionary organizations began viewing the Indians as potential converts. In 1836 the American Board of Commissioners for Foreign Missions, an umbrella group for Protestant missionaries, sponsored Marcus and Narcissa Whitman and Henry and Eliza Spalding on a mission to the Nez Perce and other Sahaptian-speaking tribes of the Columbia Plateau. Following old fur-trading routes, they became the first families to take wagons across the Snake River Plain, setting a precedent for the later Oregon Trail migrants. The Whitmans established a mission near what is now Walla Walla, Washington, and the Spaldings settled in Lapwai, about 13 miles east of Lewiston. The Spaldings started Idaho's first irrigated farm and built a school, church, gristmill, and water-powered sawmill. The couple's daughter, Eliza Spalding, was the first white child born in Idaho.

A 1904 Alfred Russell drawing depicts Sacajawea, a Lemhi Shoshone woman, guiding the Lewis and Clark expedition on its journey west a century earlier. The slave wife of a French fur trader, Sacajawea was instrumental to the expedition's success, enabling Lewis and Clark to document western lands for the United States. Their success, however, proved ominous for local tribes, whose way of life would be forever altered.

The Mission of the Sacred Heart, or Old Mission, stands on a grassy knoll overlooking the Coeur d'Alene River in Cataldo. Begun in 1848, it represents the combined efforts of Jesuit missionaries and Coeur d'Alene Indians. Impressed with what they had heard about the white man's religion, the Coeur d'Alenes invited the "Blackrobes" to the area in the early 1840s. The structure, built ingeniously with available materials to resemble Italian churches of the period, holds great significance for the tribe today.

Roman Catholic missionaries also based their efforts in northern Idaho, with Fathers Pierre Jean deSmet, Anthony Ravalli, and Nicholas Point establishing missions. Using an architectural plan Father Ravalli designed, members of the Coeur d'Alene tribe constructed the Cataldo mission. Today it is the oldest extant building in Idaho.

Members of the Church of Jesus Christ of Latter-day Saints (LDS) built Lemhi Mission, named in honor of King Limhi of the Book of Mormon, in 1855 on the Lemhi River, 20 miles upstream of its confluence with the Salmon River. Grasshoppers and conflicts with the local Shoshone plagued this first white farming community in Idaho, and the Mormons returned to Utah.

The famous Oregon Trail immigration route crossed the southern portion of what is now Idaho. According to some estimates, about 53,000 people traveled the trail between 1840 and 1860. Even more traveled to the California gold fields via Fort Hall and the Raft River valley beginning in 1849. The trip was difficult in the best of circumstances. Most emigrants crossed the Snake River Plain segment from Fort Hall to Fort Boise during the hottest part of the summer. They could see the river in places, but the trail passed high above it on cliffs.

High on a hill in Idaho City, gold mining families gather on the steps of the Catholic church. The first formal place of worship in Idaho Territory, it was built to accommodate Irish Catholic miners who poured into the Boise Basin during the gold rush. The collection plate, it was said, was filled with gold nearly as often as with bills and coins. Rich with ore, water, and a saw mill to facilitate home building, Idaho City attracted more families than most mining towns.

FREIGHTING ELK CITY IDAHO

Central Idaho's Elk City
freight stop bustled with
activity during the mining
and homesteading days
of the late 1800s and
early 1900s. The 50-mile
stretch between
Harpster, on the south
fork of the Clearwater
River, and Elk City via the
busy Elk City wagon road
took two days in summer,
five in winter.
Several waystations
provided food and shel-
ter for the weary travelers.

During these early years, migrants saw the Idaho landscape as an obstacle to be overcome on the way to a final destination. There is no better evidence for this than the history of the area's congressional designations. When Washington became a territory in 1853, Congress divided Idaho between it and Oregon Territory. Oregon statehood in 1859 resulted in a recombining of the sparsely populated future states of Washington and Idaho and parts of what would become Montana and Wyoming.

The 1860 discovery of gold in the Clearwater River drainage made the region far more attractive to immigrants and challenged Nez Perce claims to their tribal homeland. Prospector Elias Davidson Pierce illegally crossed the Nez Perce reservation to reach the Clearwater near present-day Orofino and struck gold, which soon led to a full-blown mining rush. The prospectors trespassed on Nez Perce land, but their sheer numbers made ownership a moot point. Gold was valued at $16 an ounce at the time, and $3 million worth was shipped down the Columbia River during 1861.

Discoveries at Florence and Elk City, and eventually further south in the Boise Basin, followed. By 1866, $20 million in gold had come from the Boise Basin, and Idaho City had a larger population than Portland, Oregon. Eventually the mining area yielded as much as $66 million in gold and added needed funds to the coffers of the U.S. government, then embroiled in the Civil War.

The endless expanse of southern Idaho's Snake River Plain, with artemisia as far as the eye could see, lay ahead of emigrants on the Oregon Trail. Approximately 53,000 hardy souls made the journey west between 1840–60, and not surprisingly, most hoped to cross Idaho as quickly as possible. The discovery of gold, however, made the area more attractive—and ignited land feuds with local Indians.

As her train departs from the Morning Mine at Mullen, the wife of a miner waves good-bye to friends continuing on to the next town. Hard-rock lead and zinc made the Morning Mine one of the top producers in the Coeur d'Alene mining district, a region so rich in metals that its settlement helped accelerate the creation of Idaho Territory. By 1891 both the Northern Pacific and Union Pacific railroads served the district, bringing a legion of hard-driving, hard-working miners to the wilderness.

Mining activity and railroad construction reshaped Idaho's demographic landscape as well. Many of the Idaho miners in the 1800s were Chinese who had moved north after helping to complete the first transcontinental railroad to California in 1869. By 1870, 28.5 percent of the territory's population was Chinese, compared to only 9 percent of California's. In Idaho City and Boise County, the Chinese population reached nearly 50 percent. Despite consistent political persecution that included being made to pay higher taxes based solely on their ethnicity, Chinese found a wide range of opportunities in frontier Idaho. Until the mining industry shifted away from individual placer mining to an industrial, wage-labor system by the 1890s, Chinese citizens were an important and highly visible part of territorial society.

Mining boom towns came and went on the Idaho landscape, but members of the LDS founded communities meant to last. Mormon settlers established Idaho's first town, Franklin, on April 14, 1860, and began farming. Other Mormon settlements followed: Paris, Montpelier, St. Charles, Ovid, Bennington, Fish Haven, and Bloomington. The Organic Act for Utah Territory (1850) proclaimed the 42nd parallel as the territory's northern boundary. The early Franklin and Bear Lake settlers thought they were in Utah and paid taxes there until 1872, when an official survey publicized their mistake.

Mormon livestock and crops threatened Indians' claims to land, and tensions ended in violence. On January 29, 1863, in the Bear River Massacre, 200 U.S. troops under the command of Colonel Patrick Edward Connor killed as many as 368 Cache Valley Shoshone, two thirds of them women and children. The catastrophe virtually annihilated the Northwest Shoshone.

Carving Out the New Territory

Although Mormon settlement in the south probably had more long-term impact on Idaho Territory, it was the mining boom that led to its creation. President Abraham Lincoln signed the organic act creating Idaho Territory on March 4, 1863. The last large territory created, Idaho stretched for 325,000 square miles, taking in all of the area that is present-day Idaho and Montana along with most of Wyoming. Lewiston became the capital due to its access to transportation routes, even though Idaho City, in the Boise

Top: Railroad construction crews such as this Northern Pacific team laid tracks through northern Idaho in the early 1880s. Steamboats and stagecoaches had begun service to the mining districts 20 years earlier, but the arrival of Northern Pacific in 1883 alleviated many of the challenges of governing the region's isolated communities. Bottom: This 1889 stereograph shows gold prospector Archie Smith on the porch of his cabin at Eagle Creek, in Murray.

Top: A U.S. mail
stagecoach piled with
passengers is about to
set out. Before the
proliferation of railroads,
stages (and steamboats)
were the primary means
of delivering mail, and
entire families often
signed on for the trip.
Passengers sometimes
carried gold in their
strongboxes—a
dangerous proposition in
the 19th-century West.
Bottom: Travelers wait at
Greer for the Clearwater
River ferry to the Weippe
prairie and goldfields.

Basin gold mining area, had a larger population. Ironically, Lewiston was still part of Nez Perce tribal holdings. A Nez Perce treaty negotiated that year reduced tribal lands by 90 percent (to about 1,100 square miles) and added Lewiston to Idaho, but the treaty did not receive Senate ratification until April 20, 1867. By then the territorial legislature had moved the capital to Boise, where there was a greater population base.

The new territory had only 32,342 residents, yet geographically, it was larger than all of the New England states combined. At the meeting of the First Territorial Legislature in July 1863, lawmakers acknowledged that the area was simply too large for effective government and unanimously voted to petition Congress to divide it. Congress created Montana Territory on May 26, 1864, which left an Idaho Territory with boundaries close to the current ones that were finalized on July 25, 1868.

Communication and transportation challenges also hampered effective government. Commercial steamboat and stagecoach traffic serviced the mining districts in the 1860s, and U.S. mail service began in 1864. It was another 10 years before railroad construction began in Idaho—with the Utah Northern Railway to Montana—due to the sparse population and isolated communities that defined the area. The Northern Pacific Railroad began operating across northern Idaho in 1883; the Oregon Short Line of the Union Pacific Railroad, a year later. For the first rail companies, Idaho was just a stop on the way to the Pacific Coast, but mining resources and farming settlements later led them to build spur lines there. By 1891 both the Northern Pacific and the Union Pacific offered service to the Coeur d'Alene mining district.

Obligations related to the Civil War handicapped federal efforts to adequately fund the Idaho Territorial government. Of the 16 men confirmed as governor during the 27 years of territorial status, six were in Idaho for less than a year, some for only a few months. Only eight served a year or more. Incompetence and economic irresponsibility marked the period, and the territorial governors received the pejorative "carpetbagger" label.

The territorial government confronted three major issues: the growing white demand for Indian lands; the increasing influence in southern Idaho of LDS members, whose support of the Democratic Party fostered political factionalism; and a burgeoning north-south conflict.

White settlers' desire for Indian lands was assuaged through military conquest. The Nez Perce War of 1877 resulted in the exile of many Nez Perce tribal members to Oklahoma. U.S. cavalry confrontations with the Bannocks and Paiutes in southern Idaho in 1878 led to a reduction in the size of their reservation, which had been established at Fort Hall in 1867, to one-fourth its former area. The remainder was opened to white settlement.

Anti-Mormonism was a recurring theme throughout the Idaho territorial period. Those outside the church clashed with LDS members over Mormon cooperative economic initiatives (the tendency toward church control of various aspects of the economy), political factionalism, and the practice of plural marriage. Although most estimates show that only about 3 percent of Idaho Mormons actually practiced polygamy, outsiders focused on it to indict the church and its individual members. Fred T. Dubois, a U.S. marshal, was the catalyst for converting general anti-Mormon sentiment into a full-blown political movement that led the Idaho legislature to pass, in 1885, the administration of a test oath. The test oath required those suspected of being Mormon to swear they were not, in order to qualify for certain rights. The law thus deprived all Mormons, not just practitioners of plural marriage, of the right to vote, hold office, or serve on a jury.

Top: An 1899 illustration of U.S. Army infantry exchanging fire with Indians near the Owyhee River highlights a haunting issue of the territorial period: the extreme antagonism that arose as settlers' hunger for Indian lands grew. Bottom: U.S. marshal Fred T. Dubois was the force behind a politically motivated movement to disenfranchise LDS members, thereby eliminating the possibility of Democratic factionalism.

The expansion of both population and economy exacerbated divisions between northern and southern Idaho. Prospectors in the Coeur d'Alene mining district, in the north, unearthed gold, silver, and other metals that led the area to become one of the most significant mining districts in the world. Mining discoveries in central Idaho's Wood River area, near the present-day Sun Valley resort, yielded $6 million between 1884 and 1887. Miners' political concerns differed from those of Mormon farmers in the south.

Politics of Statehood

The territory's growth and development caused Idahoans to work for statehood, and this involved party politics. Republicans thought at the time that they would never gain Mormon support, which helped to create pressure for boundary readjustment. Mine owners in the Idaho Panhandle believed they shared more of a community of interest with residents of eastern Washington and Montana than with those of southern Idaho. Non-Mormons in the south feared becoming a voting minority.

Top: Ostensibly because of objections to the practice of polygamy, the legislature passed the Idaho Test Oath in 1885, requiring those suspected of being Mormon to swear they were not or lose their rights. The Church of Jesus Christ of Latter-day Saints rescinded its support of the practice (or at least of new plural unions) in 1890, ahead of Idaho's approval for statehood. Bottom: An 1879 territorial map by the U.S. Department of the Interior's land office shows an Idaho slimmer than the original, which at 325,000 square miles was far too large to govern effectively.

Forces outside of Idaho, especially in Washington, D.C., played the key role in defining territorial boundaries. Four sessions of the Idaho Territorial Legislature petitioned Congress to annex the Idaho Panhandle to either Washington or Montana, but national party politics and a Congress split between a Democratic House and a Republican Senate kept Idaho's boundaries intact. President Grover Cleveland pocket vetoed legislation in 1887 that would have annexed the southern part of Idaho to Nevada and the north to Washington, partially due to the opposition of the territorial governor, Edward Stevenson, and other Boise politicians. Territorial Council Bill Number 20 determined that Idaho's land grant university, provided for by the Morrill Act, would be located in Moscow in northern Idaho's Latah County. The bill had virtually no opposition. Once the site for the University of Idaho was established, county voters stopped supporting annexation efforts.

Amid these regional differences in Idaho and political uncertainty on the national scene, Idahoans elected delegates—38 Republicans, 33 Democrats, and one Labor Party member—to a constitutional convention that met in Boise on July 4, 1899. Half of the delegates represented the five largest counties: Ada (which included Boise), Shoshone (the Coeur d'Alene mining district), Bingham (created around Blackfoot in 1884 to counteract Mormon influence), Alturas (the Wood River mining district), and Latah (Moscow and the University of Idaho). Many of the delegates would play significant roles in later Idaho politics.

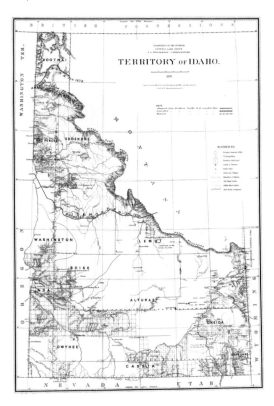

The delegates grappled with organizational issues, water rights (undoubtedly one of the most contentious and important western issues), and the legal system. One central question, however, was who had the right to vote, and therefore who could participate in government. The Idaho convention delegates heard addresses for and against women's suffrage and voted 36–20 against it. "Chinese and persons of Mongolian descent" who were not born in the United States and Indians who were "not taxed [and] who have not severed their tribal relations and adopted the habits of civilization" were denied voting rights (there seems to have been no vote on these issues), as were LDS members by a vote of 42–10. Mormon disenfranchisement benefited Republicans and probably facilitated Idaho statehood, since the Republican-controlled Congress might have balked at adding a potential Democratic state to the Union.

Idahoans sought statehood as a path to greater representation in the national government, particularly in terms of economic development. Conventional wisdom was that an Idaho voice in Washington could influence tariff policy and irrigation

Cadets from the University of Idaho in Moscow (Latah County) leave for the Spanish-American War in 1898. Before the Territorial Council selected the northern Idaho town as the site of the land-grant university, intense regional differences had caused the legislature to repeatedly petition Congress to adjust the boundaries by annexing the north to Washington and the south to Nevada. Locating the university in Moscow satisfied northern angst, and the pressure for annexation ended.

The First Idaho
Territorial Legislature
met in this wooden build-
ing in Lewiston in 1863.
Technically the town was
still part of the Nez
Perce tribal holdings, but
its location—at the
confluence of the Snake
and Clearwater rivers
with access to the
mighty Columbia River—
led to its selection as
the capital anyway.
When an 1863 treaty that
would have added
Lewiston to Idaho failed
to be quickly ratified by
the U.S. Senate, the
legislature moved the
capital to Boise.

investments—thus appealing to both mining and agricultural interests. Idaho voters ratified the state constitution on November 5, 1889, by a vote of 12,398 to 1,776.

Idaho statehood faced two barriers in the nation's capital. First, a number of other territories (North Dakota, South Dakota, Montana, Washington, Wyoming, New Mexico, and Arizona) were seeking statehood at about the same time, and politicians in the nation's capital were wary of the impact the new states would have on each political party's strength in the Congress. Second, the U.S. Supreme Court was hearing *Davis v. Beason*, a case that claimed the Mormon Test Oath was a violation of the First Amendment. When the Idaho statehood bill was presented to the House, the LDS issue was a major topic of conversation. Although the House approved admitting Idaho by a vote of 129–1, 57 Democrats present abstained due to this issue. President Benjamin Harrison signed the Idaho bill on July 3, 1890, and Idaho territorial representative Fred Dubois telegraphed officials in the territory: "Turn the eagle loose."

The new state of Idaho was indeed "parceled from many." As statehood began, Idaho was a crossroads of economic influences, cultural forces, and ethnicities.

The interaction of the Nez Perce, or Nimíipuu (the People), with the Lewis and Clark expedition on the Weippe Prairie in 1805 marked the beginning of a complex and, from the Indian perspective, often devastating history. After the Northwest became part of the United States in 1846, the Nez Perce agreed to a treaty at the Walla Walla Council of 1855. The Clearwater gold rush precipitated an 1863 renegotiation of reservation boundaries, one that many Nez Perce refused to acknowledge.

One group of nontreaty Nez Perce, led by Young Chief Joseph, remained in the Wallowa Valley in Oregon. At first the federal government acquiesced to this arrangement, but complaints from whites who coveted Nez Perce land led the government to direct Joseph and his people to move to the Nez Perce reservation on the Clearwater River in Idaho. Joseph and his band ignored this request for nearly two years. In May 1877, U.S. Army General Oliver O. Howard commanded Joseph to move within 30 days. During the relocation in June, three young warriors, including one whose father had been murdered by local whites, killed four settlers, and the peace ended.

Eight hundred Indian men, women, and children, with a herd of more than 2,000 horses, fled across the Bitterroot Mountains to Montana. General Howard and his soldiers pursued the fleeing Nez Perce. At the Battle of the Big Hole River on August 9–10, the Nez Perce suffered 70 casualties; the army toll was 21 dead and 40 wounded.

After traveling over 1,500 miles, by September 30 the Nez Perce were only 40 miles from safety in Canada when Colonel Nelson Miles and 383 troopers overtook them. Following a day of fighting and five days of siege in the extreme cold, the soldiers were victorious. Joseph surrendered on October 5 and made his famous declaration: "Hear me, my chiefs! I am tired. My heart is sick and sad. From where the sun now stands I will fight no more forever."

The army took 87 men, 184 women, and 147 children prisoner. The federal government transported them to Kansas and then Oklahoma. They remained in Oklahoma until 1885, when they were allowed to return to the Pacific Northwest.

The quiet town of Caldwell, in the irrigated countryside west of Boise, had had its share of notoriety by the time this photograph was taken in 1910. Five years earlier, Governor Frank Steunenberg had been killed at his home by a bomb blast, the work of a radical miners' union that, ironically, had supported him in his bid for governor.

Identity Formation

Frank Steunenberg, former governor of Idaho, returned to his Caldwell home from a business outing late in the afternoon of a snowy December 30, 1905, opened his garden gate, and was blown apart by a bomb. His legs gone, Steunenberg was carried into his house and died less than an hour later. The investigation of the crime and subsequent trial rocked the nation. During their investigation, officials focused on Harry Orchard (whose given name was Albert E. Horsley). Orchard's careless actions, including leaving incriminating evidence in his hotel room, suggested that he did not seek to avoid arrest. Orchard confessed to the crime and similar bombings in California and Colorado, all of which, he claimed, were carried out at the behest of leaders of the radical Western Federation of Miners union.

Residents of Caldwell, a quiet town founded in 1883 by the Idaho and Oregon Land Improvement Company, looked with horror on an event that surely signaled the encroachment of urban problems on the irrigated countryside. The explosion that pierced the cold air in Caldwell that afternoon had connections to a national struggle. The events that followed Steunenberg's death brought Idaho into focus for the nation as a place of competing visions regarding the roles of labor, industry, and immigration in a modern democracy. The blast had its roots in an outbreak of labor violence more than 500 miles away in northern Idaho's Coeur d'Alene mining district, an area very different from booster-laden railroad and irrigation communities in southern Idaho. Fed up with dangerous conditions and low wages in Rocky Mountain mines, miners throughout the West—many of them Irish and eastern European immigrants—formed the Western Federation of Miners in Butte in 1893, partially in response to violent conflicts with mine owners in the Coeur d'Alenes the previous year. The group's first president, Edward Boyce, an Idaho miner and aggressive union activist, led the union's participation in highly publicized strikes in Colorado (including at Cripple Creek in 1894) before turning his attention to Idaho's silver district. In 1899, when Coeur d'Alene owners ignored union demands and used Pinkerton detectives to infiltrate union meetings, miners took action against the largest mine in the region, the Bunker Hill and Sullivan. Rowdy miners commandeered a Northern Pacific passenger train and used it to transport 3,000 pounds of dynamite to Kellogg, where Harry Orchard and others blew up the Bunker Hill office and concentrating mill. In response, then governor Steunenberg declared martial law and asked for federal assistance. A company of African-American troops fresh from the Spanish-American War arrived in the region and placed more than 600 people—including local professionals—in makeshift jails, or bull pens. Unsanitary conditions and racial prejudice compounded the miners' anger at Steunenberg. Martial law remained in place for two years.

Orchard's confession reopened the bitter wounds of the Coeur d'Alene dispute and implicated Western Federation officials, including William "Big Bill" Haywood—also an Idaho miner—who held the secretary/treasurer post for the union. Many in Idaho's Republican Party blamed Steunenberg's assassination on a conspiracy to pay back the former governor for his role in subduing the Coeur d'Alene miners.

Shortly after Steunenberg's death, state officials and members of Boise's elite met in Caldwell and planned their pursuit of three key suspects: Haywood; Charles Moyer, the Western Federation president; and George Pettibone, a former Coeur d'Alene miner and Colorado merchant.

Frank Steunenberg (top), shown circa 1900, was elected governor on a Democratic and Populist platform. Miners thought he represented them, but when—fed up with mine owners' deaf ears—they dynamited the region's largest mine, Steunenberg declared martial law. Supportive federal troops threw the miners (and many others) into unsanitary, makeshift jails (bottom), where their anger continued to fester.

Pinkerton detectives illegally seized the three in Denver and transported them to Boise aboard a special train chartered by Idaho's mine owners. Because of the high-handed action of Idaho officials in kidnapping federation officials, the episode was thrust onto the national stage. The case launched the careers of William Borah, the prosecuting attorney and newly elected U.S. Senator from Idaho, and Clarence Darrow, hired by the unions to defend Haywood, who was first to be tried. (Darrow would later defend Tennessee teacher John Scopes in the famous "Monkey Trial" of 1912, in which Scopes was found guilty of violating state law by teaching evolution in a biology class.) Darrow won the Haywood case. The jury acquitted his client, after which the cases against Moyer and Pettibone fell apart. Harry Orchard, because of his confession, spent the rest of his life in the state penitentiary in Boise.

Dramatic Change

Idaho's brief national exposure ended, but the bitter fear evoked by the assassination and trial continued to ripple through the state. The inscription on the monument to Frank Steunenberg, located in front of the state capitol in Boise, reflects the

The 1906 Steunenberg murder trial launched the career of attorney Clarence Darrow (standing), who was hired by the Western Federation of Miners to defend one of their leaders, "Big Bill" Haywood (indicated by the "2" above his head). Idaho officials had illegally seized Haywood and his codefendants in Denver to bring them to trial, and the case against the miners fell apart.

After 1890, Idaho's population grew exponentially, fueling the expansion of urban centers in the new state. Signs of the times included (both pages, clockwise from top left) the Old Courthouse in Pocatello; Boise's "street railroad," discharging passengers at the city fairgrounds; downtown Boise circa 1909; and Boise itself, in a view looking northeast from the capitol, on a 1913 postcard.

BOISE IDAHO

This page: Troops patrol the Silver Valley mining town of Wallace in July 1892 after a conflict between mine owners and laborers. Opposite page: In the hopes of preserving their land base, Indians such as these Coeur d'Alenes assimilated, adopting a non-Indian style of farming. In the end, they were forced to negotiate with the federal government anyway.

sentiment of Idahoans who viewed labor strife as a threat to the social order: "When in 1899 organized lawlessness challenged the power of Idaho, he upheld the dignity of the state, enforced its authority and restored LAW AND ORDER within its boundaries, for which he was assassinated in 1905."

Like those in the rest of the country, some Idaho residents looked askance at the dramatic social and cultural changes then under way. In the span of only a few decades, Idaho's native peoples had relinquished their aboriginal territory to the federal government; mines in the state had become big business, and Idaho's mining communities, company towns rife with labor violence; and irrigation on the southern sagebrush steppes had opened thousands of square miles to agriculture and settlement.

When statehood was granted in 1890, most people in Idaho lived in small communities scattered throughout the state. Mormons, miners , and Indians divided along religious, political, and geographic lines: Mormon settlements in southern Idaho, miner communities in northern and central parts of the state, reservations of the Nez Perce at Lapwai, Coeur d'Alene at DeSmet, and Shoshone-Bannock at Fort Hall. Yet between 1890 and World War I, Idaho settled into an identity of its own.

Boise's population in 1890 was only 4,000, and Montpelier, in the east, was the only other town to exceed a population of 1,000. In 1890 Idaho's largest counties were Bingham, with 13,575 people, and Ada, with 8,368. By 1930 Ada County had mushroomed to 37,925 people, and Canyon County, which did not exist in 1890, had swelled to 30,930. Population growth, statehood, and economic development fueled the expansion of Idaho's urban centers—particularly Boise and Pocatello—and attracted immigrants who worked in mines and on farms.

While Coeur d'Alene miners protested their treatment by company owners, Coeur d'Alene Indians (Schitsu'umsh) fought to retain their land base in northern Idaho. The Schitsu'umsh homeland had once encompassed more than five million acres centered on the Spokane River drainage system, Lake Coeur d'Alene, and the Coeur d'Alene River. Jesuit missionaries had arrived in the region in the 1840s; Euro-American pioneers came throughout the 19th century to farm in the Palouse hills or mine in the Coeur d'Alene valley. The Coeur d'Alene Indian Reservation, created by presidential executive order in 1873, encompassed 600,000 acres. By the 1880s, it was under constant assault by mining, lumbering, and steamboat traffic.

Chief Andrew Seltice, a Catholic respected by other tribes and non-Indians alike, advanced a policy of assimilation—including adoption of non-Indian–style farming and Catholicism—to argue for the preservation of the tribe's remaining land base. Despite these efforts and the considerable expansion of native farms, the Coeur d'Alenes were forced to negotiate with federal officials in 1887 and 1889. During the latter negotiations, tribal leaders agreed to the transfer of approximately two-thirds of the reservation to the federal government. In 1909 the reservation was divided into parcels for private ownership by individual members of the tribe under authority of the Dawes Severalty Act (1887), despite the strident opposition of the tribal leadership.

Severalty grew out of an effort in the late-19th century to reform the government's Indian Office, which oversaw U.S. relations with the tribes. Adherents of severalty supported the idea that land ownership—based on the model of 160-acre farms established by the 1862 Homestead Act—was the answer to the problem of native poverty and cultural decline on reservations. Many Coeur d'Alene farmers already cultivated more than the standard 40-, 80-, and 160-acre allotments allowed under severalty and actually lost farmland as a result. Following allotment, the U.S. Land Office sold the land to non-Indians, often on a first-come, first-served basis. By the time Congress ended the practice of severalty in 1934 with the passage of the Indian Reorganization Act, Coeur d'Alene tribal holdings had been reduced to 62,400 acres—45,120 of which were leased to non-Indians.

Similar negotiations and the imposition of severalty reduced the tribal holdings of the Nez Perce, the Coeur d'Alene's southern neighbor, and the Shoshone-Bannock, in southeastern Idaho. President Grover Cleveland ordered the allotment of the Nez Perce reservation in 1895. As late as the 1960s, Nez Perce ownership reflected the legacy of the misguided institution of severalty. The Nez Perce controlled a very small percentage of their reservation; the rest was either owned or leased by nontribal members. Under extreme pressure from white settlers in the Pocatello area, federal negotiators in 1888 purchased the Pocatello town site—1,840 acres—from the Shoshone-Bannock peoples at Fort Hall. By 1896 relentless pressure on the Indian Office and Congress for the cession of additional land from the Fort Hall reservation prompted the negotiation of a new round of agreements, and three Indian commissioners purchased 418,560 acres for $600,000 in 1898. In June 1902 the cession area was opened to pioneers, or "sagebrush sooners," in a land rush. Lands within a five-mile radius of Pocatello were sold in 40-acre units at a public auction. The Fort Hall reservation was allotted in 1911, and its "additional lands" were sold to the public. Between 1885 and 1914, negotiated agreements and severalty reduced the Fort Hall reservation holdings to half their original size.

Emergence of Communities

With the forced cession from the Shoshone-Bannock tribes, Pocatello soon emerged as a center of non-Indian activity and a crossroads for the Upper Snake and Great Basin regions. Its position at the junction of the Oregon Short Line and the Utah and Northern railroads made Pocatello a railroad town of the first order. The Oregon Short Line, also responsible for the settlement of towns like Caldwell, revolutionized travel in the West by linking Wyoming to Oregon and bypassing California. By 1900 Pocatello could claim a population of 4,096 and billed itself as the Gate City to the Northwest. As a transportation hub, the town attracted the state's most diverse population. One traveler in the early 1900s observed, "I saw more nationalities in an hour than the capital of the state can produce in its directory."

The state legislature chose Pocatello as the site of the Academy of Idaho in 1901. The academy began as a secondary school, was renamed the Idaho Technical Institute in 1915, reorganized as the southern branch of the

This page and opposite page, left: "Sagebrush sooners" rush to claim land ceded by the Shoshone-Bannock at Fort Hall. Opposite page, top: Land investors crowd outside an attorney's office in Pocatello, at the crossing of the Oregon Short Line. Opposite, page, bottom: Idaho's first African-Americans included this Pocatello lawman. The city, at the crossroads of the Upper Snake and Great Basin regions, drew the state's most diverse population.

University of Idaho in 1927, evolved into Idaho State College in 1947, and became Idaho State University in 1963.

Pocatello's neighborhoods developed in the early 20th century, in an eclectic mix of architectural styles that included classical revival, Tudor, and craftsman. The city's master builder, Frank Paradice, built a number of impressive structures within the downtown core. His 1915 Franklin Building, an Italian Renaissance revival–style structure housing the Bannock National Bank, was, in Paradice's words, "the first real terra-cotta job in Pocatello." Paradice's neoclassic revival Valentine Building, built the next year for First National Bank, today is the state's best example of a terra-cotta facade. Travelers passing through Pocatello in the early 1900s could dine at a local establishment, sleep at the Monarch Hotel, and walk along new streets teeming with construction. Pocatello's raucous red-light district maintained a precarious existence along the railroad tracks.

Railroad access, along with the ceding of native lands, made Idaho's forest products available to a national market. Frederick Weyerhaeuser, a German immigrant involved in the Minnesota timber industry, became the most important of a number of timber entrepreneurs who converged on northern Idaho during the early 20th century. Beginning in 1900, Weyerhaeuser and his associates quickly bought up timber lands in northern and central Idaho and by 1908 controlled seven Idaho ventures, representing the majority of the state's pre–WWI production.

This page, top: The Academy of Idaho, which eventually became Idaho State University, opened in 1902 in booming Pocatello. Bottom: Loggers transport white pine to the mill at Cataldo Mission, one of 72 major mills in the region in the early 1900s. Opposite page: Rick's Academy in Rexburg, today's Brigham Young University–Idaho, has set the pace for Mormon students in Idaho since its opening in 1888.

In 1905 a two-year-old Weyerhaeuser subsidiary, the Potlatch Lumber Company, established a company town, Potlatch, in the white-pine forests north of Moscow. The company built the world's largest white-pine sawmill there in 1906, and between 1908–27, it produced an annual average of 131 million board feet of high quality lumber. The town attracted a largely male, transient population. Potlatch Lumber hired only young men to work in the mill and forced retirees to leave its town. Families who stayed participated in a wide array of community-oriented functions sponsored by the company. With no access to work, the town's female population established a tight social network characterized by club meetings and social gatherings.

In contrast to the state's boom-and-bust mining communities, timber company towns, and emergent railroad centers, Idaho's Mormon farming towns followed a development model characterized by order, function, and urban planning. The Mormon Church, centered in Salt Lake City, instituted a settlement system for southern Idaho and sent faithful families into the region to establish Mormon communities. Rexburg, founded in 1883 by Mormon pioneers from Utah, boasted a tabernacle, a precursor to the modern LDS stake center, within three decades of settlement. An impressive structure of pink and gray stone, the building is now listed on the National Register of Historic Places. Thomas E. Ricks, one of the region's earliest Mormon settlers, founded Ricks Academy (formerly the Bannock Stake Academy) in Rexburg in 1888. Today the four-year Brigham Young University–Idaho, Ricks was the first junior college in the Intermountain region.

In the central Snake River Plain's "Magic Valley," fast-growing communities sprouted as federal and corporate enterprises made irrigation water available. Ira Burton Perrine's Twin Falls Land and Water Company, formed with investors Peter L. Kimberly, Frank H. Buhl, and Stanley B. Milner, financed the construction of Milner Dam in 1905. Twin Falls—a community that billed itself as the Chicago of Idaho for its commercial possibilities— rose from the sagebrush flats along the Snake River canyon soon after. The Twin Falls project, subsidized by the federal Carey Act of 1894 (giving participating states up to one million acres of federal land if they produced plans for irrigating it), irrigated more than 130,000 acres by 1908, making it one of the most successful Carey Act projects in the nation. Other communities, including Buhl and Kimberly, emerged as new canal systems opened desert land to settlement. Between 1895–1930, Idaho had 65 such projects come up for consideration. More than 600,000 acres were patented, making Idaho the most successful Carey Act state in the nation.

This page and opposite left: Milner Dam, completed in 1905, was among the irrigation systems that opened arid southern central Idaho to development. The community of Twin Falls blossomed as a result, and others soon followed in the thriving "Magic" Valley. Opposite page, right: By the late 19th century, Boise was well on the road to providing an outstanding quality of life for its residents with such amenities as a natatorium. The facility had a geothermal pool, dance floor, and even an amusement park.

Boise, the capital, engaged in an ambitious civic building program of its own. Its natatorium, an indoor geothermal swimming pool and recreation center, opened to the public in 1892. Designed by John C. Paulsen, the impressive structure had Moorish towers, a 125-foot pool, a wooden dance floor that could be extended across the pool, and an amusement park—dubbed The White City—complete with the state's only roller coaster. Boise's elite neighborhoods, developing along Warm Springs Avenue and Harrison Boulevard, had easy access to the natatorium via the electric trolley along Warm Springs Avenue. Boise replaced its "sand walks" with concrete by the end of the 1890s and acquired Julia Davis Park, a gift of 43 acres from Boise developer Tom Davis, in 1907.

The Political Landscape

The opening of new agricultural tracts coupled with mining interests to create significant support in Idaho for the 1890s third-party movement known as Populism. The Populist platform included a graduated income tax, government ownership of railroads and telephone lines, and the "free" and unlimited coinage

This page: Workers on the Minidoka Project in 1905 drill a diversion channel for water from the Snake River. The project was Idaho's first reclamation attempt using funds earmarked by the federal government for such large-scale irrigation projects. Opposite page: With Populism gaining support throughout the nation, a young marcher in Boise carries the banner of one of the party's main platforms in a parade supporting presidential candidate William Jennings Bryan.

of silver by the Treasury Department, a platform thought by its advocates to create an inflationary economic environment favorable to agrarian debtors. The People's Party attracted support from farm interests throughout the nation and free-silver advocates in Rocky Mountain mining regions who desired a change from the nation's gold standard. Populist support in Idaho peaked in 1896, when the state's voters abandoned the national trend and supported Populist and Democratic candidate William Jennings Bryan for president. Ironically, it was a Populist voting trend that sent Populist and Democratic candidate Frank Steunenberg to the governor's mansion the same year.

By 1902, fuel for the third party had dissipated throughout the nation. A new political movement, Progressivism, dominated American politics during the early 1900s and 1910s. Progressives supported a variety of local, state, and national reforms, including universal women's suffrage, child and women's labor laws, childhood programs, neighborhood parks, and urban beautification. Women's suffrage had been a reality in Idaho since 1896, when it was granted in part to enlist voting support for free silver. It had passed in every western state except New Mexico by 1914. The nation's women did not receive the vote as a whole until the 19th amendment to the constitution was ratified in 1920.

It was partly through women's activism that Progressive reform made itself felt in Idaho. Women's clubs in Moscow, Boise, Caldwell, Twin Falls, Rupert, and Pocatello successfully lobbied for city beautification, antisaloon measures, and cultural reforms, including the institution of city theaters, traveling libraries, and public lounges (restrooms) for women. Elizabeth Layton DeMary's South Boise Improvement Society fought for parks, sidewalks, and schools.

The U.S. Reclamation Service, created by the Newlands Act of 1902 to provide federal funding for large-scale irrigation projects in the West, created government towns along the Snake River. In 1905 DeMary and her family moved to the newly platted town of Rupert, founded by the Reclamation Service as part of the Minidoka Project, the state's first reclamation project. There she established the Rupert Culture Club and continued her commitment to Progressive reform. The Culture Club began a lyceum lecture series, held art exhibits, and secured Rupert's place on the traveling library itinerary of what may have been the most important women's group in the state, the Boise Columbian Club.

The Culture Club was effective in other ways, as well. It helped, for example, to eliminate Rupert's red-light district. The town newspaper, the *Rupert Pioneer,* reported in September 1906 that, after receiving warnings of imminent arrest from a large group of angry citizens and city trustees, the town's "social evil" had departed on the night train. In 1909, Rupert, along with the Minidoka project's other settlement communities, Heyburn and Acequia, outlawed the sale of alcoholic beverages. The influence of DeMary's club also resulted in laws unique to Rupert. The community illegalized sidewalk spitting and horse teams in the business district, so the ladies could have relatively clean paths as they walked through town.

Top: The midwestern-style town square in Rupert was the only one of its kind in Idaho, thanks to the town's progressive, culture-oriented women. Bottom: Industrial Workers of the World, including this young man at a 1914 rally, fought for abolition of the wage system as the solution to workers' woes. In response, the group was targeted as Communist during the Red scare that swept the nation.

Based on its population today—around 5,000, according to the 2000 census—Rupert has been the nation's most successful reclamation settlement community.

DeMary's Culture Club and many other women's clubs throughout the state disbanded or changed their priorities with the outbreak of the First World War in 1914. Women's groups met to prepare bandages to send overseas or to raise money for the American Red Cross.

The U.S. entrance into the war and the Bolshevik Revolution in Russia coincided in 1917 to set off a "Red" scare in the United States. All organizations, but particularly labor and reform groups, came under federal and state suspicion as potential sources of socialist or communist support. The International Workers of the World (IWW), or Wobblies, a radical union that Big Bill Haywood helped to form in 1905, had garnered strong support in north Idaho's mining districts and logging camps. The IWW became a particular target for Red-scare

Even before Progressivism took hold, women were reshaping state history. Top: By 1899, the Boise Columbian Club—whose members are shown inaugurating their traveling library—was Idaho's most effective culture club. Bottom left: With the U.S. entry into WWI, women focused on activities such as collecting money for the Red Cross. Bottom right: An all-female surveyors team works on the Minidoka Project in 1918.

tactics. After the United States declared war on Germany, Idaho became the first state to pass a criminal syndicalism law, which outlawed the overthrow of the government or any activity advocating an antigovernment position. Aimed at the Wobblies, Idaho's statute became the model for similar legislation in other states. Although the IWW's campaign for the eight-hour workday nearly shut down the state's lumber industry in 1917, the union and others like it disintegrated in Idaho—and throughout the country—as a result of prosecutions under federal and state espionage, sedition, and criminal syndicalism laws. Indeed, although IWW leader Bill Haywood had been found innocent by an Idaho jury in 1906, in 1918 he was convicted of violating a federal espionage and sedition act by calling a strike during wartime.

The First World War dealt a blow to Idaho's unions and reform organizations, but it provided additional markets for the state's agriculture just as irrigated communities were beginning to expand production. The resulting boom was short-lived, but it prompted many in agricultural Idaho to adopt a progressive, optimistic view of the future.

Support for the military, expressed in numerous parades, was strong throughout the state long before the nation entered the war in 1918. Top: A military band marches in a parade in Boise on July 17, 1915. Bottom: Spectators thrill to the sight of a tank rolling down the street in another Boise parade, most likely on the Fourth of July, sometime between 1917 and 1920.

Idaho's National Guard units were mobilized for war as part of the 41st Division and spent time on the front in France in 1918. According to historian Carlos A. Schwantes, the ratio of military servicemen and -women to population in Idaho during WWI was one in 18; nationally, it was one in 22.

When the war ended with armistice on November 11, 1918, Pocatello residents converged on the city's newly paved streets, Twin Falls held a parade, and the town of Challis burned the German kaiser in effigy. But the celebrations masked the invasion of a silent killer: Spanish flu. The optimism of the boom years would be no match for a pandemic and a depression. The twenties would be brittle, mean years.

Edward Pulaski

Edward Pulaski's migration to northern Idaho during the late 19th century followed the pattern of that of many residents of the state's mining and logging country. The gold rush of 1884 brought Pulaski from Ohio to the booming town of Murray, where he worked as a packer. Later he labored in Montana's hard-rock mines at Butte and Anaconda, and then returned to Idaho, where he spent time prospecting in the Salmon and Clearwater river regions. For two years, he served as a foreman on a southern Idaho ranch.

Described by historian Stephen J. Pyne as "a tall, hardened, plainspoken but kindly man," Pulaski was "gifted with his hands," comfortable with the wilderness life, and skilled in every category important to frontier survival. At the age of 40, after decades of mining, prospecting, packing, and ranching, Pulaski signed on as a ranger with a new agency, the U.S. Forest Service, in 1908. His appointment as ranger of the Wallace District placed him in what was known in the service as the Great Lone Land, or District One. The year he joined, it encompassed 22 national forests—41 million acres—in four states. Its eastern boundary was South Dakota, its western boundary, Washington.

The division head, Bill Greeley, estimated that by early August 1910, 3,000 fires were burning in his district, and he had on hand fewer than one man per fire. On August 20, hurricane-force winds blew across northern Idaho and western Montana. The fires became raging storms, fueled by thousands of acres of dry trees and brush. When it became clear to Pulaski that his men could not escape the flames, he herded them into an abandoned mine shaft and guarded the door with his pistol lest anyone try to escape. Pulaski suffered temporary blindness and smoke inhalation, but his actions made him a hero. Seven of his 45-member crew were lost, but all would have been incinerated except for his efforts. The fires, which constituted the largest forest fire in U.S. history, eventually burned three million acres of forest in northern Idaho and western Montana and killed 86 people.

Pulaski worked for the Forest Service for another 20 years. The service named the combination axe and hoe, a standard wildland fire tool, in honor of Pulaski, who is believed to be its inventor. The Pulaski tool remains in wide use today.

Workers on the H. E. Chaffer farm, six miles west of Twin Falls, take a break from digging potatoes in the early 1920s. The combustible engine tractor had not yet come to the farm, whose 40-bushels-per-acre yield was harvested by the power of man and horse.

THE FARM CRASH, 1917–1932

Lean Times

Idaho's servicemen returned to a young state that had experienced two decades of steady growth. The end of WWI, however, ushered in a decade of struggle, especially for Idaho's farm families. While the state experienced a bit of the nation's 1920s boom—particularly in automobile ownership—the twenties served as a harbinger of an economic depression that, by the end of the decade, would confront the entire country. Idaho's 1920s social landscape, moreover, represented a variety of patterns arising from homesteading, immigration, and politics. During a decade characterized elsewhere as roaring, Idahoans were plagued by suffering.

Like ghostly apparitions, these doctors, army officers, and reporters have covered themselves in masks and gowns in preparation for a hospital tour of Spanish influenza patients in 1918. The first outbreak in the state was reported on September 30, 1918, in Canyon County. Although final numbers are not known, many Idaho towns reported as many as 50 percent of their populations lost in the pandemic.

A deadly pandemic, Spanish influenza, accompanied the end of the First World War. The virus infected as many as 28 percent of all Americans; at least 675,000 people in the United States died of it. By contrast, WWI claimed 112,432 lives, and more than half of those deaths were attributable to disease, including flu. Worldwide, 1918's lethal flu strain killed between 20 and 40 million people.

Idaho newspapers reported the arrival of the flu virus in October 1918. Responding to recommendations issued by the U.S. surgeon general, the Idaho State Board of Health prohibited public assemblies. Schools, church gatherings, theater productions, town meetings—even election-year rallies—were shut down to avoid the spread of the flu. City officials in the new sagebrush community of Kimberly, in Idaho's irrigated Magic Valley, prohibited passengers from disembarking at the train station and set up roadblocks to prevent vehicle traffic in and out of the community. Minidoka, Gooding, and Bonneville counties guarded their roads and diverted, often by force, those who attempted to circumvent the blocks. Idaho's hospitals strained to service large numbers of very ill patients, many of them 20–40 years old, the age range most affected by the pandemic. Women's groups that had been busy preparing bandages for the Red Cross now turned to cooking meals, scrubbing floors, and hauling water for families stricken by the disease. Idaho communities continued their quarantine efforts until spring 1919, when the worst of the pandemic had passed. No numbers are available for Idaho, but the disease touched every community, large and small, and claimed family and friends from every corner of the state.

An Economic Scourge

While Idahoans recovered from the world's worst pandemic since the black death of the 14th century, the state's farmers experienced a different kind of scourge, an economic one. Increased production during the war years had created a boom for Idaho's farmers. Many had expanded their operations by borrowing money from local banks to buy new equipment or additional land. Dry farms—those in arid locations without irrigation—had proliferated in southern Idaho and throughout the West in areas previously rejected by homesteaders as too dry for agriculture without irrigation. Dry farming's proponents—particularly Hardy Campbell, whose bestselling 1902 *Soil Culture Manual* became the bible of nonirrigated agriculture—argued that with the proper techniques, water could be gleaned from the soil, and what little rain fell could be preserved. Believing the dictate that "rain followed the plow," homesteaders had staked claims in parched areas such as Cassia County's sagebrush canyons in the Sublett Range, with as little as eight inches of rain per year.

With their parents struck down by the flu, children line up at stations manned by volunteers who have prepared meals for them. The pandemic interrupted the day-to-day lives of Idahoans as schools, churches, theaters, restaurants, and other gathering places were closed.

Farming was a solitary, backbreaking existence for Idaho pioneers in the early 1900s. Here, a woman tills the soil while her husband looks on from the door of their one-room cabin in Homedale, west of Caldwell. Farmers in southern Idaho practiced dry farming, wherein crops were planted only every other year (and sometimes even every three years); in the interim years, the soil was turned to keep in as much moisture as possible in preparation for the next year's crop.

With the war over, European farms became operational again and demand for U.S. agricultural products dropped. At the same time, local banks found themselves in trouble when their farm mortgages suddenly declined in value. The worth of the nation's farm exports plummeted from their wartime peak of $4 billion in 1919 to less than $2 billion in 1922. Idaho's famed potato—one of the state's top cash crops, renowned for quality and yield as early as the 1890s—harvested at $1.51 per bushel in 1919 but could garner only $.31 in 1922. In a desperate effort to promote sales of Idaho potatoes nationwide, local chambers of commerce sent samples across the country and the state incorporated the slogan "Famous Potatoes" on license plates in 1926 (a brief effort that returned in 1948). As prices for farm products plunged, a serious depression gripped the state. Prices for board lumber also dropped, and the state's timber-dependent communities grappled with unemployment.

The farm depression meant that most Idaho residents did not experience the explosion of domestic convenience that those in the urban United States enjoyed during this period. While cities like Chicago, St. Louis, and Denver became electrified and their upper- and middle-class families acquired at least limited running water, many Idahoans remained in rural locations without electricity, indoor plumbing, or the comforts afforded by new appliances like washing machines. In dry-farming wheat communities like Heglar, south of the Snake River in Cassia County, scattered residents hauled water, heated their houses with wood or coal stoves, and shared their limited appliances. Children in rural areas throughout the state rode horses or walked to their community's one-room schoolhouse, while urban dwellers grew accustomed to the convenience of trolley cars and electric commuter trains.

Desperate for relief from unrelenting drought, blowing dust, inadequate prices, and low yields, many dry farmers simply abandoned their homesteads. Some left the state or relocated to Boise, Pocatello, or Twin Falls; others moved onto newly opened irrigation projects. By the end of the 1930s, Heglar had lost its post office, schools, and most of its residents. The families that remained bought up abandoned homesteads for around $5 per acre.

The farm downturn also hurt the state's most vulnerable agrarian population, its new Hispanic migrants. The Mexican Revolution (1910–20) created upheaval in the countryside, driving Mexican citizens north across the U.S. border to seek opportunities in the American West. Migrant laborers found work in Idaho's infant sugar beet industry in the plants Amalgamated Sugar Company built in Rupert, Burley, and Twin Falls during the 1910s. Mexican migrants also worked in the fields, but as farmers struggled, they failed to pay or adequately support such workers. Long hours, low wages, and substandard housing were the norm. Mexican citizens living in Idaho often faced bigotry and fear. In 1920 Burley police shot a Mexican laborer to death, but the action was never justified by the law. While the Mexican consulate in Salt Lake City demanded answers, none was forthcoming, and no charges were ever filed against the police department.

Top: Migrant workers from Mexico, many of whom fled their country during the Mexican Revolution of 1910–20, found work in the state's sugar beet industry and on other farms. Bigotry, low wages, and substandard housing were just a few of the many problems they faced. Bottom: Mexicans were just one group targeted by the Ku Klux Klan. Here, carrying a burning cross and an American flag, Knights of the Ku Klux Klan hold a meeting in the 1920s, at the height of their influence.

The kind of xenophobia that led to anti-Mexican sentiment exhibited itself in Idaho's participation in a national resurgence of the Ku Klux Klan. The organization formerly linked to the Reconstruction era in the American Southeast reemerged during the 1910s. By the 1920s, this second incarnation of the KKK had reached its zenith with more than three million members, many of them from the Pacific Northwest, the American South, and the Midwest. The group opposed Jewish people, African-Americans, Roman Catholics, Mexicans, and nearly anyone or anything that did not represent white, Protestant nativism. Local branches of the KKK, known as klaverns, emerged in Idaho cities with significant Mexican immigrant populations, including Caldwell, Nampa, Twin Falls, Burley, and Pocatello. By the end of the decade, the Klan lost its support in Idaho and elsewhere due to the highly publicized murder trial and conviction of its Grand Dragon, David C. Stephenson. Stephenson, a political leader in Indiana, had taken a young female secretary on a train ride after a bootleg liquor party and repeatedly raped and assaulted her. When the young woman killed herself by swallowing poison, Stephenson went to trial, and then to jail.

Technological Advances

Despite the difficulties of life for migrant laborers and farmers in 1920s Idaho, technological advances slowly changed the rural and urban landscapes of the state. While dry farming communities lost population, the Reclamation Service (known as the Bureau of Reclamation after 1924) breathed new life into Idaho's irrigated

The current American Falls Dam was built between 1974 and 1978. Located downstream from the original, the second incarnation of the dam became necessary when the first one, completed in 1927, deteriorated such that by the 1970s, its capacity had decreased by one-third. The new dam continues the work of the original, providing water for much of southern Idaho's farmlands.

Downtown Pocatello,
seen here in the early
20th century, reflects the
transition from
horse-drawn carriage to
automobile that was
occurring throughout the
country, as both modes
of transportation share
the road. By the 1920s,
Pocatello was offering
an auto stage, which
transported residents
from outlying towns into
the city. Today Pocatello
remains a transportation
hub of eastern Idaho.

settlements along the Snake River. The 1927 completion of American Falls Dam and Reservoir, characterized by noted Idaho historian Leonard J. Arrington as the most important Snake River project in the 20th century, provided water storage and additional late-season water to farmers from Fort Hall to Twin Falls. It took two years and an average of 400 men, working day and night, to build the concrete gravity dam. The 1.7 million acre-foot reservoir also provided water for the opening of the Gooding Division, a 115,000 acre tract on the Minidoka Project. The dam and reservoir posed a problem for American Falls, whose downtown core was situated in what would become the bed of the reservoir. As a result, the Bureau of Reclamation moved the town to its present location. Only a grain elevator and concrete foundations were left beneath the reservoir's waters; these come to light in late summer when water levels drop, revealing the ghostly outline of the old town site.

Thankful for a buoyant respite from the relentless work of the 1920s homestead, farm families from throughout southern Idaho flocked to the American Falls dedication ceremonies. They came on horseback, in horse-drawn wagons, and in new automobiles.

The increasingly widespread availability of the automobile began to transform transportation and communication throughout the rural West. The car would come to define mobility in states character- ized by widely dispersed settlements and rugged terrain. The first automobiles had been far too expen- sive for average Americans, but by the 1920s, Henry Ford's mass-production innovations had put the car within reach of Idaho residents. In 1927 the Idaho legislature passed the Uniform Motor Vehicle Anti- theft Act, which required owners to register their vehicles. In 1928, the first year the law required reg- istration, the Motor Vehicle Bureau issued more than 107,000 titles for automobiles, trucks, and trailers.

The eerie, barren land- scape of Craters of the Moon National Monument (left) is the result of volcanic erup- tions as far back as 15,000 years. The most recent eruption is thought to have occurred approximately 2,100 years ago. Robert W. Limbert (right), a taxider- mist, was also a writer, explorer, and naturalist. His photographs of Craters of the Moon, which appeared in a 1924 issue of *National Geographic* magazine, were instrumental in convincing President Calvin Coolidge to declare the site a national monument.

The accessibility of motor vehicles enabled Idahoans to traverse their state like never before. By the mid-1920s, elongated vehicles called motorbuses, or stages, were operating throughout the state. In eastern Idaho, for example, Ashton residents could catch an elegant auto stage to Pocatello's downtown business and shopping district. Northern Idaho, meanwhile, became a tourist attraction for neighboring states. Excursionists from nearby Spokane, Washington, were among those who employed stages or used their own vehicles to go to Lake Coeur d'Alene's Slide City, a water amusement park, or picnic or camp in the St. Joe and Coeur d'Alene river valleys.

As personal automobile ownership in the state and nation soared, so did interest in scenic excursions and the preservation of open space. Idaho's chambers of commerce, descendants of the early community clubs, embraced the idea of tourism and lobbied for federal and state recognition of their areas' unique natural attractions. Business leaders in Arco, a desert commu- nity in the southeastern portion of the state, looked with fresh eyes on a neighboring expanse of stark lava flows known as Devil's Playground. Explorer Robert Limbert completed a 17-day, 80-mile survey of the area in 1920, photographing the landscape and naming features, including Yellowjacket Water Hole and Bridge of Tears. Limbert returned to the region in 1921 with geologists and local leaders and argued for its preservation. Limbert's prediction that it would "some day attract tourists from all America, for its lava flows are as interesting as those of Vesuvius, Mauna Loa, or Kilauea" convinced Arco leaders to change the name to Craters of the Moon and lobby for national monument status. The proposal met with little resistance locally, since ranchers and farmers alike avoided the seemingly barren lava beds. Limbert's crusade caught the attention of the White House when *National Geographic* magazine featured the explorer's stunning photos in a 1924 article. Within months, President Calvin Coolidge set aside an 83 square-mile area for the Craters of the Moon National Monument. In 1929 the new monument hosted 220 visitors in 58 vehicles. Today the site welcomes nearly 200,000 visitors annually.

Shifting Sentiment

Idaho politics during the 1920s reflected the nation's shift from an era of Progressive reform to a period of conservatism characterized by a focus on foreign affairs and American economic opportunity abroad. Idaho's incumbent Republicans enjoyed repetitious ascendancy. Senator William Borah, first elected in 1907, represented Idaho continuously until his death in 1940. Moscow's Burton French, who had served in the U.S. House of Representatives between 1903 and 1915, successfully sought reelection in 1916. His second tenure in the House lasted until 1933.

As chair of the Senate's Committee on Foreign Relations between 1924 and 1933, Borah gave Idaho a high profile in international affairs by becoming, in some countries, "the most famous living American." In foreign affairs, Borah advocated diplomatic recognition of the Soviet Union, a controversial measure that did not reach fruition until 1933. At home Borah dissented from the national Republican Party to champion measures aimed at providing aid to the nation's ailing farm economy.

Top: William E. Borah, fourth from right, presides over a meeting of the Senate Foreign Relations Committee in 1933. Borah, who chaired the committee from 1924 through 1933, became known in many countries as "the most famous living American" for his work in international relations. Bottom: Senator Borah attends the Republican National Convention in Chicago in 1912. Borah served in the Idaho House from 1907 until his death in 1940.

Idaho's 1920s governors reflected the state's economic struggles. Republican Charles C. Moore, presented by his supporters as a true "dirt farmer," came to the governor's office in 1923 and served two terms. Moore's legendary thriftiness—he used up his predecessor's stationery before he ordered his own and vetoed a bill to build a governor's mansion—and his support of low freight rates, high tariff duties, and new irrigation projects made him popular with the state's agrarian interests.

Despite the efforts of Borah, Moore, and others to assist farmers, the agriculture industry remained mired in debt and struggle. Then in 1929, the stock market crashed, setting off bank failures, unemployment, and foreclosures in a nationwide domino effect. Idaho's farmers had not prospered during the 1920s; now industrial segments, including mines, faltered as well. The Great Depression, coupled with a severe drought in the early 1930s, convinced many Idahoans to change their political allegiance. In the 1930 election, they chose former Pocatello mayor Charles Benjamin Ross as the governor, the first Democrat to hold that office since WWI. Idahoans began the 1930s—a decade that promised more hardship—with a commitment to reform and a hope for relief.

Annie Pike Greenwood

When Annie Pike Greenwood's husband, Charley, announced his dream to move to Idaho and farm, she "almost went on a hunger-strike, through horror." Charles Greenwood had fallen under the spell of booster literature about new Carey Act communities in Idaho. The couple enjoyed a comfortable life in Kansas, where Greenwood drew a good salary from the local sugar beet factory, "but Charley brought home a certain magazine published for city farmers, who love to make fortunes on the imaginary acres in their heads." Produced by the Oregon Short Line Railroad or local commercial clubs, such publications represented the Snake River Plain as a Garden of Eden, where man's command of the rivers meant farmers never had to concern themselves with vagaries of weather. Annie remained unconvinced by the boosters, but, despite this being an era in which women achieved greater rights than ever before—including universal suffrage with the 19th Amendment in 1920—she believed that she had no choice but to accompany her husband. Charles Greenwood's desire for a farm life, regardless of his apparent job stability, typified the attraction of irrigated settlement for middle-class, educated individuals: independence from the endless monotony of wage labor.

We Sagebrush Folks, Annie Pike Greenwood's lyrical memoir of her family's experience on a homestead near Hazelton, made it clear that 20th-century irrigated homesteading was no panacea. First published in 1934, the book detailed the difficulties of waiting for irrigation projects to deliver water, shivering in tar-paper shacks poorly insulated against southern Idaho's harsh winter winds, and fearing the very real possibility of losing a child in the project's myriad of swift-running canals. Yet Greenwood embraced the homesteading life and fell in love with the Idaho landscape, where she could view "a million stars in the dark-blue sky—a million stars, seen at a breath." Annie Pike Greenwood opened the only school in the region and actively participated in political campaigns. Her one-room schoolhouse still stands, just off of Interstate 84 between Paul and Twin Falls.

The Greenwoods lost their farm, despite the advantages of class and education they enjoyed. Annie's account of their struggle gave voice to countless others who did not possess the privileges or the literacy of the Greenwoods, and whose failures remain lost to history.

Children on an Oneida County farm in May 1936 manage a smile, but the submarginal land they stand on tells the real story. Drought and the Great Depression combined to desecrate agriculture in Idaho, bringing average annual farm income down by more than 36 percent. Nearly half the state's population made a living farming, but with a $22.4 million crop loss early in the decade, unemployment and foreclosures became the norm.

The World Rushes In

Mining companies in Idaho's Silver Valley had successfully combated workers' attempts to form effective unions since the Coeur d'Alene mining wars of the 1890s. The onset of the Great Depression and President Franklin D. Roosevelt's New Deal programs provided catalysts for change, and workers flocked to sign union cards. When asked to explain this action, one worker proclaimed that he only wanted "to help the president in his recovery program."

4

The shell of a car on the barren Snake River Plain stands as a testament to the difficulties the nation experienced during the thirties. Dust Bowl refugees from the Great Plains continued to pack up their cars and pour into Idaho hoping for a better life, but by March 1937, wind erosion had transformed even this once-luxuriant bunchgrass country to nothing more than a dusty desert.

This perceived personal connection to official Washington, D.C., represented a sea change in attitudes in the state. During Idaho's early history, the state had been a crossroads for people and ideas, and residents were wary of federal interference. But 1932–45, the years of the twin crises of depression and war, marked a literal onslaught of federal initiatives and involvement in the state. Idaho, like the rest of the West, was transformed from a hinterland to a focal point of the nation's capital, and the attention was welcomed.

Idaho may have been the hardest hit of the Pacific Northwest states during the Great Depression. By 1932 a bushel of potatoes sold for 10–25 cents, down from a high of $1.51 in 1919. Average annual farm income in 1932 was $250, down from $686 in 1929—the continuation of a downturn in agricultural income that had plagued the state since World War I. The Snake River Plain, along with other parts of the country, experienced a drought in the early 1930s; 1934 was the driest year in southern Idaho since record-keeping began in 1909. The water supply was down by about 50 percent, resulting in an estimated $22.4 million in crop loss during the first years of the decade. About half of Idaho's residents depended on agriculture for their livelihood.

Other sectors of the economy also suffered. Demand for Idaho's lumber products became practically nonexistent, since few people could afford to build houses. Between 1929 and 1933, silver fell from $1.39 to 24 cents an ounce, the lowest price in state history. Total metal production dropped from $32 million to less than $10 million. Thirty-eight of Idaho's 106 banks closed. In 1931 arsonists set fire to Idaho's forests so they could seek employment as firefighters. Governor C. Ben Ross responded by declaring martial law and bringing in the National Guard to protect the forestlands. By winter 1932–33, more than 20,000 Idahoans were unemployed, and banks had foreclosed on more than 1,000 mortgages in the state. Still Dust Bowl refugees came from the Midwest seeking a better life. Idaho's population actually increased during the 1930s, resulting in even more demand for relief programs.

Two years after Democratic governor Ross was elected in 1930, James P. Pope became the first Democratic U.S. senator from Idaho in 14 years, and Democrat Franklin D. Roosevelt carried every Idaho county except Bear Lake to defeat incumbent president Herbert Hoover. In 1928, when Hoover had received 64 percent of the popular vote, only

Top: Firefighters line up for food as fire rages through Selway Falls, in northern Idaho's Kaniksu National Forest, in 1934. Young men like these, part of FDR's Civilian Conservation Corps, not only fought fires but built infrastructure and conserved forests.
Bottom: Governor C. Ben Ross, Idaho's first Democratic governor since World War I, was swept into office in 1930 as voters demanded relief and reform.

President Franklin D. Roosevelt, shown during a radio broadcast in November 1938, precipitated a sea change in Idahoans' attitudes toward the federal government. His New Deal economic recovery programs brought hundreds of millions of dollars to the state, stabilized commodity prices, and put people to work. Idaho ranked fifth in the nation in per capita New Deal expenditures.

Freemont County had failed to support him. In 1936 Idahoans continued their long history of political unpredictability and willingness to cross party lines. When Ross challenged William E. Borah for his seat in the U.S. Senate, he received only 74,444 votes to Borah's 128,723. In the presidential contest that year, Franklin Roosevelt defeated Republican Alf Landon 125,683 to 66,232 among Idaho voters.

Government Intervention

Roosevelt's New Deal economic recovery programs significantly altered the relationship between Idaho and the federal government. In 1933 the state paid Washington $904,000 in internal revenue taxes and received $39.9 million in relief. From 1933 to 1939, Idaho ranked fifth in the nation in per capita New Deal expenditures.

Not surprisingly, agricultural programs were the most prominent New Deal initiatives in Idaho. As part of the effort to stabilize commodity prices, the Agricultural Adjustment Administration (AAA) made payments to farmers who were willing to reduce the number of acres they planted. The Farm Security Administration loaned $76 million to nearly 20,000 Idaho residents to help save their farms from foreclosure. The passage of the Taylor Grazing Act in 1934 assured western cattle operators a system of allotment of federal grazing land. Approximately 80 million acres of public land were set aside for cattle and sheep grazing, and the secretary of the interior issued 10-year permits for use of the land at low fees. Idaho sheep and cattle ranchers applauded the act and continue, even today, to rely on federal grazing land.

Senators Borah, Burton K. Wheeler of Montana, and Key Pitman of Nevada were vocal advocates for silver miners and instrumental in convincing the U.S. Senate to act on their behalf. The Silver Purchase Act of 1934 required the Treasury Department to purchase silver until it either reached a price of $1.29 an ounce or accounted for one fourth of the federal monetary reserve. The act was, in actuality, a subsidy for the western mining industry, and as such, provided a tremendous boost to Idaho metal production, particularly in the Coeur d'Alenes.

Top: Cattle graze on public land near Payette National Forest. As part of the 1934 Taylor Grazing Act, ranchers in the state were given access to nearly 12 million acres. Bottom: Farmers are about to take a load of logs to a cooperative mill they opened in Ola with the help of a Farm Security Administration loan. By October 1939, when this photo was taken, the plight of farmers had improved dramatically.

New Deal programs paid for construction of courthouses, post offices, and roads; facilitated rural electrification (only 30 percent of Idaho farms had electricity in 1936, but by the early 1950s that number was close to 97 percent); and put people to work in numerous other ways. When the Federal Writers' Project hired unemployed authors to prepare state guidebooks, Vardis Fisher took on the task. His 1937 *Idaho: A Guide in Word and Picture* was the first of the state guides to be completed; it set a standard for all the others and remains an important source of information on the state. The Civilian Conservation Corps (CCC) was responsible for many improvements to Idaho forestlands. Works Progress Administration (WPA) and Public Works Administration (PWA) projects funded the construction of 25 airports, 78 schools, and more than 100 public buildings in the state.

Idahoans, however, were not always willing to embrace New Deal efforts at greater federal control. One example occurred in 1935, when Senator Pope helped sponsor a bill to create a comprehensive Columbia Valley Authority (CVA). Modeled after the Tennessee Valley Authority, the new federal agency would oversee the management of all water in the Columbia and Snake river systems. Idaho Power Company and other private utility companies successfully fought this measure, as well as the establishment of public utility districts in Idaho. The majority of Idahoans favored private power over public, a reflection of long-held fears of government control.

Top: In the late 1930s, the new Boundary County Courthouse, a product of the Work Projects Administration, rose next to the old one in Bonners Ferry. Its builders earned an average $41.57 a month. Bottom: A couple discusses employment possibilities with an Idaho representative at the Farm Security Administration migratory labor camp mobile unit in Wilder in 1941.

President Roosevelt's 1933 National Industrial Recovery Act (NIRA), which gave workers the right to collective bargaining through representatives of their own choosing, motivated Idahoans to renew their efforts to organize labor unions. The Committee for Industrial Organization (CIO; later renamed the Congress for Industrial Organization)—a splinter group of the American Federation of Labor (AFL)—actively recruited new members, especially among Silver Valley miners. In Pocatello, a union stronghold, the Central Labor Union frequently supported the CIO in its battles against the more traditional AFL.

Workers' attempts to voice their demands sometimes met with resistance, as in April 1934, when workers at the Sunshine mine near Kellogg demanded a $1.50 per day raise. Mine operators appealed to Governor Ross to intervene, as the state had in the 1890s, but he refused. Sunshine miners eventually won their wage increase, the first unambiguous union victory in Shoshone County since the 1890s. In another incident, however, in August 1935, the workers did not prevail. As many as 2,000 Mexicans who were employed in a pea harvest near Driggs, in Teton County, demanded a pay increase, and when they did not receive it they went on strike. Violence erupted, and local authorities called on Governor Ross for assistance. This time the governor did intervene, declaring martial law and sending the Idaho National Guard to restore order. Brigadier General M. C. McConnel, adjutant general of the guard, oversaw the arrest of about 150 Mexicans, who were escorted to the county line and told not to come back. The next day, the remaining workers returned to the fields.

FDR's National Industrial Recovery Act empowered workers such as these Mexican-American laborers, harvesting peas in Nampa in 1941, to fight for their rights through collective bargaining. The process was not always well received, however; in 1935 when pea pickers in Driggs demanded a pay raise, violence erupted, and Governor Ross declared martial law.

Business Visionaries

The 1930s are most often associated with economic downturn, but there are notable exceptions. Harry Morrison, an Illinois farm boy, and Morris Hans Knudsen, a Danish immigrant, had formed their own construction firm, the Morrison-Knudsen Company (M-K), in Boise in 1912. M-K was one of six companies commissioned in 1931 to build Boulder Dam (now Hoover Dam), which was completed on the lower Colorado River in 1935, and numerous other PWA–financed projects. Between 1933 and 1940, M-K built 20 major dams and hydroelectric works. Operating today as Washington Group International, the company has become a global leader in engineering and construction.

Joe Albertson also challenged the economic hard times of the 1930s when he opened his first grocery store on State Street in Boise in summer 1939. From its beginnings, Albertson's offered the size and variety now familiar to modern shoppers, with free parking and multiple departments under one roof.

Inroads were made in the hospitality industry, as well. Under the direction of chairman of the board W. Averell Harriman, the Union Pacific Railroad purchased a 3,888-acre ranch near the former mining town of Ketchum and constructed a 220-room lodge there. Opening on New Year's Eve 1936, the lodge marked the beginning of Sun Valley's development as a top resort destination. The area featured the world's first chair lift, a swimming pool, and an ice rink. In the years that followed, tourism became an increasingly significant part of Idaho's economic profile.

A few Idaho entrepreneurs thrived despite the dark days of the 1930s. Top: Harry Morrison, at the site of Hoover Dam with his wife, Ann, would form Morrison-Knudsen Construction Company and build 20 dams and hydroelectric projects by 1940. Bottom: Employees of mail-order religion Psychiana helped Frank Bruce Robinson become Latah County's largest employer.

Another successful depression-era venture was that of Frank Bruce Robinson, a Moscow (Idaho) druggist who had come to the United States from England via Canada. His search for spiritual fulfillment and religious truth led him to form Psychiana, a philosophy he spread through advertising. Psychiana became the world's largest mail-order religion, and the founder's company became Latah County's largest private employer. Robinson wrote 20 books, and his employees, numbering as many as 100, processed approximately 50,000 pieces of mail each day.

Sun Valley opened near Ketchum in 1936 as the nation's first "fabulous" winter resort, courtesy of geniuses including Averell Harriman—who, as the Union Pacific Railroad chairman, dreamed of bringing trainloads of people to a dream vacation spot—and publicist Steve Hannagan, credited with creating Miami Beach's image. Sun Valley paved the way for a new era in Idaho tourism.

Both pages: Although Lake Pend Oreille lies more than 300 miles from the nearest seaport, its broad waters and safety from coastal attack made it an ideal place to train sailors during World War II. The Farragut Naval Training Station, whose five camps made it the state's largest city during the war, processed some 300,000 men between April 1942 and June 1946.

Pressures of War

Idahoans were as shocked as other Americans when Japanese forces launched a surprise attack on Pearl Harbor on December 7, 1941. While World War II meant dislocation for families and the loss of loved ones (1,784 Idahoans were killed while serving in the armed forces), it also inaugurated a period of prosperity for the state. The U.S. Department of Defense hired Morrison-Knudsen to construct airfields and roads in the Pacific theater, while industries in the state produced raw materials that were essential to the war effort—particularly timber products, metal, and various foodstuffs.

More than 60,000 Idaho residents served in various branches of the armed forces during World War II. Over 1,000 Morrison-Knudsen employees were captured when the Japanese occupied Wake Island, Guam, and Midway, and many remained prisoners there until 1945.

Idaho served as training ground for many thousands of American soldiers. Gowen Field, an air base in Boise constructed in 1941, was used as a major base for B-24 bombers. Named for Lieutenant Paul Gowen of Caldwell, who died in an air crash while on duty in Panama in 1938, Gowen Field was a final training center for units assigned to both the European and Pacific theaters. Air bases were also built in

Pocatello to train fighter pilots and in Mountain Home to train bomber crews. The Pocatello Naval Ordnance Plant, which featured a huge lathe and a 150-ton-capacity crane to accommodate guns with up to 18-inch barrels, was built in Pocatello in an effort to have a facility away from the West Coast, yet close to major transportation routes. Farragut Naval Training Station, on Lake Pend Oreille, was the largest inland naval base in the world. Built to train 30,000 troops at one time, it became the largest "city" in Idaho, eventually containing 800 buildings. In 1942–43, Farragut trained 293,381 sailors. The federal government spent $64 million on the base.

Idaho industries also responded to the wartime emergency. J. R. "Jack" Simplot, who by 1942 was the state's largest shipper of potatoes and onions, had a small dehydration operation at Caldwell. After the invasion of Pearl Harbor he expanded it, and he soon became the armed forces' largest supplier of dehydrated potatoes. His dehydration method reduced 100 pounds of potatoes to 15, facilitating shipment overseas. Between 1942 and 1945, Simplot shipped more than 33 million pounds of dried potatoes for the government each year. The Boise company today is one of the world's top processors of frozen potatoes.

This page: Lt. Col. Leo Leeburn inspects female air personnel at Gowen Field near Boise in May 1943. Opposite page: J. R. Simplot turned his Caldwell potato dryer into a gold mine, preparing millions of pounds of dehydrated potatoes for the U.S. military during the 1940s. His company today is the primary supplier of frozen french fries for McDonald's, Burger King, and other fast-food chains.

In February 1942, President Franklin D. Roosevelt issued an executive order calling for the evacuation of approximately 120,000 West Coast Japanese. Idaho governor Chase Clark was a vocal advocate of internment. The Minidoka Relocation Center in Hunt, just northeast of Twin Falls, was one of 10 such centers the federal government built that year. (Morrison-Knudsen received the Minidoka construction contract.) Nearly 10,000 Japanese, primarily from Oregon and Washington, were incarcerated at the camp, which stretched over 68,000 acres of desert land. Most of the internees were second- and third-generation Japanese-Americans and, therefore, were American citizens. Some volunteered to work on Idaho farms during the war. More than 800 eventually served in the armed forces, many in the segregated Japanese-American 442nd Combat Battalion. Ironically, the 1,200 Japanese who resided in Idaho in 1941 were not subject to relocation.

In addition to the Minidoka Relocation Center, Idaho had a relocation camp at Kooskia, a prisoner-of-war camp at Farragut (with branches throughout the state), and a camp for conscientious objectors at Downey. The U.S. government has since apologized for this wholesale attack upon citizens of one race, and in 1988 Congress allocated $20,000 reparation for each survivor of the camps.

This page: West Coast
Japanese-Americans
pose in front of barracks
at the Minidoka
Relocation Center in
1943. Opposite page:
Civilian Conservation
Corps (CCC) firefighters
head out to a blaze in
Kaniksu National Forest
in August 1934. The CCC
also built bridges,
drained swamps, planted
trees, and laid 3,000
miles of telephone lines
in the state.

Since many Idahoans found lucrative employment in war-related production plants on the West Coast and elsewhere, and thousands more joined the military, farmers in the state faced a severe labor shortage. They recruited migrant workers from Mexico through the bracero program, in which Mexican farm workers were permitted to enter the country but were obligated to return after six months of work.

By 1947 at least 15,600 Mexican-Americans had become part of the Idaho workforce. On farms, they often experienced discrimination and exploitation. The demand for labor, however, opened more jobs to them. As railroaders in Pocatello, they enjoyed more opportunities and higher-paying jobs than farm workers. The same was true of Mexican-Americans employed in Silver Valley mines and smelters.

The war also brought women into the workforce. They held jobs in almost every industry in Idaho, standing in for men in small businesses, on farms, and in many other capacities. They organized the Red Cross and other relief efforts, as well.

As the war ended, members of the armed forces and thousands of erstwhile war-industries workers returned home, where they found an Idaho that was vastly different from the one they had left. The war succeeded in doing what the New Deal had been unable to: return prosperity to Idaho. Wartime labor shortages had resulted in a more diverse labor force; the state boasted significant manufacturing concerns; and the traditional economic base—the agriculture, timber, and mining industries—had experienced tremendous growth. The federal government now played a role in nearly every aspect of the Idaho economy. The depression and war had irrevocably changed the landscape.

The Civilian Conservation Corps in Idaho

Probably none of President Franklin D. Roosevelt's New Deal programs enjoyed the level of popularity that the Civilian Conservation Corps (CCC) did. Established April 5, 1933, the CCC was designed to aid unemployed young men, particularly those from urban areas, and at the same time, conserve the nation's forests and other outdoor resources. Males between the ages of 18 and 25 who were admitted to the corps by the Department of Labor received $30 per month (of which $25 went to their families) plus room and board and medical care. Nationwide more than 2.75 million men found jobs in the CCC.

By 1935 there were 82 CCC camps in Idaho—more than in any other state except California. Most of the enrollees were not Idaho natives but came from New York, New England, Pennsylvania, New Jersey, Kentucky, Tennessee, and the Midwest. Although most of the camps were south of the Salmon River, the CCC was noteworthy for its efforts in the north, where it battled blister rust—a fungus that threatened to wipe out Idaho's famous white-pine forests. The corps controlled the disease and saved 700,000 acres.

A separate corps for Indians living on reservations was also started in 1933. It employed about 1,000 Idaho Indians until it ended in 1942.

CCC members in Idaho fought fires, planted millions of trees, installed telephone lines, and built lookout towers, houses, roads, bridges, and even thousands of picnic tables, benches, fireplaces, and shelters in the state's forests. During the FDR years, the U.S. Forest Service spent $57 million on the CCC in Idaho, more than it had in any other state. Few places exist in the woods where the results are not still evident. The state received the benefit of the corps, but at the same time, thousands of young men from other parts of the country were able to experience life in Idaho.

Forging nuclear energy technology has been the mission of the Idaho National Laboratory for half a century. Its Materials Test Reactor (seen here) operated from 1952 to 1970 and provided crucial data that has been used to design every reactor in America since. The laboratory is now home to the largest test reactor in the world, where researchers are able to simulate years of radiation exposure in order to study how materials perform.

Idaho on the National Stage

On December 20, 1951, in the desert 40 miles west of Idaho Falls, scientists from Chicago-based Argonne National Laboratory set a global precedent by producing electricity from a nuclear reaction. A few years later, on July 17, 1955, the town of Arco became the first community in the world electrified by nuclear power when 12 light bulbs burned for two hours. These were two of the many accomplishments in nuclear engineering pioneered by scientists at the federal government's National Reactor Testing Station.

This page: In 1955 Arco made history when it became the first city to be lit by nuclear power. With the Idaho National Laboratory nearby, nuclear energy continues to play an important role in the community, now in the form of job opportunities. Opposite page: The Food Machinery and Chemical Corporation (FMC)'s phosphorus plant in Pocatello was the country's largest for 52 years. FMC dismantled the plant in 2001.

The Atomic Energy Commission established the "site"—as the testing station would become known to local communities— in 1949 to test nuclear reactors and contribute scientific research to American efforts in the global Cold War with the Soviet Union. The federal government chose eastern Idaho because of its geographic isolation in case of a nuclear accident, as well as the fact that cities in the area could absorb the many thousands of new residents expected to come to work at the facilities. Over the next several decades, more than 50 reactors were built at the site, which had previously served as a World War II testing ground for weapons built at Pocatello's Naval Ordnance Plant. Idahoans participated in the Cold War through developments at the National Reactor Testing Station and in many other ways. In turn, the global conflict deeply shaped the state during the decades following World War II.

The National Reactor Testing Station, which after a series of name changes became the Idaho National Laboratory in 2005, was one of the most significant large-scale industrial developments in the state. To this day, it has employed tens of thousands of Idahoans. Historically, the site reflects the trends in Idaho during the last half of the 20th century: a growing manufacturing economy, the increasing presence of the federal government, the state's prickly and contradictory relations with the federal authorities, and a rising concern about the environmental costs of development.

Boom Times

In the heady days after World War II, Idaho shared in the nation's prosperity. After several decades of stagnant or declining population, the state saw an influx of immigrants, mostly to urban areas. Statewide, the population grew more than 12 percent per decade from 1940 to 1960. Although the 1960s saw a smaller gain, during the 1970s the population grew by 32 percent to a total of nearly one million people. New manufacturing companies arose in a wider variety of industries, while established businesses expanded.

On the northern edge of Pocatello, the J. R. Simplot Company created a factory in 1944 to manufacture fertilizer and other chemicals, part of its expansion into a large, integrated corporation. In 1949 the Food Machinery and Chemical Corporation (FMC) set up an elemental phosphorus processing plant adjacent to the Simplot enterprise that became the largest facility of its kind in the world. Postwar growth continued in Pocatello as FMC and other companies recruited workers from distant states. As a result of this general growth trend, the two-year southern branch of the University of Idaho became the independent, four-year Idaho State College in 1947 (today's Idaho State University).

Simplot's presence in Pocatello was one sign of the company's growing corporate empire. Jack Simplot used his entrepreneurial talents and the opportunities federal wartime contracts presented to build Idaho's largest company as of the 1950s. After developing new techniques for processing frozen french fries and dehydrated potatoes, Simplot became the main supplier of fries to McDonald's, one of postwar America's cultural icons.

As a nationwide construction boom fueled the demand for timber, the lumber industry in Idaho grew. The Lewiston-based Potlatch Lumber Company had survived decades of inconsistent profits since its founding in 1903, and this continued after its merger with four other Idaho firms into Potlatch Forests in 1931. Yet in the 1950s, the company experienced an era of unprecedented growth and diversification. Farther south, the Boise Payette Lumber Company merged with the Washington-based Cascade Lumber Company in 1957 to form Boise Cascade Corporation, the state's largest timber products company in the post–World War II era.

The U.S. Forest Service, a federal agency that faced heavy criticism in Idaho for its perceived domineering presence and obstruction to private development when it was founded to manage the country's national forests in 1905, transformed itself after World War II to become the dominant supplier of timber. As the largest land manager in Idaho, the Forest Service fueled much of the state's timber economy by building roads and selling cutting rights to public timber. To many Idahoans, federal foresters now stood as icons of efficient management and development of natural resources. Although instability continued to plague the lumber industry, expanding federal support and corporate diversification allowed timber to remain an important part of Idaho's economy.

The mining industry also experienced a time of growth and diversification, though one not without its challenges. The powerful Bunker Hill and Sullivan Mining Company, which had dominated the silver and lead mining operations in the Coeur d'Alene region since 1887, greatly expanded all aspects of its operations after the war and developed a new sulfuric acid plant capable of producing 250 tons per day. For a number of years in the 1950s, it sold most of its acid product to Simplot's fertilizer plant in Pocatello. The company worked during these years to reduce the clout of the local labor union, which had represented Idaho's silver miners since its foundation as part of the Western Federation of Miners in 1893. Bunker Hill divested itself of company housing in Kellogg, a cost-saving measure also practiced by Potlatch Forests, which gradually sold its company town, Potlatch. The town became independent in 1952, though the lumber mill remained the major employer.

Throughout the years of growth from World War II to the late 1970s, the federal government increased its role in Idaho's economy and politics. Federal agencies like the Forest Service and the Bureau of Land Management controlled the majority of land in the state.

Federal influence has been a dominant theme in Idaho history—from the Lewis and Clark expedition to the establishment of Idaho's awkward borders to negotiations with the state's Indian tribes to construction of the irrigation infrastructure in the Snake River Plain. After the war, however, the scale of federal influence and dollars rose sharply. Following decades of work regulating grazing lands, the Forest Service began focusing on

This page: A flurry of timber harvesting after World War II radically changed the composition of Idaho's forests. Between 1952 and 1987, 44 percent of the state's ponderosa pines, once the most common tree in Idaho, were logged or burned for fire suppression. Opposite page: The Bunker Hill mine in Kellogg, nicknamed "Uncle Bunker" by miners, was one of the most important mines in the Silver Valley until it closed in 1981.

This page: When it was
completed in 1950,
Anderson Ranch Dam
was the highest earth-
filled dam in the world.
Opposite page, top: Pull-
offs along the Payette
River Scenic Byway
bring motorists like this
one in 1966 closer to
the river's wild habitat.
Bottom: Sun Valley's
exquisite scenery has
attracted politicians,
royalty, and Hollywood
stars since it opened
in 1936. Shown is the
Kennedy family vacation-
ing at the resort in 1966.

expanding the sale of Idaho timber. The Bureau of Reclamation continued its large-scale expansion of infrastructure in south-ern Idaho. It built storage dams on the south fork of the Boise River at Anderson Ranch—the earth-filled dam was the largest of its kind in the world when it opened in 1950—and on the south fork of the Snake River at Palisades in 1957. The Army Corps of Engineers engaged in massive flood-control projects, completing Lucky Peak Dam on the Boise River in 1954 and Dworshak Dam—the highest concrete dam of its type in the Western Hemisphere—on the north fork of the Clearwater River near Orofino in 1972.

Although the federal government had been building roads through Idaho since 1857, when Frederick West Lander completed Lander Road between South Pass in Wyoming and City of Rocks in southern Idaho, federal transportation dollars had their biggest impact after World War II. As part of the broader defense strategies of the Cold War, the interstate highway system—first approved by Congress in 1956—greatly improved connections between Idaho's major cities.

Competing Visions

Although the natural resource industries of timber, mining, and agriculture remained important to the state's economy, tourism and outdoor recreation were growing in popularity. They rose to offer a competing vision of Idaho's landscape, one that placed aesthetic beauty and recreation on a par with resource extraction. The collision between the two would increasingly dominate political debates in Idaho after 1950.

Idaho's spectacular scenery became a magnet for tourists, and the state's skiing industry came of age during this time. Sun Valley Resort, which the Union Pacific Railroad had developed as a hideaway for the rich and famous during the depths of the Great Depression, was sold in 1968 to Bill Janss, who remodeled it into a family facility and greatly expanded the skiing capacity on Baldy Mountain.

Sun Valley has often taken the spotlight in the Idaho recreation industry, but dozens of other ski areas arose in the decades from World War II through the 1970s. One was the town of McCall, along the shores of Payette Lake. Long a mountain retreat for Boise residents, in the 1950s its offered only the Little Ski Hill for winter recreation. At the instigation and financial backing of one of Boise's most prominent residents, Jack Simplot, local ski instructor Corey Engen designed a larger skiing facility on Brundage Mountain. The resort opened for business in fall 1961, with Governor Robert Smylie in attendance to help dedicate the new facility.

The Selkirk Mountains, long a source of trees and furs for north Idaho, followed a similar course, becoming the site of a resort in 1963. Two Spokane, Washington, residents—Jack Fowler, a dentist, and Grant Groesbech, an architect—joined Jim Brown, a skier and investor from Sandpoint, to develop Schweitzer Mountain resort on the Selkirk peaks overlooking Lake Pend Oreille. Although Brown and other locals had skied these mountains for several decades, that year Schweitzer Mountain opened as a commercial venture with a lodge and chairlift.

The development of most of the ski areas scattered throughout the state reflected the growth of both Idaho and its tourist economy in these decades. Because these resorts generally leased their property from the Forest Service, they also reflected the increasing role played by the federal government.

The rapid growth in recreational use of public land was a year-round phenomenon that affected all parts of the state. Growing prosperity, the general population shift to cities, rising automobile ownership, and the expansion of roads all contributed to increasing the participation in outdoor recreation.

The Forest Service responded by developing campgrounds and other facilities throughout the state. The agency optimistically felt it could dramatically boost both its timber harvesting and recreation programs. By the 1960s, the Forest Service had deeply alienated state and national conservationists, who felt that logging had been given excessive priority over recreational tourism, aesthetic enjoyment, and the health of the land. Senator Frank Church used his frustration against "the concentration of power" in the Forest Service to help lead congressional approval of the Wilderness Act of 1964, which ended the agency's absolute control over boundary decisions and opened the issue of establishing protected wilderness areas to public debate. Idaho, with more undeveloped public land than any other state outside of Alaska, was center stage for the national conflicts between resource extraction and preservation.

Much of the Idaho landscape today is a product of those debates. The proliferation of logging roads in central and northern Idaho and large, open-pit phosphate mines in the southeast demonstrate the continued clout of resource extraction interests. The rapid expansion of the state park system, led by Governor Smylie in the 1960s, creation of the Sawtooth National Recreation Area in 1972, and the federal designation of four million acres of wilderness areas in Idaho by 1980 demonstrate the growing support for recreation and preservation.

In Hells Canyon, debates in the 1950s pitted those who felt that Idaho Power Company should be able to develop a series of private hydroelectric dams against supporters of a federal initiative to build a single, high dam to service

This page: Generations of Idahoans, including these young campers in 1955, have enjoyed the vast wilderness of the Boise National Forest, which was created in 1908. Opposite page: The White Cloud Mountains were the focus of a fierce conservation battle between 1968 and 1972, after an open-pit molybdenum mine was proposed at Castle Peak, pictured here in 1960. Governor Cecil Andrus and Senator Frank Church were integral to saving the mountain from mining.

This page: Largely due to the efforts of Senator Frank Church, Hell's Canyon, North America's deepest river gorge, became part of a National Recreation Area in 1975. Opposite page, top: The first Democratic Senator to be elected to two consecutive terms in Idaho, Church worked tirelessly to preserve the state's wild lands. Bottom: Len Jordan, who served both as Idaho governor and as a state senator, played a role in creating the Sawtooth National Recreation Area in 1972.

regional needs for electricity and flood control. The traditional split between advocates of private power and those of public power grew more complex when Idaho conservationists and the U.S. Supreme Court suggested that the Snake River and the canyon should be protected from any development. Additional concerns were aroused by the Oxbow Incident in fall 1958, when some 11,000 returning salmon in Hells Canyon died due to the failure of attempts to transport them around the Oxbow Dam, then under construction. The economic and ecological devastation at Oxbow led many to question the costs of dams. The final result of the conflict was a series of three dams, including Oxbow, owned by Idaho Power in the upper canyon, and the creation of the Hells Canyon Wilderness Area in the central core of the nation's deepest gorge. Senator Church, who supported a federal dam when he was first elected in 1956—in part to supply power for phosphate mining in southeast Idaho—switched his position over the decades to increasingly support environmental concerns.

Senator Church's evolution on the questions of how to manage Idaho's backcountry lands and his corresponding long-term political success as a Democratic senator for 24 years in a Republican-dominated state demonstrate that Idaho voters continued to cross party lines to elect individuals based on policy and character.

Maverick Statesmen

A variety of maverick personalities characterized Idaho politics in the postwar years. Len Jordan was one of them. A Grangeville businessman and former sheep rancher in Hells Canyon, Jordan was elected to the Idaho Legislature in 1946 as a Republican representing Democratic-dominated Idaho County. He became governor in 1951 and stood against the growing influence of federal policies and the national "rush to collectivism." Jordan served one term as governor and later was appointed to the U.S. Senate after the death of Henry Dworshak in 1962. Grace Edgington Jordan, a prolific writer and professor at Boise Junior College while her husband served as governor, chronicled his senatorial career in the 1972 book *The Unintentional Senator.* Jordan served 11 years in the Senate, where in 1968 he proposed a moratorium on dam construction in Hells Canyon, a step that eventually placed his family's former home into a national recreation area managed by the Forest Service. He also helped create the Sawtooth National Recreation Area in 1972.

In contrast to Len Jordan, Glen Taylor, the "singing cowboy," represented the other side of the state's ambivalent relationship with the federal government. Taylor, a Democrat elected to the U.S. Senate in 1944, supported a wide range of federal development projects, including the National Reactor Testing Station, new irrigation dams such as Palisades, and the controversial Columbia Valley Authority. Although the CVA never materialized, for most Idahoans the idea represented too much centralized control of the state's precious water, and Taylor lasted only one term in office.

Gracie Pfost, of Nampa, served in Congress from 1952 to 1962 as the representative of Idaho's First Congressional District, the first Idaho woman elected to Congress and the longest tenured. With the slogan "tie your vote to a solid Pfost," she aggressively campaigned through the small logging and mining towns scattered across the far-flung First District of western and northern Idaho. In 1954 she competed against her male Republican

opponent in a log-rolling contest at Orofino's Lumberjack Days; the result was a draw. Pfost joined the fray over Hells Canyon with her strong support for a publicly owned dam, a position that earned her the nickname "Hell's Belle."

Church was not the only one elected based on his environmental policies. In the governor's election of 1970, Democratic challenger Cecil Andrus supported efforts to stop the American Smelting and Refining Company (ASARCO) plan to mine molybdenum on national forest land in the White Cloud Mountains. He soundly defeated sitting governor Don Samuelson, who defended the company's development rights. Andrus served two terms, characterized by pragmatic politics and an emphasis on quality-of-life issues, before he resigned to become U.S. Secretary of the Interior in 1977. He would be elected to two additional terms as governor, serving from 1987 to 1995. Andrus represented the state's challenge to growing federal authority when he took on the Department of Energy—which managed the Idaho National Engineering Laboratory—for both reactor testing and dumping nuclear waste. Like Church, who became frustrated with federal arrogance in the Forest Service, Andrus faced a federal bureaucracy that refused to answer his questions, claiming that the governor did not have the right to know about every activity at the federal facility. Much of the classified information regarding operations at the site would eventually be released, including the story of the nation's first fatal nuclear accident in 1961 and many accounts of leaking or missing radioactive waste.

By the end of the 1970s, Idaho had diversified economically and politically from its previous reliance on rural, natural resource–based communities. The state's growth rate outpaced the nation's during this time. Federal policies played a significant role in that development, but Idahoans increasingly questioned the costs of those policies in loss of state autonomy and environmental degradation. Although the years 1945–79 saw overall economic progress, the era was punctuated by a series of downturns that briefly reminded residents of the hard times of the 1920s–30s. However, none of those downturns would be as desperate as the depression that accompanied Idaho into the 1980s.

Democrat Gracie Pfost (sixth from right, seen at the U.S. Capitol in 1955) represented Idaho's first congressional district from 1953 to 1963. In 1962, she made an unsuccessful bid for the senate, losing to Republican Len Jordan. The following year, however, President John F. Kennedy appointed Pfost administrator of Public Housing for the Elderly in the Federal Housing Administration.

Joseph Garry

Idaho veterans returning from the battlefields of World War II had high expectations for their home state, and they contributed in countless ways to its growth in the postwar years. Sergeant Joe Garry, who served in World War II and the Korean War, came home with additional expectations for the rights and dignity of his people, the Coeur d'Alene Indians. Garry was one of the state's nationally prominent political leaders in the 1950s–60s, and his accomplishments helped to reestablish tribal people as leading players in Idaho politics.

Born in 1910 on the Coeur d'Alene Indian Reservation, Joe Garry was a great-grandson of Spokane Garry, the region's most prominent tribal leader in the 1830s–40s. Reflecting Idaho's long history as a cultural crossroads, he was born into a Catholic family of Coeur d'Alene, Kalispell, Spokane, and Irish ancestry.

Garry's experience in World War II was a catalyst for his commitment to improve the lives of his people. He was convinced that Native Americans needed to regain control over tribal issues from federal bureaucrats, reclaim their lands, establish a stronger economic foundation, and provide education for tribal children.

His political career began on a local level. He was elected chairman of the Coeur d'Alene Tribal Council in 1948 and president of the Affiliated Tribes of Northwest Indians a year later. Active in local politics off the reservation as well, Garry was voted to the Idaho State Legislature in 1956, the first Native American to hold such an office. He retained the seat for two terms before waging an unsuccessful campaign for the U.S. Senate in 1960.

Garry's greatest influence came during his six terms (1953–59) as president of the National Congress of American Indians, the nation's leading voice for native concerns. He focused on fighting the federal policy of termination for Indian tribes across the country. The policy, pushed by a handful of congressmen and officials in the Bureau of Indian Affairs in 1953, was designed to eliminate tribal governments, sell off reservation lands, and end federal obligations to treaties and agreements negotiated during the 1800s. Garry condemned the policy as the ultimate step in a long series of actions by a paternalistic federal government and demanded that Indians be offered basic consent to any law that affected them. His tireless lobbying paid off in 1958, when federal officials agreed not to pursue termination without the consent of the tribes involved. Congress later abandoned the policy and recognized the rights of Indians to govern themselves.

Joe Garry left a legacy that promoted greater self-determination and economic development among all tribes. Idaho tribes have continued to follow his lead by playing an increasingly influential role in the state's economic, political, and legal developments.

Engineers at Micron Technology's microchip manufacturing plant in Boise, shown in 1983, examine photolithographs and silicon wafers for flaws. A homegrown success story, Micron Technology accounts for 24,000 jobs in Idaho. The firm began manufacturing DRAM, a computer memory product, in 1981, and by 1998 it had become one of the largest memory producers in the world. As Micron expanded, it diversified into components such as flash memory and image sensors.

GROWING PAINS AT THE TURN
OF THE CENTURY

Contemporary Idaho

In fall 1980, Idaho effected a momentous shift in its political history. Frank Church, who had served as the state's U.S. senator since 1957 and had run for president in 1976, lost his bid for reelection to Steve Symms of Caldwell, who had served in the House of Representatives since 1973. Idaho, like much of the nation, was taking a strong step towards more conservative politics. But this was only one of many rapid changes to reshape the state in the final decades of the 20th century. By the turn of the 21st century, Idaho's economic strength had shifted from natural resource extraction to high-tech manufacturing and tourism. The state's population growth continued to increase far more rapidly than the national average. Idaho attained the sixth-fastest growth rate of any state from 2000 to 2005. The demographic and economic changes created both instability and opportunity in a state trying to redefine itself as the new century dawned.

This page: Republican Senator James McClure (far left, with President Reagan in 1982) became chairman of the Senate Energy and Natural Resources Committee in 1981. Opposite page, top: Cattle cross federal land that became the subject of the Sagebrush Rebellion, in which rural westerners urged the government to "give back" land it managed in the region. Bottom: After the Bunker Hill mine closed in 1981, all that remained was desolate land in need of environmental cleanup.

Church had long been a liberal maverick, a self-described Don Quixote of Idaho politics who pursued idealistic visions with a savvy brand of political pragmatism and an abiding faith in political compromise. He championed wilderness preservation in a state that deeply distrusted federal conservation measures, yet Idaho voters repeatedly reelected him. In some ways he represented a passing era in national politics, one of bipartisan consensus and compromise, and was a casualty of a brand of politics characterized by divisive partisan attacks. By the turn of the century, Idaho would be known as the most conservative state in the union, with Republican representatives holding nearly all statewide political offices, including almost 90 percent of the seats in the state legislature in 2001.

Church's support for U.S. divestment of the Panama Canal and his leadership in the Congressional creation of the Gospel-Hump Wilderness Area in 1978 and the River of No Return Wilderness Area in 1980 cost him political support and exposed him to a rising tide of conservative criticism. By 1979 an organization had emerged calling itself Anybody but Church. Together with the National Conservative Political Action Committee, it funded a series of media ads attacking Senator Church.

Much of his opposition united around growing frustration over federal land management laws. In Grangeville in 1978, local activists hung Church in effigy in response to his push to preserve the Gospel-Hump. A regional movement dubbing itself the "sagebrush rebellion" began in 1979, when Nevada passed a law insisting that the federal government "return" 49 million acres of land it managed within that state. The movement spread to other public land states, including Idaho, galvanizing rural westerners into organized political opposition to conservation laws and environmental preservation groups such as the Idaho Conservation League and the Sierra Club. Unlike most western states, however, the Idaho legislature never passed a measure similar to Nevada's.

Economic Diversification

To some degree, the rebellion represented a growing rural-urban split within Idaho and the West, although more accurately it reflected anxiety over the shift from an economy dependent on natural resource industries toward a more diversified manufacturing and service economy. Representative Helen Chenoweth defeated Democratic incumbent Larry LaRocco in 1994 for the First District Congressional seat, partly on a platform that opposed federal environmental regulations to preserve salmon and other resources. Although the Sagebrush Rebellion waned as an organized political front, replaced in the 1990s by the Wise Use Movement and off-road vehicle lobbyists, the core dispute remains vital between a new West and an old West.

The late 1970s and early 1980s constituted the lowest point since the Great Depression for the economy of the rural West. Throughout Idaho the natural resource economy had always been fraught with cycles of boom and bust, but in north Idaho many mines and mills closed permanently. After 75 years in operation, the mill in Potlatch closed its doors in 1981, its massive timbers later sold as salvage lumber. That same year, the Bunker Hill mine near Kellogg locked its gates, shutting down the world's largest lead smelter and 15 percent of the U.S. production of refined silver. Dogged by global competition, Gulf Resources, the Texas-based owner of the mine since 1968, moved its capital overseas and filed for bankruptcy, leaving a legacy of resentment among former workers and one of the nation's largest environmental cleanup sites. The city of Kellogg faced a precipitous drop in population and later remade itself as a destination resort, home to the Silver Mountain ski area.

This page: An engineering technician runs photo experiments in the class 1 fabrication facility of AMI Semiconductors in Pocatello. Since moving its headquarters from Santa Clara, California, in 1988, the company has become one of Pocatello's largest employers. About 950 people in the city work for the company. Opposite page: With its diamond blade spinning at about 45,000 RPM, a Micron wafer saw will cut a slice of silicon, mounted on ultraviolet-sensitive adhesive tape, into individual die.

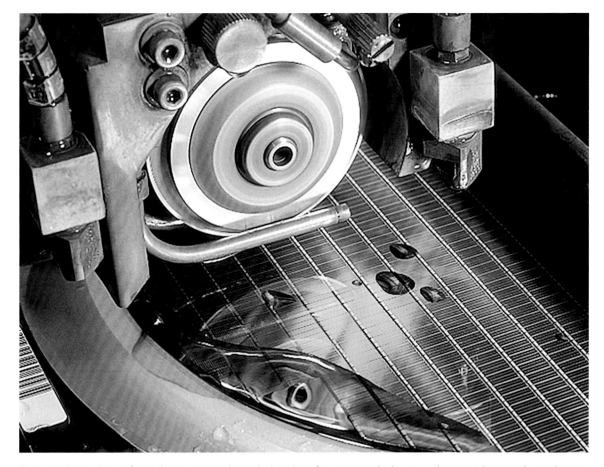

Although Kellogg's transformation was more dramatic than that of most towns in the state, the general economic trends were toward high technology and tourism. Micron Technology, established in Boise in 1978 and boosted by financial help from Jack Simplot, became the biggest employer in the region in the 1990s, providing jobs for several thousand people. The company began by designing semiconductors and later expanded its production line. Historian Carlos Schwantes points out that by 1988, Micron itself earned more revenue than the entire sheep industry, which had once dominated the Idaho ranching economy. By 2004 Micron employed 10,000 workers, and a 2005 economic study commissioned by the company estimated that Micron was responsible for 3.7 percent of the state's entire economy. Before the growth of Micron, Hewlett-Packard was the largest employer in the Boise area and by 2004 still maintained a payroll of 4,000. AMI Semiconductors began operations in Pocatello in 1970 and in 1988 moved its headquarters there from California, becoming the city's largest private employer. In 2005 only Idaho State University had a larger workforce in Pocatello than AMI.

This page: Idaho's diverse landscape provides a plethora of recreational opportunities, including canoeing at the Coeur d'Alene Resort (top left), strolling in the pastures along Coeur d'Alene Lake (top right), and skiing on Castle Peak (bottom). Opposite page: The Coeur d'Alene Resort Golf Course offers a unique golfing experience—the 14th hole is on a floating island green in Coeur d'Alene Lake.

Coeur d'Alene emerged from the closure of some of its lumber mills in the 1980s to become a nationally known resort community. *U.S. News and World Report* titled a 1982 article about the city "An Outdoor Paradise," and in 1994, *Ski Magazine* rated it as America's best ski town. Real estate investor Duane Hagadone developed a luxury resort and golf course on the shores of Lake Coeur d'Alene; the course won accolades in 1992 from *Golf Digest* magazine, which called it America's most beautiful resort course.

The region developed an opposite and damaging image nationwide in the 1980s–90s as home to white supremacist groups centered at the Aryan Nations compound at Hayden Lake, just north of Coeur d'Alene. Richard Butler moved to the area from southern California in the early 1970s to establish the center and recruit like-minded extremists to his "white homeland." Violent harassment of area residents and a series of bombs set off in homes and businesses in Coeur d'Alene in 1986 helped to galvanize support for local human rights activists and business leaders who opposed the neo-Nazi presence. An attack in 1998 on a mother and her son by Aryan Nations security guards proved to be the last straw. The family won a civil lawsuit against Butler for $6.3 million, which bankrupted his entire operation. An Idaho philanthropist later purchased the compound and donated it to Coeur d'Alene's North Idaho College.

The economic growth in recent decades has been impressive, although much of it occurred in only a few locations. Many rural areas continue to lose population. As a result, the state has become far more urban, with nearly half its population concentrated in the Treasure Valley around Boise. Though it still remains a strongly rural area, the spectacular Teton Valley, along the Wyoming border, has grown rapidly due to "lifestyle refugees" seeking a quieter life among inspiring scenery. In 2005 McCall, on the opposite side of the state, requested planning help from the Environmental Protection Agency after the town's rapid growth rate caused housing prices to double in one year. One of the engines driving McCall's growth was the 2004 opening of Tamarack Resort, the first new, full-service ski resort built in North America in several decades.

Among the migrants to Idaho in the last few decades are a large number of Mexican nationals who are pursuing jobs in the service and agricultural industries. By 2000 over half the foreign-born population in the state was Mexican, concentrated mainly into the urban and suburban counties in southern Idaho. Mexican immigration in the state is not new, but the emphasis of this new generation on service jobs over agricultural work is, and reflects broader changes in the state.

Challenges, Past and Future

The last years of the century also saw a resurgence in the influence and visibility of the state's Native American population, building on the work of earlier tribal leaders like Joe Garry. With growing economic clout from a series of Indian-managed casinos and an aggressive defense of treaty rights, Idaho's tribes became major political players. The Coeur d'Alene Casino drew visitors from several states and Canada, and the tribe used the revenues to recover ownership of lands within the reservation boundary. The Coeur d'Alenes also

This page: Quiet and secluded, the Teton River is a haven for fly fishers looking to catch rainbow, cutthroat, cutt-bow, and brook trout. Opposite page, top: Mexican migrant workers, who primarily work in manual labor jobs, have become an important part of Idaho's economy. Bottom: The Coeur d'Alene Casino has grown into a $100 million resort since it opened in 1993.

This page, top: Revered by Native Americans, gray wolves had been exterminated from the lower 48 states when the Endangered Species Act passed in 1973. Today some 240 wolves live in Idaho, Montana, and Wyoming. Bottom: Water rights have been an ongoing concern for Idaho farmers whose livelihoods are impacted by unstable water supplies. Opposite page: The Swan Falls Dam was at the center of controversy in 1977, when Idaho Power ratepayers sued the company for not defending its water rights at the dam.

won jurisdiction over the southern third of Lake Coeur d'Alene, an interpretation of a century-old agreement upheld by the U.S. Supreme Court in 1998. The Nez Perce, Idaho's largest tribe, won authority to manage the state's population of wolves and pursued water rights claims in most of the Snake River Basin. In a monumental agreement, the state, the tribe, and the federal government in 2005 approved a $193 million comprehensive resolution to the water claims, an essential step in the volatile and complicated Snake River Basin Adjudication.

At least in southern Idaho, no issue has generated as much concern in recent years as the adjudication of water rights throughout the Snake River Basin. In 1977 a group of Idaho Power ratepayers sued the company for not fully defending its water rights at Swan Falls Dam, on the Snake River above Boise. To protect itself, the company demanded in court that the state guarantee minimum flows at Swan Falls. In 1982 the state supreme court unanimously sided with the company, calling into question the water rights of hundreds of farmers who developed their irrigation after 1915, when Idaho Power began operating the dam. The company agreed to accept lower amounts of water than it was legally entitled to and negotiated with the state to develop the Swan Falls Agreement in 1984. The compromise established the Snake River Basin Adjudication Court in 1987 to define priority among all water-rights owners in southern Idaho.

The Swan Falls controversy simply exposed a far greater source of conflict, a basic lack of sufficient water supply to cover all the water rights held in the region. After World War II, new irrigation developments depended heavily on the Snake River Aquifer, a massive underground body of water that extends from St. Anthony to Hagerman. Mining of the aquifer caused water levels to drop and reduced the supply for users of surface water from the Snake River, setting the stage for conflict. Devastating drought returned to the region in the first years of the 21st century, sparking a crisis among farmers who feared having their water shut off. Wetter years since 2004 have brought more abundant water supplies and temporary reprieve to the

conflicts, but as Idaho Department of Water Resources director Karl Dreher said in 2004, "There are more water rights out there than we have water to fill them."

In the new century, some familiar issues have reemerged. Among these is a new effort to define boundaries between competing land-use interests in the White Cloud Mountains. In the governor's race of 1970, Cecil Andrus defeated incumbent Don Samuelson with a campaign to stop a proposed mine at Castle Peak in the White Clouds. Much of the area later became part of the Sawtooth National Recreation Area, but conflicts remained. In recent decades, the contest has no longer been between recreational users and mining companies, but among recreational users with conflicting agendas. Use of Idaho's mountain areas by hikers, bicyclists, and all-terrain vehicle riders has skyrocketed since 1970. It is telling of the Idaho economy that mining and logging are not significant factors in this latest round of debates.

Congressman Mike Simpson is spearheading the current efforts to designate a wilderness area in the region—off-limits by law to all vehicles—and clearly define areas for motorized use. His proposed legislation, introduced to Congress in 2004, would also guarantee federal payments and land to rural Custer County. This type of trade-off is the historical norm for such land-use debates, but what is unique and generating significant national attention is the process by which the plan was developed. A wide range of competing users sat down for several years to develop the original proposal. A similarly broad coalition formed to propose land-use solutions for a much larger land area in the Owyhee Mountains of southwest Idaho. Although many question whether this process will resolve old tensions of land use in the state, it is seen as a model of collaboration. Congressman Simpson has said "Things are different now."

Certainly Idaho has changed remarkably and rapidly. It is now far more of a destination than the geographic waypoint it was through much of its history, but many themes remain consistent. The battle for the White Clouds may have new tactics and new voices, but how to use the state's vast public domain has always been at the center of the Idaho roundtable. In north

Top: The adrenaline rush of large drops and fast water draws kayakers and rafters to the Lochsa River, which was once part of the Lewis and Clark exploration route. Bottom: Young riders consider the Timber Terror roller-coaster a highlight of their day at Athol's Silverwood Theme Park, the largest amusement park in the Northwest.

Idaho, the pattern of attracting outside investors to the resources of the mountains—once logging and mining, now recreation and tourism—continues. For southern Idaho, use and distribution of the precious waters of the Snake River Basin remain central. In the rapidly urbanizing modern era, increasing amounts of that water supply go to domestic and manufacturing uses, although agriculture still consumes the vast majority of it. And political and social conflicts in both the north and the south demonstrate that Idahoans still struggle over the definitions of who they are. Yet shaped by the challenges of a consistent series of geographical, social, and political crossroads, Idaho has retained the luster and promise implied by one of the state's oldest nicknames, the Gem of the Mountains.

Bill Wassmuth

In the late-night hours of September 15, 1986, Bill Wassmuth, the priest of St. Pius X Catholic parish in Coeur d'Alene, was at home when an explosion ripped off a corner of his house and slammed him against the wall. The bomb was set by three members of the Aryan Nations compound, based nearby in Hayden Lake. Founded by Richard Butler, the group organized campaigns for white supremacy and neo-Nazi propaganda. As Butler's followers increased their visibility and harassment of local residents in the 1980s, Wassmuth stood up with dozens of other citizens to expose Butler's operations, organizing the Kootenai County Human Rights Task Force. Although the task force gained the support of the local chamber of commerce and elected leaders, many in the area preferred that it ignore the extremists. Wassmuth refused to quietly accept either the apathy or the bigotry. Other Americans who openly challenged the Aryan Nation were murdered, but Wassmuth refused to back down. "If someone wants to get me," he said shortly after the bombing, "I won't live in fear."

In the 1980s, white supremacists dominated the impression most Americans had of Idaho, often replacing the link with famous potatoes. Wassmuth and many others worked tirelessly organizing rallies, parades, and press conferences to present these neo-Nazis as unwelcome outsiders and their messages as unacceptable.

Wassmuth, who was born in 1941 in the tiny Camas Prairie hamlet of Greencreek, near Grangeville, had both the Idaho pedigree and the courage to challenge the bigotry of the newcomers. His great-grandfather had settled in the region along with other German Catholics in the 1890s. He decided as a teenager to join the priesthood and served in Catholic parishes in Boise, Caldwell, Twin Falls, and McCall. "Father Bill" moved to Coeur d'Alene in 1979, around the same time that Butler's Aryan Nations began to attract a following. He opened his church to community organizing and effectively developed broad-based community support for human rights. After expanding his efforts as executive director of the Northwest Coalition against Malicious Harassment, Wassmuth succumbed to Lou Gehrig's disease in 2002.

PART TWO

PORTRAITS OF SUCCESS

Profiles of Companies and Organizations

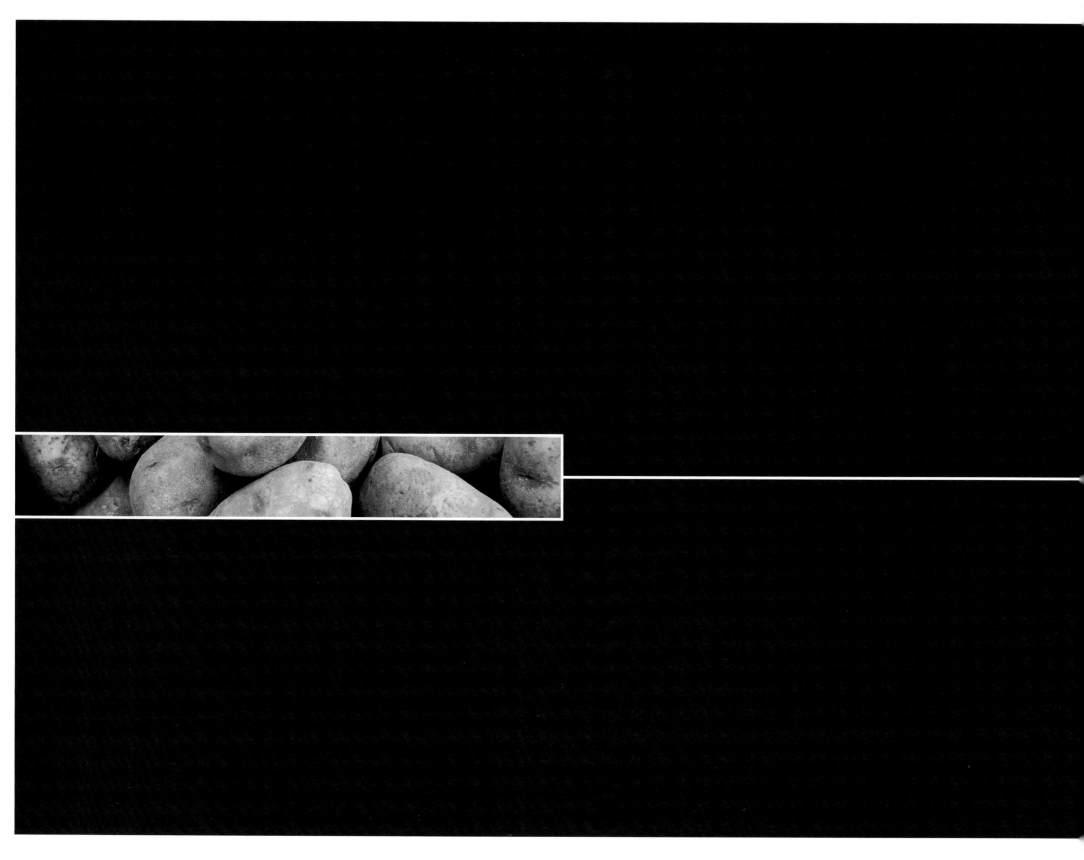

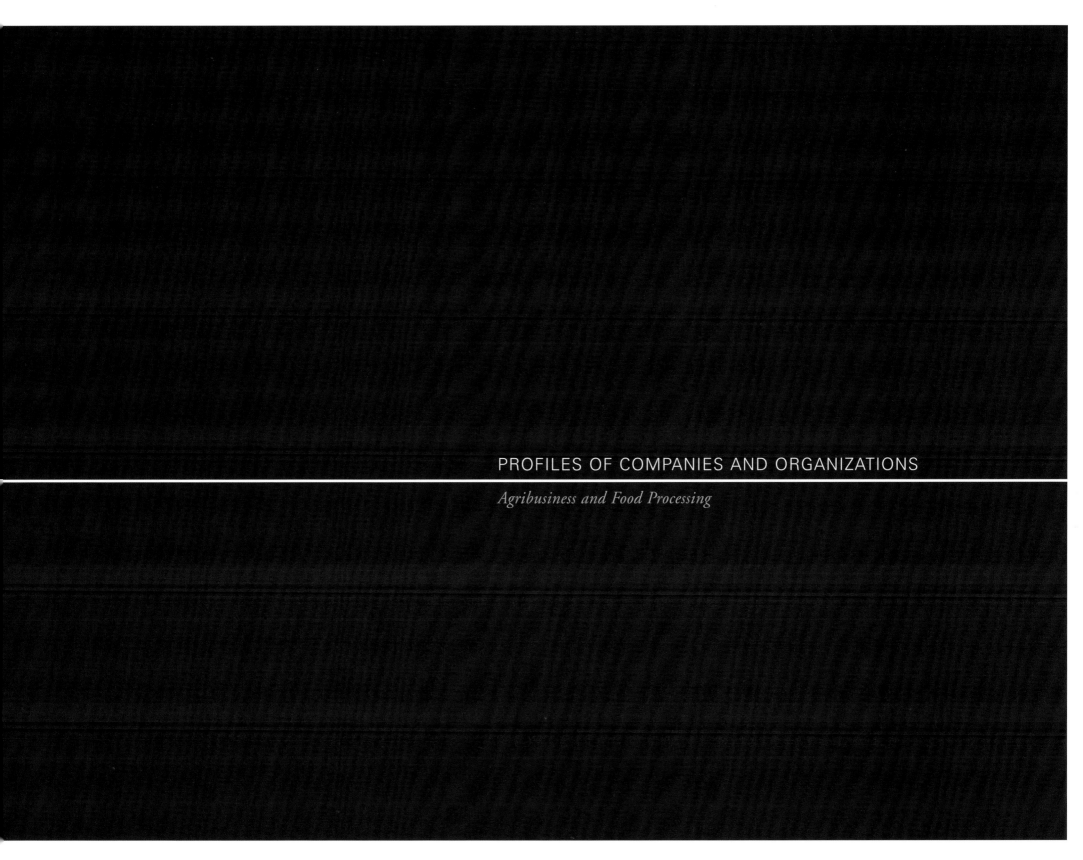

PROFILES OF COMPANIES AND ORGANIZATIONS

Agribusiness and Food Processing

J. R. Simplot Company

One of the nation's largest privately held corporations, this Idaho-based, global food and agribusiness company 'molds Earth's raw materials into items that sustain and enhance life,' focusing on production efficiency, good stewardship of natural resources, and support for its communities.

The J. R. Simplot Company is a diverse, privately held food and agribusiness company headquartered in Boise, Idaho, employing more than 10,000 people in the United States, Canada, Mexico, and Australia. It generates annual sales of more than $3 billion.

The company's philosophy is reflected in its mission statement, "Bringing Earth's Resources to Life." Through its core businesses—food processing, fertilizer manufacturing, and cattle feeding—Simplot takes raw materials and creates a wide variety of products that are marketed in the United States and many other countries.

Above left: J. R. Simplot founded the company that bears his name and was its president for many years. Above right: In addition to operating its own farms, the Simplot Company assists other growers by manufacturing and marketing the fertilizers needed to increase crop yields. The firm also processes raw potatoes and other vegetables and distributes the products around the world.

Simplot is one of the world's largest frozen-potato processors, annually turning out approximately 3 billion pounds of french fries and other products.

The company is a major manufacturer of agricultural fertilizers and professional turf products and also is among the nation's biggest producers of beef cattle.

In the early 1950s, Simplot created and marketed the first commercially viable

frozen french fries. Since then, the company has maintained a strong tradition of innovation and operational excellence. In 2004, it became one of the first to market a high quality frozen french fry with zero grams of trans fat to the foodservice industry.

The company that is now one of the largest privately held corporations in the nation rose from humble beginnings.

Its founder, J. R. "Jack" Simplot, left his parents' home in Declo, Idaho, at age 14 and earned enough money to buy 500 hogs at depressed prices in 1923. He fattened and sold the

hogs when the market improved, then used the profits to start a larger farming operation.

By 1941, Simplot's company had become the nation's largest shipper of potatoes and onions. He supplied dehydrated food to the military during World War II and subsequently built

and acquired food and fertilizer plants in the western United States and Canada.

Simplot continued to maintain a role in his company's growth until 1994 when he resigned as chairman of the board of directors. His children and a professional management team are now responsible for the company's future.

Photos: © J. R. Simplot Company

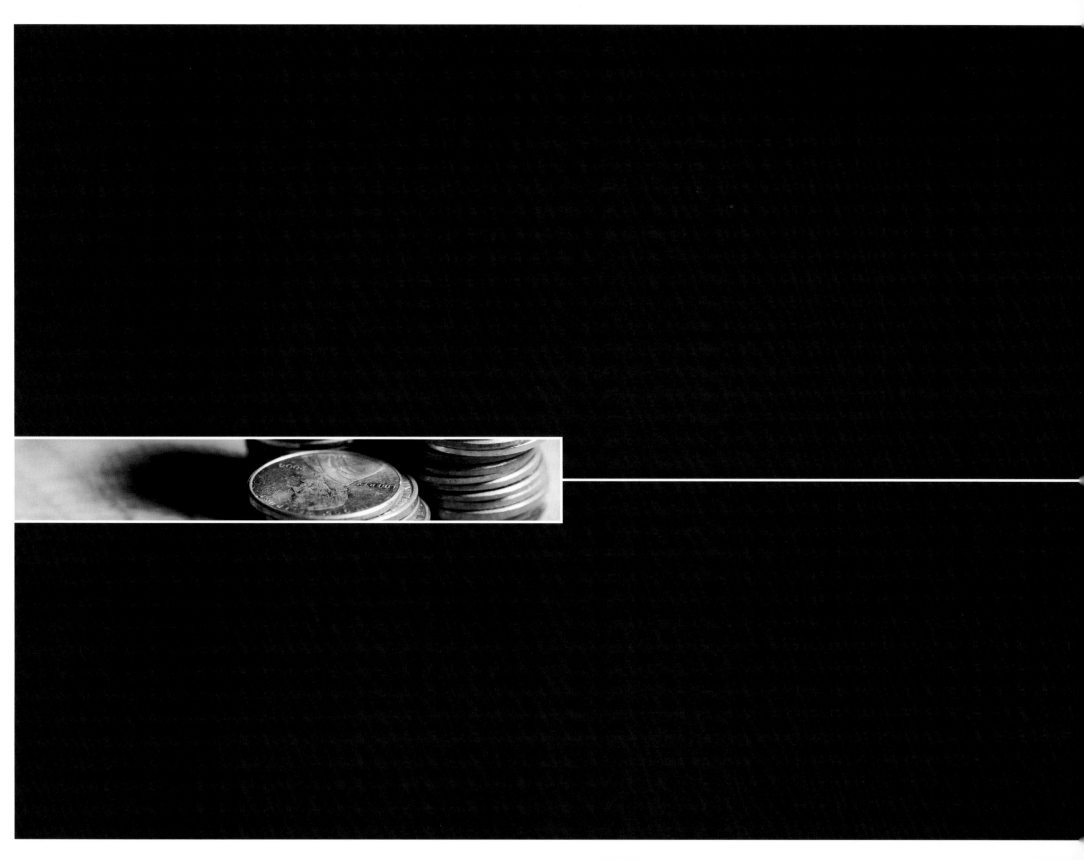

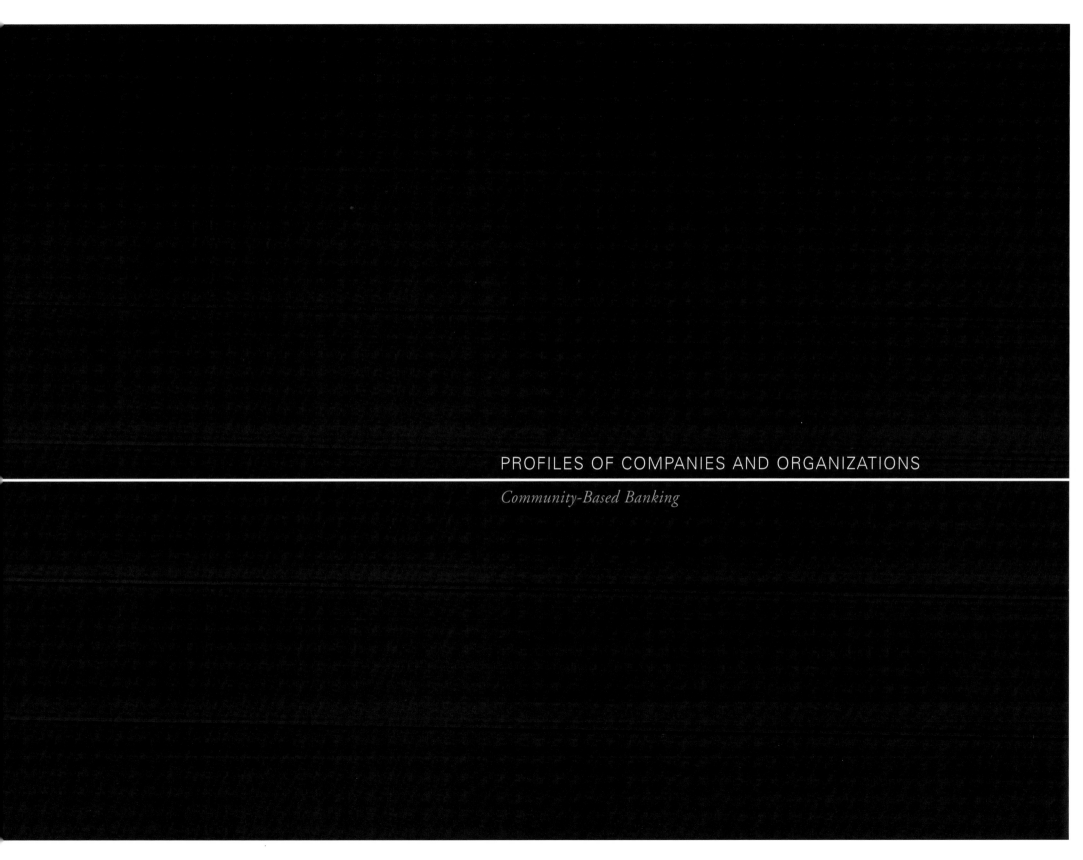

PROFILES OF COMPANIES AND ORGANIZATIONS

Community-Based Banking

Home Federal Bank

Headquartered in Nampa, Idaho, this federally chartered stock savings bank serves the Treasure Valley region of southwestern Idaho with 15 full-service banking offices and two mortgage loan centers, offering a variety of checking and savings products, home and personal loans, commercial lending solutions, and investment services.

In 1920, Home Federal Bank opened its doors in Nampa, Idaho, with a single purpose: to help residents build and buy homes. A steady stream of newcomers to the area prompted a housing crunch followed by a building boom. With few options for financing available to local residents, a group of businessmen recognized an opportunity to found a bank that would help their community and foster its growth.

Banking on the Future

In 1900, Nampa had a population of about 800. Today, with a population of 78,000, Nampa is the second-largest city in the state, the largest in Canyon County, and one of Idaho's fastest growing cities. It is nestled in the Treasure Valley region in southwestern Idaho, one of the premier economic growth areas in the nation because of its thriving business climate, strong workforce, and outstanding quality of life. Long known for its agricultural operations, since the 1990s the Nampa economy has dramatically shifted to technology.

Just as Nampa looks very different now than it did in the 1920s, so does Home Federal Bank. In today's vibrant economic climate, Home Federal Bank continues to help people buy homes and meet their financial goals. Yet it too has gone through a transformation—to not only keep pace with the changing economy but also better serve the community. Perhaps the most significant change occurred in 2004 when Home Federal Bank become a federally chartered stock savings bank. Today, the company is held by Home Federal Bancorp, a publicly traded bank holding company (Nasdaq: HOME).

Still headquartered in Nampa, where it began, Home Federal Bank now has 15 full-service retail locations and two mortgage loan centers throughout the Treasure Valley. Six of the full-service locations are in Wal-Mart stores. The company's growth is evident in its fiscal year performance as well. In 2005, Home Federal Bank reported a 13 percent increase in net income to $5.3 million; a 15 percent increase in total deposits to $396.3 million; and a 9.8 percent increase in loan receivables to $430.9 million.

Capitalizing on Assets

Home Federal Bank credits its success over the years not to mere luck but to the strategic development of a full line of banking services coupled with innovation and personal service in a friendly environment.

To meet the needs of its customers, Home Federal offers a broad spectrum of financial services for both personal and business accounts. Topping the list is a variety of checking account plans ranging from free accounts to no-fee, interest-bearing accounts, to interest-bearing accounts

with CD-type interest rates on higher balances. Each plan features easy-to-balance monthly statements, an optional VISA check card, free eBanking, and free ePay online with selected accounts.

Home Federal Bank also offers three types of savings accounts to help customers accomplish their financial goals: basic savings accounts, money market accounts, and retirement accounts. All are FDIC insured.

Having helped buyers achieve their dreams of homeownership since

1920, it is safe to say that few understand real estate lending better than Home Federal Bank. The bank offers streamlined application processing and fast, local loan approval, along with an experienced staff that can help home buyers find the best loan to suit their specific needs.

In 1996, Home Federal was one of the first financial institutions in the nation to provide medical savings accounts (MSAs) with debit card access. Since then, customers have come to realize what Home Federal has known for more than a decade: that MSAs, and now health savings accounts (HSAs), have put the consumer in control of the health care

they receive. Today, Home Federal provides an HSA that not only is one of the best in the nation but also provides numerous options and customer benefits with no initial sign-up fee.

In addition to its banking services for individuals, Home Federal offers an extensive portfolio of business banking products and services. From checking accounts for small businesses to commercial real estate loans and business lines of credit, Home Federal helps local businesses enhance their competitive edge and leverage local connections, while also helping them to meet their financial needs and grow.

This page, left: Each Home Federal Bank lobby features an Internet Café, where customers can bank online or just browse the Web. This page, right: In early 2000, Home Federal Bank branched out into Wal-Mart supercenters to provide customers with convenient branch access. Opposite page: Established in 1920, Home Federal Bank has corporate offices in downtown Nampa.

Above: Each Home Federal
Bank branch is designed
to make the customer feel
welcome. This tastefully
appointed investment center
offers comfortable seating and
a relaxing environment.

Throughout its history, Home Federal Bank consistently has demonstrated an innovative approach in its products and services. In 2000, it replaced the traditional style of its branch offices with a new, friendly "store" concept. Each store now has an Internet Café and an Investment Center. Investment Centers feature big-screen television broadcasting financial news, Internet access to the Web site of the *Wall Street Journal* and other Web sites of interest to investors, and various financial publications. While taking advantage of these resources, customers can also enjoy free coffee.

Credit Where Credit is Due

From personal to commercial banking, from checking accounts to investment services, Home Federal Bank's experienced, professional staff takes a friendly, individual approach to service. This approach coupled with employee dedication and innovation have contributed to the bank's success and longevity.

The bank's personal service has not gone unnoticed. In 2005, the Nampa Chamber of Commerce named Home Federal Bank "Business of the Year." In 2002, 2003, and 2005, readers of the *Idaho Press-Tribune* rated Home Federal Bank the "best bank."

Compounding Interest in the Community

While Home Federal Bank clearly has enjoyed the opportunity and growth afforded by the Treasure Valley area, it also recognizes its responsibility to help meet the expanding needs of local communities. In 2004, it established the Home Federal Foundation to support charitable causes in the regions served by the bank.

At its inaugural meeting in 2006, the foundation approved donations totaling $88,775 to various local community organizations. These include Albertson College, the Nampa chapter of Boys & Girls Clubs of Idaho, the Greater Idaho Chapter of the American Red Cross, Mercy Housing Idaho, Mercy Medical Center, Nampa Family Shelter Coalition, Saint Alphonsus Regional Medical Center, United Way of Treasure Valley, and Sage Community Resources. In addition, Home Federal Bank provides direct funding for numerous local civic and charitable organizations. Among these are the Idaho Food Bank, the YMCA, Neighborhood Housing Services in Boise, the Boise Philharmonic, the Women's and Children's Alliance, the Boise Schools Foundation, Syringa House, and several state universities and colleges.

Since 1920, Home Federal Bank has cultivated its customers, its services, and its personal approach to banking. As an independent, community-based financial institution, the bank is dedicated to serving the needs of its customers and local communities. It is meeting this goal by providing exceptional service and quality products and services. Today, Home Federal is a cornerstone in Treasure Valley's financial community, where it is poised to continue to grow and help Idahoans achieve their financial goals.

Above: Home Federal Bank's branches—also referred to as stores—are designed by local architects to be aesthetically pleasing and inviting.

D. L. Evans Bank

With a legacy in Idaho stretching back more than a century, this family-owned bank has grown to more than $600 million in assets, 18 full-service banking locations, and two mortgage lending offices in southern Idaho, truly making it 'Idaho's Hometown Community Bank.'

D. L. Evans Bank has a rich history in Idaho. Right: In this photo, taken in the early 1900s, D. L. Evans, the bank's founder, namesake, and first president, sits in the rear seat on the far left. Next to him are J. N. Ireland (center), founder and namesake of Ireland Bank, headquartered in Malad; and R. J. Harding (right). In the front seat are the founder's son, D. L. Evans Jr. (left), and the founder's brother, L. L. Evans (right). Far right: This two-story stone building in Albion, Idaho (shown here in 1910), served as the headquarters for D. L. Evans Bank from 1910 until 1970.

A pioneering group of southern Idaho businessmen founded D. L. Evans Bank on September 15, 1904, in Albion, Idaho. Located in a one-story frame building, it was Cassia County's first bank. State Senator D. L. Evans called the first stockholders meeting to order, and the stockholders elected the bank's first directors and officers. D. L. Evans was elected president; A. Lounsbury, vice president; and J. A. Givens, treasurer and cashier. The directors were D. L. Evans, L. L. Evans, and W. G. Jenkins, all of Malad City, Idaho, and Judge Drew W. Standrod of Pocatello, Idaho. The bank was capitalized for $25,000.

Communities developed in the following years, and with more people, the demand for bank services grew. In 1910, the bank moved to a two-story stone building in Albion, where it stayed for 60 years. The recession of the 1930s closed most banks in Idaho, but D. L. Evans Bank survived, continuing to provide customers with essential financial services. In 1970 the Albion branch moved to its current location, a modern building on the corner of Market and Main streets. (The bank has since moved its headquarters to Burley, Idaho.)

The Burley branch opened in 1979, with John V. Evans Jr., a great-grandson of the founder, as manager. On December 31, 1986, he became CEO and announced that his father, then-governor John V. Evans Sr., would join the bank as president after his term as governor was completed. John Sr., fondly known as "the Gov," held public office for more than 35 years. He ended his second term as governor on January 5, 1987, having held the office for 10 years. His background in banking, farming, ranching, and government helped him lead D. L. Evans Bank into the 21st century.

From 1904 to 1986, the Evans and Jenkins families of Malad were the bank's principal stockholders. D. L. Evans Jr., G. L. Jenkins, and McKinley L. Jenkins were principal officers for over 60 years, from about 1915 until their

deaths. After World War II, Roland T. Evans became chairman of the board; Don S. Evans Sr., vice chairman; and W. G. Jenkins, president. The three presided until Jenkins died in 1978 and Roland Evans retired in 1976. Don S. Evans Sr. became chairman in 1976 and continues to serve the bank in that office. In 1986, the Evans family bought the Jenkins' interest and assumed ownership and control of the bank.

Today, three generations of the Evans family participate in the bank's daily operations and on the board of directors. President John V. Evans Sr. leads the bank with his executive managers: John V. Evans Jr., CEO; John V. Evans III, executive vice president of the Treasure Valley region; H. Scott Horsley, executive vice president and chief credit officer;

and Brenda Sanford, chief financial officer. The current board of directors includes chairman Don S. Evans Sr., John V. Evans Sr., John V. Evans Jr., M. DeLell Evans, Don S. Evans Jr., Larry L. Evans, Paula D. Evans, Martha Evans Gilgen, Glen R. Kunau, Lex H. Kunau, James J. Lynch, Susan D. Evans Scarlett, and David L. Evans IV.

D. L. Evans Bank has expanded tremendously since 2000. It maintains that "Hometown Community Bank Spirit" as it grows by blending a "High-Tech High-Touch" philosophy along with the personal service the bank has prided itself on since the first branch opened in Albion in 1904. The bank has grown to more than $600 million in assets with 18 full-service branches and two mortgage lending offices across southern Idaho.

D. L. Evans lived by the principles of integrity, charity, friendliness, compassion, and hard work. D. L. Evans Bank directors and officers emulate these principles and encourage employees to do the same. While times have changed, the bank has never lost sight of the founder's vision, that banking is really just about one thing: helping people. That is the strength of a family-owned community bank—meaningful, long-term relationships. For more than 100 years, D. L. Evans Bank has taken pride in helping Idaho's families grow and prosper. Its roots are firmly planted in Idaho, and as a community bank with headquarters in Burley and branch offices in Albion, Rupert, Twin Falls, Jerome, Boise, Meridian, Nampa, Ketchum, Hailey, Pocatello, and Idaho Falls, it has truly become "Idaho's Hometown Community Bank."

Above left: Former Idaho governor John V. Evans Sr., the founder's great-grandson, is president of D. L. Evans Bank. Above right: The board members of the family-owned bank include (back row, from left) James J. Lynch, Glen R. Kunau, Don S. Evans Jr., Don S. Evans Sr., John V. Evans Sr., Larry L. Evans, John V. Evans Jr., (front row, from left) M. DeLell Evans, Susan D. Evans Scarlett, Martha E. Gilgen, David L. Evans IV, and Paula D. Evans.

Bank of Idaho

With a strong local focus, the Bank of Idaho has served eastern Idaho for 20 years with an unwavering commitment to meet its customers' needs, complete dedication to its staff, and constant support of the communities it serves.

Above: The Bank of Idaho's main office building, shown here, is proudly located at 399 North Capital Avenue, in Idaho Falls, Idaho.

The Bank of Idaho, originally known as the Bank of Eastern Idaho, was chartered by the Idaho Department of Finance and the Federal Deposit Insurance Corporation in September 1985 and opened for business in the downtown area of Idaho Falls at 500 North Capital Avenue. The bank was formed by a group of local businessmen who felt a community bank was needed in this area to provide service and boost financial competition among local institutions.

The second Idaho Falls location was opened in August 1990 on the east side and is known as the Channing office. Due to the bank's significant growth, it became necessary in 1991 to move the bank's headquarters from 500 North Capital Avenue to a larger facility, at 399 North Capital Avenue, which is now the bank's main office.

Under the leadership of Chairman and CEO William F. Rigby, who is also one of the bank's founders, the Bank of Idaho has become a leader in serving small businesses and professional customers. The bank has grown to $200 million in assets, and at times has sustained growth of up to 20 percent annually. In addition, the mortgage market has made a significant contribution to the bank's performance through the years.

April 1995 brought the bank's first move into a new city: Pocatello, Idaho. The Pocatello area did not have a community bank at the time, which made it an appealing market to the Bank of Idaho. As larger banks continued to merge and consolidate, the hometown customer service of a community bank was greatly needed in Pocatello.

The bank continued its expansion in February 1997 by opening a branch in Ashton, Idaho. A trust department was formed in June, enabling the bank to offer trust services including IRAs, trusts, and other investment opportunities, and it has grown to $100 million in assets. Also in 1997, the Bank of Idaho Holding Company was organized as a parent company for the Bank of Idaho.

Two additional branches were opened in 1998, in St. Anthony and in Island Park, as the bank expanded its market area north.

The administrative offices of the Bank of Idaho were relocated to 151 North Ridge in the O. E. Bell Center in the fall of 1999 to allow for staff expansion at the main office on Capital Avenue.

The Bank of Idaho offers a wide range of services, including commercial and agricultural loans, consumer loans, and mortgage loans. In addition, deposit products include checking accounts, savings accounts, CDs, and money market accounts. The bank's electronic banking services include online banking and bill payment. The bank also offers ATM services, 24-hour telephone banking, and some of the best customer service around. The bank's Web site offers a large

menu of services and references, including online loan applications with prompt turnaround.

The bank has become a leader in electronic cash letters through the Federal Reserve and is now offering remote deposit capture services to those customers with large check volumes or locations outside the bank's service area.

According to the bank's mission statement: "The Bank of Idaho, your community bank, will be the preferred

financial institution providing exceptional service for shared success." The bank prides itself on its commitment to help its customers be successful. The bank's philosophy has always been to contribute to and support the people and communities in its market area, with a focus on its service to its communities, and in doing so, the bank believes it is on the road to continued growth and success.

The bank's president, Park Price, continued expansion in the Pocatello market by moving the existing

Pocatello branch to a larger building in 2004. Another new branch will be built and opened in Pocatello in 2006.

"We are fortunate to be centered in a vibrant, growing part of Idaho," says Price. According to Price, the bank has identified several communities for expansion in the foreseeable

future. The Bank of Idaho remains committed to the reason it was opened 20 years ago: to be an independent, locally focused, and community-involved bank.

Additional information, as well as banking services, is available online at www.bankofidaho.com.

Above left: This view of the Grand Tetons, from the Idaho side, speaks to the Bank of Idaho's expansive focus and statewide reach in providing products and services.
Above: The Bank of Idaho's Pocatello branch is located at 1230 Yellowstone Avenue.

Farmers & Merchants

This hometown bank began in 1967 and grew into a full-service financial resource for loans, mortgages, investment management, and more, giving its customers down-to-earth service premised on the belief that Treasure Valley citizens—businesspeople, farmers, and families—deserve a great bank.

Above: Founded in 1967, Farmers & Merchants is headquartered in Boise, Idaho, and operates 12 branch offices serving the Treasure Valley area.

Farmers & Merchants began with a vision: a hometown bank in downtown Meridian that could provide local residents and the surrounding farm communities with the exceptional service and personal attention that only a locally owned bank could offer.

While the seven individuals who founded the bank in 1967 likely envisioned success, they probably could not have foreseen that several decades later Farmers & Merchants would not only be the oldest community bank in southwestern Idaho but also rank as one of the region's most rapidly growing financial institutions.

In many ways, the Farmers & Merchants story tracks closely with the evolution of the modern Treasure Valley. Growth began under Idaho entrepreneurial icon J. R. Simplot, who purchased the bank with a partner in the late 1970s. Under Simplot's ownership, the bank opened its first Boise branch office in 1985.

Though Simplot sold his interest in 1993, expansion continued, with a branch office opening in Nampa in 1995. Branches in Garden City (1997) and Caldwell (1998) followed, as well as an Overland Park office (1998) and Trust Services (1998). In the 1990s, Clarence Jones led the bank as its president and CEO until Mike Mooney, who joined the team in 2003, replaced him as chief executive in 2005.

Expansion accelerated; starting in 2003, the bank opened five new offices, added 70 jobs, and increased its assets by more than $250 million— all in just three years. In April 2006, Farmers & Merchants joined forces with Bank of the Cascades, based in Bend, Oregon.

The bank's momentum comes from a deeply ingrained service ethic that often gives Farmers & Merchants an edge compared to larger banks or to out-of-state banks. President Mike Mooney says, "Our decision-making process is local, which allows us to be quick, flexible, and creative in providing custom-designed financial solutions for our customers."

With growing market share, opportunities for continued expansion, and a reputation for customer service that any business would envy, Farmers & Merchants is now poised to serve even greater numbers of Idaho businesses, farmers, and families.

While the bank has grown into a financial powerhouse offering complete services, success can be traced back to its mission: "Delivering the best in banking for the financial well-being of our customers and shareholders."

Mountain West Bank

This innovative bank was founded to serve the local community, providing individuals, small-to-midsize businesses, and organizations and institutions in Idaho, Washington, and Utah with flexible financial solutions to help them succeed in their goals.

Above left: Mountain West Bank is based in Coeur d'Alene and has branches across Idaho, Washington, and Utah. Shown here is a branch in Coeur d'Alene that was opened in 2006.
Above right: Customers find a friendly atmosphere at Mountain West, whose slogan is "Love Where You Bank."

It is an Idaho success story. In little more than a decade, Mountain West Bank has grown from just a dream to become one of the region's leading community banks. Founder Jon W. Hippler set out in 1993 to redefine what banking should be.

Today Mountain West has 21 branches across Idaho, Washington, and Utah. Based in Coeur d'Alene, it is one of Idaho's most innovative companies and the number one Small Business Administration (SBA) lender in Idaho in volume of loans.

At Mountain West, banking is anything but "business as usual." Customers can sip coffee, access the Internet, and relax by the fire. They can find the financial products they need to help them succeed. Mountain West believes in providing banking services to fit each person's unique goals.

"Mountain West provides financial services to fit people's needs at every stage of life," says Hippler, president and CEO. "Relationships are vital here. People find a warm, friendly atmosphere in every Mountain West Bank office they visit. We want customers to really love their bank."

The bank contributes to Idaho's booming economy with lending for businesses, construction, and home-owners. Mountain West has national preferred status through the SBA and provides more SBA loans than any other state-chartered bank.

"Growing Idaho by providing small businesses with the opportunity to start up or expand and to hire people is good business for our state," Hippler says.

With the bank's flexible financing solutions, thousands of Idahoans have seen their dreams of home ownership come true. Mountain West's residential lending centers provide a variety of mortgage products to meet people's needs "from the ground up," including all-in-one lending, which allows fluid financing from the beginning of a project, throughout construction, to the completion of the loan process.

In 2000 the bank joined Glacier Bancorp, Inc. (Nasdaq: GBCI), a holding company headquartered in Kalispell, Montana. Mountain West retains its original state charter and its own board of directors. Its senior management team directs the bank in each market it serves.

Being a good neighbor is one of Mountain West's founding principles. Its people volunteer at community events, make donations to charitable causes, and participate actively in the communities where they live, work, and play.

The more than 300 employees of Mountain West Bank take great pride in being a part of Idaho's successful present—and its future.

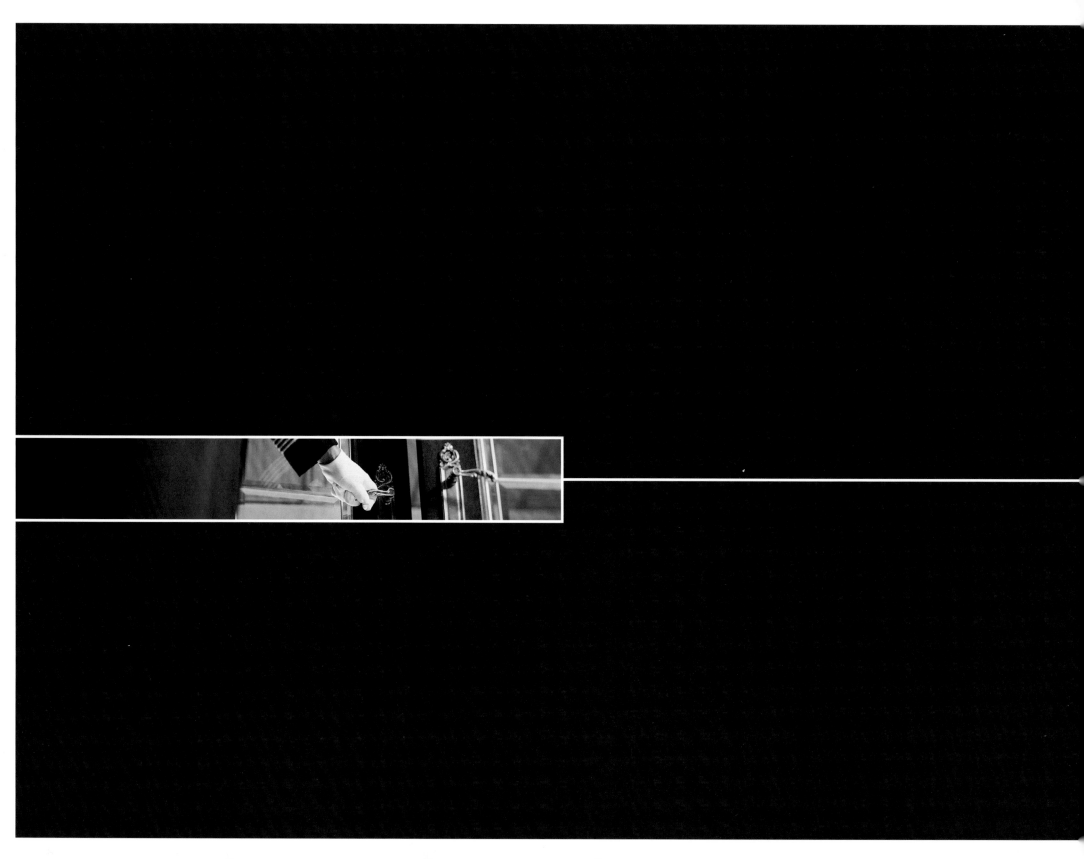

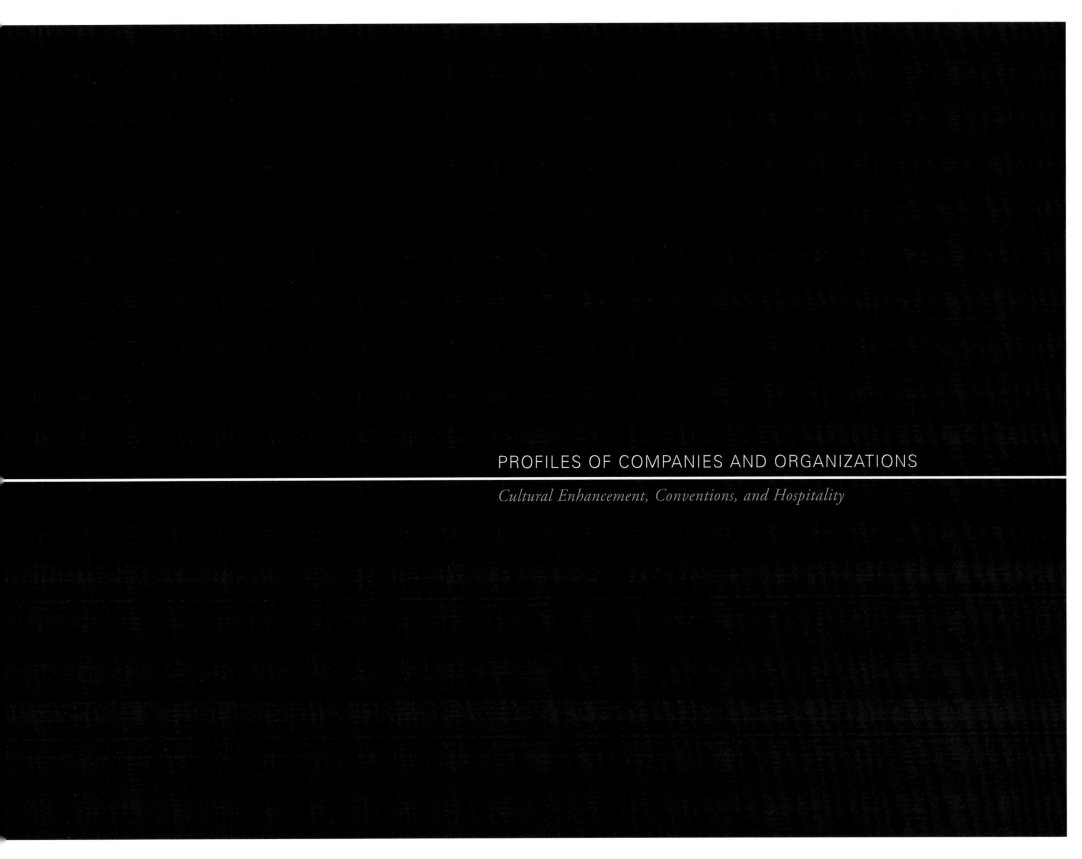

PROFILES OF COMPANIES AND ORGANIZATIONS

Cultural Enhancement, Conventions, and Hospitality

The Grove Hotel

Centrally located in downtown Boise, this four-star, four-diamond hotel offers some of the finest dining, hospitality, and comfort in the city, and it has first-class facilities for business meetings, conventions, trade shows, weddings, or any other special occasion.

Above left: The Grove Hotel has elegant guest rooms, suites, condominiums, and meeting spaces. Its services, amenities, and class have made it Boise's only four-star, four-diamond hotel. Above center: The hotel lobby exudes European refinement. Above right: Spacious guest rooms include Internet access, workstations, and comfortable furnishings.

Downtown Boise, a dynamic cultural and business hub at the center of the Treasure Valley, is home to the luxurious Grove Hotel, Boise's only hotel with a four-diamond rating for quality and service from the American Automobile Association (AAA). From its elegant lobby, featuring neoclassical chandeliers and cherry-paneled walls, to its full-service fitness club and fine dining establishment, The Grove Hotel offers a first-class experience distinguished by luxury, convenience, and

the highest standards in amenities and guest services.

The Grove Hotel's complex of 250 guest rooms, suites, and high-rise residential condominiums is attached to the 5,000-seat Qwest Arena of Idaho, a multipurpose event center where sporting events, concerts, and trade shows are held. Known as one of Idaho's premier event and attractions showplaces, Qwest Arena is one of the newest indoor sports and event centers in the Northwest. It features bowl seating for 5,000 people and 39 entertainment suites and is home to the Idaho Steelheads

hockey team, the Idaho Stampede basketball team, and Arena Football. Guests of The Grove Hotel may contact the concierge to arrange for preferred seating at any arena event.

Located at the center of a vibrant downtown, the hotel is adjacent to the Boise Centre on the Grove convention center and only 10 minutes from the Boise Airport, three blocks from the Idaho State Capitol, and minutes from the downtown financial community. Also within walking distance are retail shops, restaurants, theaters, art galleries, and many other entertainment options.

Elegant Rooms and Amenities

Guest rooms and services at The Grove Hotel are top of the line. With their elegant furnishings and spacious interiors, the hotel's rooms and suites overlook the city and foothills. In-room conveniences include mini bars, coffee and tea service, workstations, dual-line telephones with computer data jacks, high-speed wireless Internet access, television with video on demand, in-room dining, bath amenities, terrycloth robes, and laundry and valet service. The hotel also provides complimentary airport shuttle service, concierge service, and a business center with state-of-the-art fax, modem, and communications capabilities.

The Grove Hotel also features the Ultimate Fitness Facility, 14,000 square feet of state-of-the-art cardiovascular conditioning machines, free weights, and conditioning station-weights. Use of the pool, spa, and saunas is free for hotel guests, while a fee is charged for the use of exercise equipment and for personal training, massage therapy, tanning booths, and steam bath. Spacious locker rooms and private men's and women's lounges make this fifth-floor facility, managed by Gold's Gym, top notch.

Dining in Style

A variety of restaurants on The Grove gives diners many options that are within easy walking distance. Emilio's, located in the hotel's lobby, serves fresh fish, seafood, aged steaks, and locally grown produce. Renowned for its award-winning meals, excellent service, and elegant ambiance, Emilio's offers breakfast, lunch, dinner, and

Sunday brunch. For special occasions, a private dining room seats up to 10 people. The Bar is The Grove Hotel's sophisticated gathering place for travelers and local professionals. Guests may enjoy cocktails and live piano music while relaxing fireside. On Tuesdays, Wednesdays, and Thursdays, The Bar features a variety of made-to-order sushi items from Satori Sushi.

Sports enthusiasts will appreciate The Zone Bar & Grill, located in the Qwest Arena. The Zone, which is open during hockey season and for other special events, offers a casual dining atmosphere with a bird's-eye view of downtown activities and events. The Zone's many televisions, outdoor terrace dining, and rail seating for arena events give diners multiple game viewing options.

Facilities for Gatherings

For banquets, business meetings, and conventions, The Grove Hotel offers

16,000 square feet of flexible meeting space complemented by the hotel's outstanding catering services. The Grove Hotel and Qwest Arena offer a total of 36,000 square feet of meeting space. The Grove Hotel's second-floor meeting space includes the 6,800-square-foot Grand Ballroom, which consists of three separate but adjoining bays and can accommodate up to 400 guests for dining functions and 700 theater style. Executive suites accommodate from 15 to 45 people and are located side by side overlooking the event center, which makes moving between meetings convenient and efficient.

The Grove Hotel's third-floor meeting space is ideal for board meetings and breakout spaces. These rooms feature high-tech audiovisual capabilities that

can be customized to suit the user. Corporate viewing suites are available to groups during events at the center or can be used as additional breakout rooms. Two suites that open into each other provide contiguous reception space when needed.

The Grove Hotel's fourth-floor terrace is available, weather permitting, for outdoor events. Upon request, special guest room lodging prices are available for wedding and other groups, and referrals are provided for local florists, cake designers, musicians and music providers, and photographers. In addition, the hotel's executive chef can create an elegant customized menu.

Whether they are visiting Boise for business or pleasure, guests of The Grove Hotel will enjoy its great location, luxurious amenities, and high standards of service. A grand entertainment hotel, The Grove Hotel is proud of the four-diamond rating it has earned and is committed to maintaining its reputation for excellence.

Above, far left: Chef Rick Sordahl oversees The Grove Hotel's four-star, four-diamond Emilio's restaurant. Above center: The restaurant's luxury private dining room can seat 10. Above right, top and bottom: Emilio's artful New American cuisine entices discriminating diners, whether local or visiting from abroad.

Boise Centre on the Grove and Boise Convention & Visitors Bureau

This spacious, well-appointed convention center—owned by the Greater Boise Auditorium District and supported by the promotional efforts and tourism services of the convention and visitors bureau—accommodates trade shows, academic conferences, corporate meetings, banquets, and other events.

Above left: Boise Centre on the Grove is in the heart of downtown Boise, within walking distance of hotels, restaurants, museums and other cultural attractions, shopping, and entertainment. Right and above right: The Grove Plaza, in front of the Boise Centre, is the site of numerous outdoor events throughout the year.

The travel and tourism industry continues to rank as one of the top five industries in Idaho, providing nearly 50,000 jobs and accounting for approximately 5 percent of Idaho's gross state product.

Boise Centre on the Grove

Tourism is big business in Boise, too, and Boise Centre on the Grove is a keystone of that success. Convention groups infuse more than $50 million in new money into the community annually. Since the opening of Boise Centre in 1990, Boiseans and visitors alike have enjoyed its beautiful public spaces. As a primary location for meetings, conventions, fund-raising events, and large trade shows, Boise Centre has become a "living room" for the community—a place where people can trade life experiences, see great treasures, and most importantly, learn of others' ideas while sharing their own. Boise Centre's oversight board, management, and staff recognize the Boise Centre's and their own contribution to the Boise community and continually provide exemplary service to all who enter there.

Boise Convention & Visitors Bureau

Boise Convention & Visitors Bureau (CVB)—a marketing arm for the Boise Centre on the Grove—is a private, nonprofit organization founded in 1982 by the Greater Boise Auditorium District. The Boise CVB enhances Boise's economy by marketing and promoting the city and region as a site for conventions, corporate meetings, trade shows, and pleasure travel, cultural, sporting, and special events. As active participants in the economic development of the metropolitan Boise area, the organization's staff pursues convention, meeting, and tourism business aggressively and with the highest degree of professionalism and provides extensive services tailored to visitors' needs.

In essence, the Boise CVB acts as a liaison between individual customers, meeting planners, travel agents, tour operators, event organizers, media outlets, and the Boise hospitality industry. Its sales efforts are far-reaching, targeting potential travelers and groups through domestic and international marketplaces and, closer to home, via contacts with local government, educators, corporations, and others. CVB employees are proud of Boise, taking pride in the opportunity to represent Boise and to market it as a premier destination.

Outstanding meeting facilities, a vibrant downtown area, unique attractions, plentiful outdoor recreation, and Boise's wonderful quality of life point to a bright future for tourism in Idaho's capital.

Night skiing at Bogus Basin Mountain Resort, Boise

sin x
sin x/cos x

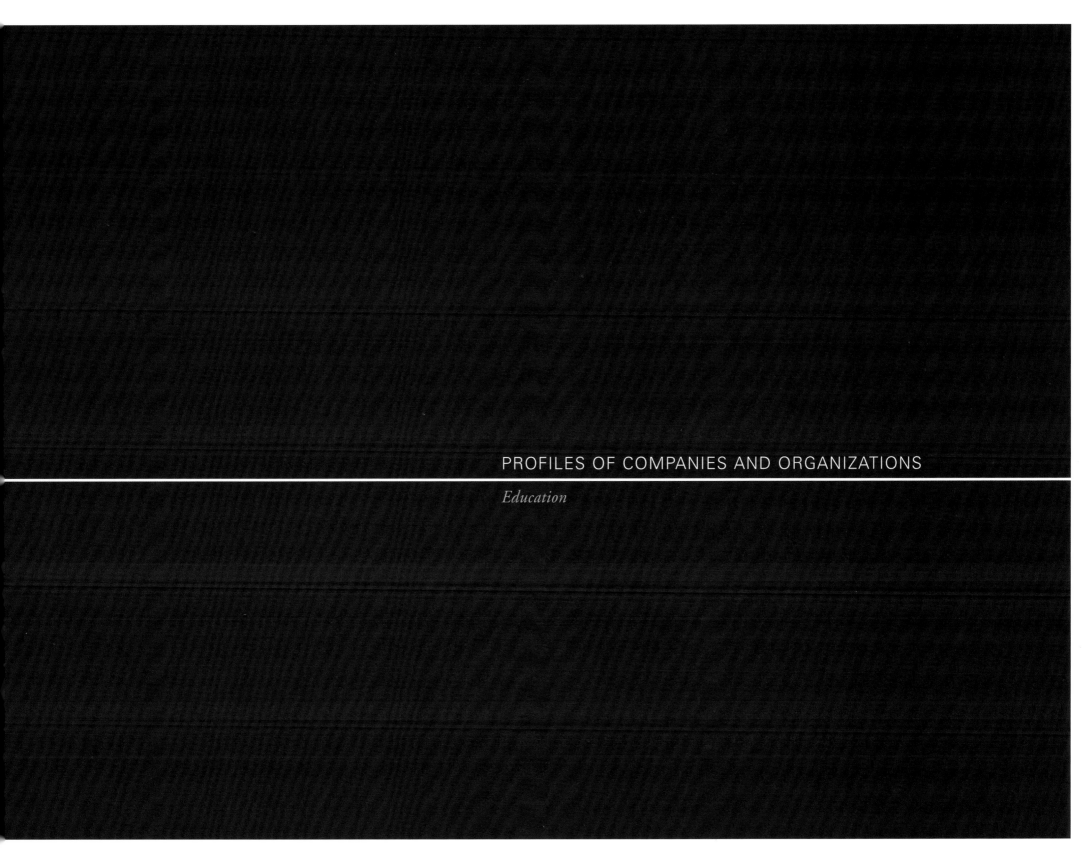

PROFILES OF COMPANIES AND ORGANIZATIONS

Education

Albertson College of Idaho

With a foremost belief that a liberal arts education teaches students to reason, imagine, inquire, and thrive in a complex, changing world, this private college, founded in 1891, offers small classes, excellent value, and a broad foundation of knowledge.

Above: According to the Princeton Review, Albertson College of Idaho professors are at the top of their game when it comes to bringing material to life. And with an average class size of 10, students are sure to receive personal attention.

Nationally recognized for its academic programs and its many accomplished alumni, Albertson College of Idaho (ACI) in Caldwell, just west of Boise, prepares students for life. Education in the liberal arts—the humanities, fine arts, social sciences, natural sciences, and mathematics—enables students to make choices grounded in knowledge. The ACI slogan, "Awaken the Mind, Encounter Truth, Contribute to Community," embodies the liberal arts tradition.

ACI believes that the liberal arts lead students to think logically, imaginatively, and independently; write and speak forcefully; frame questions and find answers; think across academic disciplines; assess values; and approach others with understanding and compassion. They prepare students for career flexibility, future jobs, and a lifetime of learning.

Even ACI's unique academic calendar contributes to its educational goals. During the fall and spring semesters, students engage in 12 weeks of traditional coursework. In between these sessions, a six-week winter term immerses them in off-campus learning opportunities, unique field experiences, independent research, and seminars. Every six weeks, students are given a one-week break. The winter term also gives students a chance to take courses in special topics or travel abroad on faculty-led trips.

Opening Doors for Others

Dr. William Judson Boone, a Presbyterian minister, founded the school in 1891 as the College of Idaho. The college's first president, Boone was also a botanist, teacher, debate coach, and avid photographer. His pictures, taken from the late 1800s until his death in 1936, chronicle the growth of ACI and the town of Caldwell. His photos now belong to the college archives. Boone's presidency spanned 45 years, and he understood that "a life well lived requires the ability to see beyond the self while also educating the self."

Joe and Kathryn Albertson, who met at the college, also became key figures in the school's history and legacy. The Great Depression cut short their education, and both left school before graduating in order to work. A tireless entrepreneur, Joe created a chain of grocery stores. In 1966 Joe and his wife established the J. A. & Kathryn Albertson Foundation to administer their charitable giving and to provide educational opportunities for others. In 1991 the college's name was changed from College of Idaho to Albertson College of Idaho to honor the family and its generosity.

Today ACI is positioned among the top 150 U.S. liberal arts colleges and universities by *U.S.News & World Report*, and is using a $17 million challenge grant from the J. A. & Kathryn

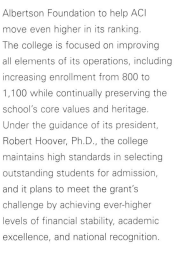

Photo, right: © Jason Jones Photography, Inc.

Albertson Foundation to help ACI move even higher in its ranking. The college is focused on improving all elements of its operations, including increasing enrollment from 800 to 1,100 while continually preserving the school's core values and heritage. Under the guidance of its president, Robert Hoover, Ph.D., the college maintains high standards in selecting outstanding students for admission, and it plans to meet the grant's challenge by achieving ever-higher levels of financial stability, academic excellence, and national recognition.

A Supportive Campus Community

Students at ACI are in a place that supports their success—as high school graduates entering college, as practiced students, and as college graduates embarking on a new life. The school's "First Year Experience" program, designed to welcome incoming freshmen, is geared toward making the transition from high school to college a positive one. The program involves social activities, classroom discussions, and student mentoring.

Small classes and more than 70 outstanding faculty members are also instrumental in fulfilling the college's mission. Selected for their academic achievements and teaching skills, ACI professors—nearly 90 percent of whom hold the highest degree in their field—are known for developing student potential, helped by a low student-faculty ratio of 11 to one and classes averaging 10 students. Dedicated to teaching, faculty members know their students by name and place a high priority on individual student-teacher interaction.

In addition to a world-class education, the college offers students excellent value with its competitive tuition rates. ACI was recognized on the list of schools offering the "Best Academic Bang for Your Buck" in *The Best 345 Colleges*, published in 2004 by the Princeton Review.

ACI also has a proven record of helping its graduates achieve their goals, whether they move on to medical school, law school, or graduate school or enter the workforce. With a liberal arts education from Albertson College of Idaho, young adults can lead productive, fulfilling lives and make great contributions to society.

Above left: Albertson College of Idaho's (ACI) beautiful campus—unbroken by roads—provides plenty of room for students to study and fosters a tight-knit community. Above right: ACI students explore all aspects of the Idaho environment, from paddling in pristine rivers through the college's Outdoor Program to biological field studies in the Owyhee desert mountains.

Northwest Nazarene University

Known nationally for excellence in its schools of education, nursing, and business, this comprehensive Christian university in Nampa has the small classes, great professors, and academic rigor to shape its students into scholars who succeed professionally and spiritually.

Photos, both pages: © Brad Elsberg, NNU

Above left: Northwest Nazarene University (NNU) is situated on a beautiful 85-acre, park-like campus in Nampa, Idaho. Seven residence halls and apartment complexes provide a variety of traditional and added-amenity housing, both offering the convenience of on-campus living. Above right: NNU's John and Orah Brandt Fine Arts and Convocation Center is home to many campus and community events.

When students graduate from Northwest Nazarene University (NNU), a liberal arts institution founded in 1913, they are prepared to be global Christians ministering around the world through their chosen professions. Together, the school's liberal arts philosophy of education and its mission to develop Christian character within the framework of scholarship create a nurturing environment that is consistently praised by students. Well-known publications also rate NNU high. *U.S.News & World Report* calls NNU one of the best values around, and the Princeton Review places it at the top of its Best Western Colleges and Universities list.

Both the faculty and academic programs at NNU focus on preparing students to model Christian character in the workplace by demonstrating ethical behavior and love and respect for others. In addition, the university strives to develop in its graduates academic excellence, creative engagement, and social responsiveness—all of which enable each student to bring inspired solutions to life's problems—in the home, the workplace,

the church, and the greater community. Among the legacy alumni of NNU are a NASA shuttle astronaut, an Oregon State Teacher of the Year, a CEO of the San Jose Sharks, two university presidents, and a host of globally dispersed Christians who are contributing to their communities and the world.

NNU serves approximately 1,700 undergraduate and graduate students

and 9,000 continuing education students on its 85-acre campus in Nampa, which includes seven residence halls and apartment complexes; baseball, softball, and soccer fields; tennis courts; and an Olympic-sized track. And the university is constantly expanding to meet the needs of its students. Since 1995, NNU has constructed and purchased eight new buildings including a fine arts facility,

a sports complex, a business center, a dormitory, and apartment complexes.

NNU offers more than 60 areas of study and master's programs in six disciplines as well as study-abroad cooperative programs in 10 countries. The university employs 105 full-time faculty members, maintaining a low student-faculty ratio and an average class size of 18 students.

In addition to bachelor's and master's degrees, NNU offers an honors program that provides an integrative learning experience for academically superior freshmen; off-campus programs coordinated through the Council for Christian Colleges and Universities; an athletics program that is part of the NCAA Division II and the Great Northwest Athletic Conference; more than 30 clubs and organizations representing a wide array of interests; and the Office of Campus Life, which encourages student involvement through leadership roles.

A Century of Teaching

The formation of NNU was inspired by the formation of the Church of the Nazarene in 1908. In the last decades of the 19th century, "holiness awakenings," which emphasized the importance of a deeper spiritual life, swept through parts of the country. The Church of the Nazarene came about as a result of this movement.

In 1913, the Idaho Holiness School opened its doors in a small unoccupied church building with a handful of grade school students and a group of adults committed to integrating learning, faith, and the Scriptures. Equipment, books, and teachers were scarce, but the founders were deeply committed to the education of Nampa's children.

The school's founder, Eugene Emerson, was a prosperous business-man who needed a "deeper religious experience" and is credited as "the moving spirit in establishing the school." The school's first president, Reverend H. Orton Wiley, served from 1916 to 1926 and was instrumental in putting together the school's basic collegiate structure and advancing the climate of learning. In NNU's formative years, Wiley served as a preacher, scholar, writer, teacher, and administrator

who faithfully upheld the school's devotion to academic drive and religious intensity. For more than 50 years, Northwest Nazarene College—the name it adopted in 1916—operated a grade school, high school, and college, and offered professional instruction in music and theology until the mid 1960s, when the college broadened its scope to the liberal arts.

Today, Northwest Nazarene University (the name adopted in 1999 as part of the institution's strategic plan) is known for excellence in all academic areas. Its business graduates have scored in the 98th percentile on the national Educational Testing Service business exam, and graduates of NNU's education department are some of the most sought-after in the Northwest. The school boasts a 95 percent acceptance rate to medical school, and its nursing department graduates have scored in the mid-to-high 90s on the National Licensing Exam. Psychology graduates have scored in the high 90s on field place-ment tests and the School of Health and Science consistently receives research grants. The Students in Free

Enterprise team has earned the distinction of Regional Champion, and the NNU forensics team has placed first in the National Forensics Conference sweepstakes competition.

NNU's accredited graduate programs also come with a long history of academic quality and innovation and faculty who are committed to helping students achieve their professional goals. Working adults may choose from many convenient and flexible ways to earn a degree in education, social work, counseling, business administration, international business administration, theology, and Christian ministries. Graduate students may pursue a degree while remaining committed to their jobs and families by scheduling courses in the evening, on weekends, or online. This level of personalized student support across the board has made NNU a favorite among its students and one of the premier Christian institutions of higher education in the Northwest.

Northwest Nazarene University welcomes visitors to its campus as well as its Web site at www.nnu.edu.

Above, far left: The expansive NNU campus is home to an Olympic-sized track, tennis courts, and baseball, softball, and soccer fields. NNU offers a rich variety of extracurricular activities and specialty programs, including NCAA Division II athletics and performing and visual arts. Above center: Students thrive in NNU's friendly, nurturing campus environment. Above right: Graduates leave NNU well prepared to meet future challenges.

Boise State University

As Idaho's largest university, Boise State University channels intellectual capital to the Gem State in the form of a heightened research agenda, service to the community, faculty and students who are devoted to learning, and graduates who are well prepared to enter the workforce.

Above: Through its eight colleges, Boise State University offers students more than 190 undergraduate, graduate, doctoral, and technical degrees.

Boise State University's established "reputational currency" as university president Bob Kustra calls it, is the driving force behind its objective to transform itself into a metropolitan research university of distinction.

Boise State is perhaps best known for its blue football field, which was named the 10th greatest sports spot in America by ESPN.com. Also widely known is the university's football team. With four consecutive Western Athletic Conference championships and six bowl appearances in the last seven years, the Broncos are a point of pride for Boise State. "Beyond the Blue," however, there is more—much more—to Boise State. The following is only a sampling.

- Enrollment: Founded as a junior college in 1932, Boise State attained four-year status in 1965 and became a university in 1974. Over the years, Boise State's enrollment has grown impressively, expanding from 11,000 students in 1986 to nearly 19,000 students today.

- Academics: Boise State offers more than 190 fields of study. Undergraduate, graduate, and technical programs are available in eight colleges: Arts and Sciences, Business and Economics, Education, Engineering, Graduate Studies, Health Sciences, Social Sciences and Public Affairs, and Applied Technology.

- New graduate programs: With the approval of two new Ph.D. programs—in electrical and computer engineering and in geosciences—during the 2005–2006 academic year, Boise State now offers four doctoral programs and more than 50 master's programs.

- Teaching: Since 1990, The Carnegie Foundation for the Advancement of Teaching has on 10 occasions named a Boise State faculty member as its Idaho "Professor of the Year." In addition, Cheryl Schrader, who serves as the dean of the university's College of Engineering, received recognition from the White House for her mentoring work in science, mathematics, and engineering.

- Student achievement: Led by forensics director Marty Most, Boise State's speech and debate team is a national powerhouse. The Talkin' Broncos are the defending Pi Kappa Delta National Tournament champions. And in spring 2006, they won the Northwest Forensics Conference's Division I title for the third straight year. The victories of the Talkin' Broncos are just a few examples of the accomplishments and excellence of Boise State's students.

- Research: In fiscal year 2005, Boise State received a school-record $24.2 million for research and sponsored projects. For fiscal year 2006, the university is on track to surpass that amount. One recent example of the infusion of research dollars is the $16 million that Boise State and other Idaho universities received from the National Institutes of Health to establish the Network of Biomedical Research Excellence.

- Facilities: Boise State's $9.5 million Caven-Williams Sports Complex, an indoor practice facility that is located next to Bronco Stadium, was completed in early 2006. Also, a $14 million, four-story Interactive Learning Center is due for completion in 2007.

These two new buildings are among the early manifestations of Boise State's ambitious long-range master plan, which was approved by the Idaho State Board of Education in fall 2005. The plan would, among many other initiatives, add 25 new structures and nearly double the size of Boise State's main campus. Complementing its master plan is Boise State's strategic vision, "Charting the Course," which is a planning process that was designed to collectively define the path and means to help the university improve its emphasis on public engagement, academic excellence, a vibrant culture, and exceptional scholarship.

- Services and resources: Boise State's offerings to the business community include the Center for Professional Development, the Center for Workforce Training, the Idaho Small Business Development Center, and the Technology and Entrepreneurial Center.

"Boise State stands uniquely positioned in Idaho as a major metropolitan university that is empowered by a dynamic, high-tech economy as well as one of the most attractive regions in the nation," says President Kustra. "Our future lies in the convergence of our metropolitan character with our excellence in higher education and faculty research. We also remain focused on contributing to the economy of our region and state, to public policy, and to the advancement of the arts and sciences."

"Beyond the Blue," Boise State University is committed to teaching excellence, life-enhancing research, and public service.

Above left: Sin Ming Loo, a Boise State professor of engineering, develops sensors to study flight-cabin air quality, a Federal Aviation Administration Center for Excellence project. Above: Boise State's 175-acre main campus is centrally located in the capital city's urban center, yet affords views of Idaho's beautiful mountains. In 2007, the university celebrates its 75th anniversary.

Idaho State University

Founded in 1901, this premier public university in southeast Idaho—a fertile region for business and quality living—today educates 14,000 diverse students, and its research programs, enrollment, capital investments, and prestige are soaring while classes stay small, personalized, and rigorous.

Above: The state-of-the-art L. E. and Thelma E. Stephens Performing Arts Center at Idaho State University houses a grand concert hall, two theatres, and the university's theatre department.

Idaho State University (ISU) is a four-year educational and research institution that attracts students and professors from around the world, and for good reason. A rich resource for students, businesses, employers, and employees, it blends academics, research facilities, and expertise with a Rocky Mountain lifestyle.

In a region largely defined by economic diversity and a fine quality of life, demand has surged for an ISU education. With its main campus in Pocatello, ISU is a leading force in meeting the growing need for everything from electronics to health care professionals, business managers, even nuclear engineers. That demand has driven remarkable growth at ISU, especially over the last two decades.

Enrollment has doubled since the mid 1980s to more than 14,000 students in seven colleges: Arts and Sciences, Business, Education, Engineering, Pharmacy, Technology, and the Kasiska College of Health Professions. Yet ISU has maintained an enviable 17-to-one student-teacher ratio.

During that same period, the number of certificate and degree programs has more than doubled and today exceeds 280. From trade and technical programs to MBAs and doctorates, ISU enables students to build solid academic foundations to meet real-world challenges.

Research funding has nearly tripled since the mid 1980s, bolstering the faculty's contributions to science, technology, and the humanities. The university's operating budget has increased nine-fold as well, reflecting ISU's expanding role in higher education in the Intermountain West.

Education at ISU extends beyond the Pocatello campus to centers in Boise, Twin Falls, and Idaho Falls. ISU has also made higher education more accessible through its statewide outreach centers, distance-learning technologies, and online programs.

ISU students come not only from high schools nationwide but also from regional small businesses, leading technology companies, and industries that compete in global arenas. In Pocatello, ISU's neighbors include AMI Semiconductor, which employs many ISU graduates and collaborates with university researchers. In Idaho Falls, ISU provides professional advancement programs for thousands of highly skilled workers affiliated with the Idaho National Laboratory, one of the nation's leading laboratories for nuclear energy research.

The ISU Biomedical Research Institute embraces the latest advances in biomedical engineering, biotechnology,

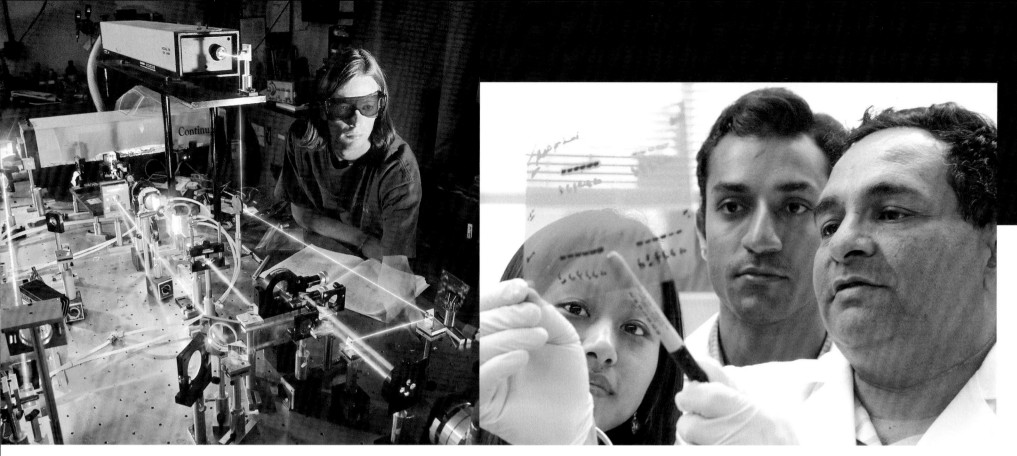

nanotechnology, neuroscience, bioinformatics, and biosignaling research in medicine, biology, and health care.

ISU is the state's leader in health professions education, as designated by the Idaho State Board of Education. At the ISU center in Boise, the fast-track nursing program is addressing the nationwide shortage of nurses. A stunning 40 percent of the nation's first-year graduate students in dental hygiene are enrolled in the university's groundbreaking online master's degree program as well. Health care institutions and businesses throughout the Intermountain West have long relied

on the Kasiska College of Health Professions at ISU and the ISU pharmacy, technology, and business colleges for skilled practitioners, managers, and other well-prepared professionals.

Growth in enrollment, opportunity, and resources has meant a flurry of capital investments—almost $180 million from the mid 1980s through 2005. On the scenic banks of the Snake River, the Center for Higher Education at University Place in Idaho Falls enrolls some 2,500 students who may choose from 30 complete degree programs. At the site, the Center for Advanced Energy Studies, an approximately

55,000-square-foot complex, is projected for completion in 2008.

On the main campus, the $43.5 million Rendezvous center, a multipurpose educational, residential, and social complex, is scheduled to open in fall 2007. Performing artists, meanwhile, have a state-of-the-art venue at ISU's $34 million L. E. and Thelma E. Stephens Performing Arts Center. At the ISU Idaho Accelerator Center, which was expanded in 2004, physicists have access to 10 operating accelerators.

Life at ISU is more than academics, research, and partnerships with

business, science, and industry. Recreational opportunities also lie at the university's doorstep. Boise and Salt Lake City are just a few hours away, as Pocatello is at the junction of two interstate highways. Yellowstone and Grand Teton national parks are nearby as well. World-class fly-fishing in some of the West's most famous waterways is right up the road, as is skiing on the legendary slopes of Jackson Hole, Wyoming, and Idaho's famous Sun Valley.

Academics, opportunity, excellent quality of life. Students have all of these at Idaho State University.

Above left: Here a student conducts an experiment in the well-equipped ISU Department of Chemistry, home to numerous and diverse advanced research programs. Above right: Students in the ISU College of Pharmacy work closely with faculty in the development of new drugs and innovative drug-delivery methods.

The University of Idaho

Students are encouraged to participate in the total college experience of classes, programs, and campus events at this university, which offers undergraduate, graduate, and specialized programs in the arts, humanities, sciences, and technology.

The University of Idaho is the state's flagship higher-education institution and its principal graduate education and research university. The Carnegie Foundation ranks University of Idaho a "research university with high research activity," the only institution in the state to achieve that elite status. The university's distinctive scholarship expands intellectual boundaries and brings insight and innovation to the state, the nation, and the world.

The University of Idaho cultivates students' practical genius through membership in a community of innovators, and students carry on a legacy of leadership. Distinguished alumni include U.S. senator Larry Craig; former U.S. ambassador Philip Habib; U.S. secretary of the interior and former U.S. senator and governor of Idaho, Dirk Kempthorne; Olympic gold medalist Dan O'Brien; Idaho supreme court justice Linda Copple Trout; NASA astronaut Jeffrey S. Ashby; and many others.

The university was founded in Moscow, Idaho, in 1889 by statute of the 15th territorial legislature as a public, land-grant institution charged with "diffusing among the people of the United States useful and practical information." In the 21st century, the university's diffusion of ideas has become global.

In the five years from 2000 to 2005 alone, University of Idaho researchers bioengineered the world's first equine clones; significantly advanced the global body of knowledge on alternative fuels and hybrid vehicles; and engineered radioactive-resistant nanotechnology that is circling Earth every 136 hours in NASA satellites. This single innovation will serve as a catalyst for radical redesigns producing smaller, less-expensive space exploration vehicles. Here on Earth, it will instigate an array of next-generation communications technologies. In 2005, undergraduate Chelan Pedrow designed the first automated growable prosthetic leg, which incorporates a sensor that allows it to grow with the child who wears it. A team of students and faculty members also designed, built, and site-tested an economical, highly effective water filter that is capable of saving hundreds of thousands of lives in third-world countries.

University of Idaho arts and humanities programs are considered world class. The Lionel Hampton International Jazz Festival, an annual tradition since 1967, brings jazz legends to campus for packed-house performances and student clinics. Students also participate in vibrant lecture series and a summer partnership with the Idaho Repertory Theatre. Kim Barnes, whose Idaho memoir *In the Wilderness* was a 1997 Pulitzer Prize finalist, and Guggenheim Fellow Robert Wrigley, whose poetry has earned four Pushcart Prizes, the Kingsley Tufts Award, and other honors, are among many outstanding members of the faculty. The University of Idaho's deep pool of faculty expertise attracts more than $100 million in grant funding annually.

The home campus in Moscow is an architectural jewel. Its ivy-covered Tudor gothic structures are set on rolling lawns surrounded by stately trees. The university also has research and education centers at Boise, Coeur d'Alene, Idaho Falls, Post Falls, and Twin Falls. University of Idaho Extension brings research-based

"At the University of Idaho, the state is our campus, and the world is our laboratory. Innovative genius thrives in this community."

—Timothy P. White, *University of Idaho President*

continues to nurture innovative leaders and productive global citizens who share their insights and discoveries.

To achieve these goals, the university strives to:

- advance core competencies in science, technology, and engineering in the areas of imaging, power and energy, biosciences, nanoscience, and materials science;
- advance the arts and sciences to strengthen and make scientific discovery, social and cultural enhancement, and progress in the applied professions relevant and accessible to all people;
- steward the environment by promoting science-based, sustainable-use practices through education, research, and extension programs;
- broaden the understanding and promotion of sustainable design and lifestyle through the integration of architecture, creative arts, and law in urban, rural, and frontier environments; and
- strengthen interdisciplinary creativity, innovation, and engagement to inspire business enterprise and technological advancement.

education with immediate, real-life application to residents of rural and urban communities in 42 Idaho counties. Some 2,300 faculty and staff members serve a diverse and high-achieving student body of more than 12,000, who come from all 50 states and some 90 countries. The university attracts many National Merit Scholars and produces students who are awarded prestigious national scholarships such as the Fulbright, Goldwater, and Udall.

U.S. News & World Report ranks University of Idaho among the top national universities that offer the widest range of undergraduate and graduate majors. More than 140 degree options are offered through 10 colleges: Agricultural and Life Sciences; Art and Architecture; Business and Economics; Education; Engineering; Letters, Arts, and Social Sciences; Natural Resources; Science; Graduate Studies; and Law. A University of Idaho education includes direct student engagement in inter-disciplinary, real-world problem solving, including research, as well as internships with organizations such as Microsoft, Boeing, NASA, and other world-leading

entities. The Princeton Review lists University of Idaho among the 150 Best Value Colleges in America, and Intel Corporation ranks it 33rd on its list of 100 "Most Unwired" College Campuses. *Outside* magazine ranks the university 29th among its top 40 colleges offering the best in outdoor adventure.

A study conducted by University of Idaho economists showed that the university created a $633.4 million statewide economic impact in 2004 and is credited with providing 13,024 jobs in Idaho. The University of Idaho

This page, far left: Says Billy Collins, the 2001–2003 U.S. Poet Laureate: "All I experienced when I was a visiting writer at the University of Idaho was a smart, devoted faculty; lively, engaging students; and a unique—sometimes breathtaking —natural environment. If there is a catch, I sure couldn't find it." This page, left: University of Idaho students and faculty members work together in state-of-the-art laboratories; their work is facilitated by a high-speed, fiber-optic, 2.4 gigabits-per-second network connection. Opposite page: The University of Idaho Administration Building, located at the heart of the Moscow campus, is listed on the National Register of Historic Places.

Lewis-Clark State College

Named after the explorers whose expeditions revealed the West, this public four-year college embodies Lewis and Clark's spirit of discovery, giving students of all backgrounds the chance to expand their frontiers with great professors, small classes, and immersion in the liberal arts, sciences, and professions.

Above and far right: On the colorful and beautiful campus of Lewis-Clark State College (LCSC), students regularly enjoy the mild climate of Lewiston, Idaho. Above center: The statues in the college's Centennial Mall depict the explorers Meriwether Lewis and William Clark meeting the Nez Perce chief Twisted Hair.

With its beautiful campus, small classes, and dedicated faculty, Lewis-Clark State College (LCSC) in Lewiston, Idaho, is often described as a public college that feels like a private one. Founded in 1893 and named after the famous explorers who scouted the area 200 years ago, LCSC is Idaho's only public four-year college. It teaches more than 3,500 diverse students from more than 20 states and 30 countries.

The location of the main Lewiston campus, at the confluence of the Clearwater and Snake rivers on the Washington-Idaho border, symbolizes LCSC's mission to connect people with their world through learning. At LCSC, education is about discovery and life.

One of the most affordable colleges in Idaho, LCSC teaches undergraduate courses in the liberal arts, sciences, professions, and applied technologies. The college has six academic divisions: nursing and health sciences, education, business, humanities, natural sciences, and social sciences. Overall, LCSC offers more than 80 programs that award bachelor or associate degrees or certificates. LCSC's student-faculty ratio of 17 to one—which is the smallest undergraduate ratio among Idaho public four-year institutions—gives students more chances for hands-on learning. Only professors—not graduate assistants—teach courses at LCSC. Beyond Lewiston, LCSC holds classes at four outreach centers in small nearby communities, and it teaches upper-division classes in Coeur d'Alene.

For five consecutive years (2001–2005), *U.S.News & World Report* ranked LCSC third or better among the West's top comprehensive bachelor's degree–granting public colleges; LCSC ranked first in 2002 and 2005. And the school's athletic teams, the Warriors, usually place at or near the top of the National Association of Intercollegiate Athletics (NAIA) standings. In the 2004–05 and 2005–06 school years, nine of the college's 10 sports teams were ranked in the NAIA Top 25, and since 1984 LCSC's baseball teams have won 14 NAIA World Series titles—an NAIA best.

At Lewis-Clark State College, students reap the benefits of a smaller campus that maintains big opportunities for practical experience and research that are related to their studies.

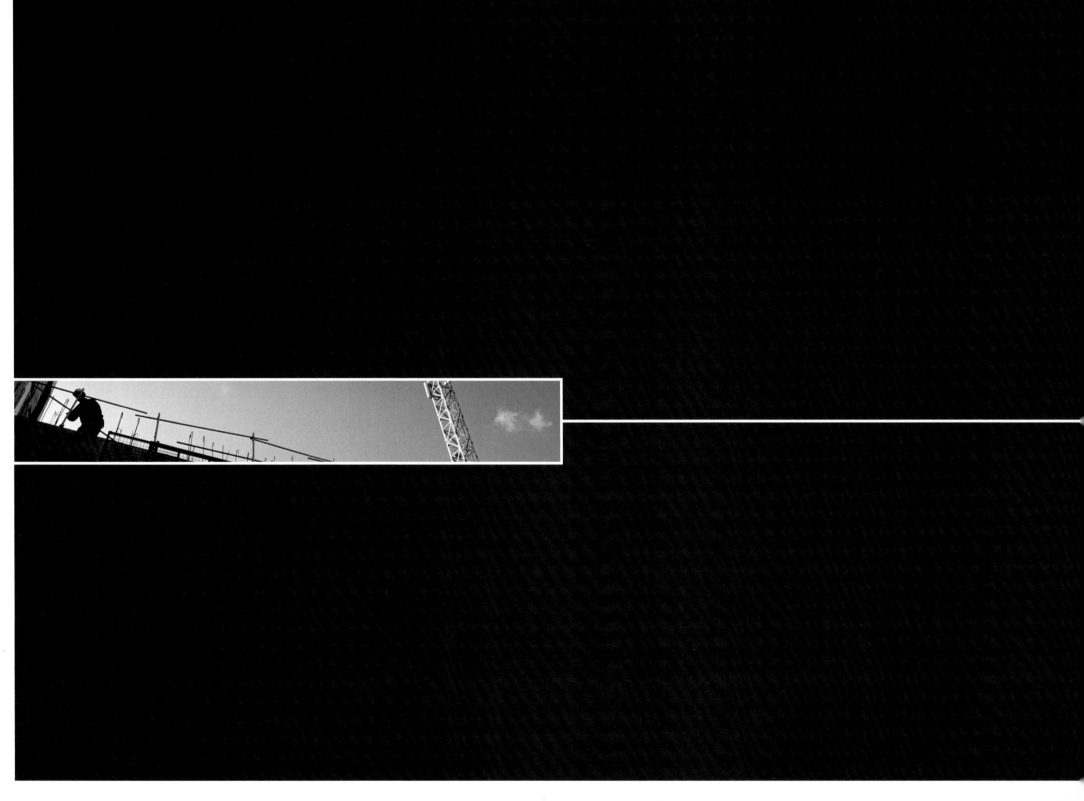

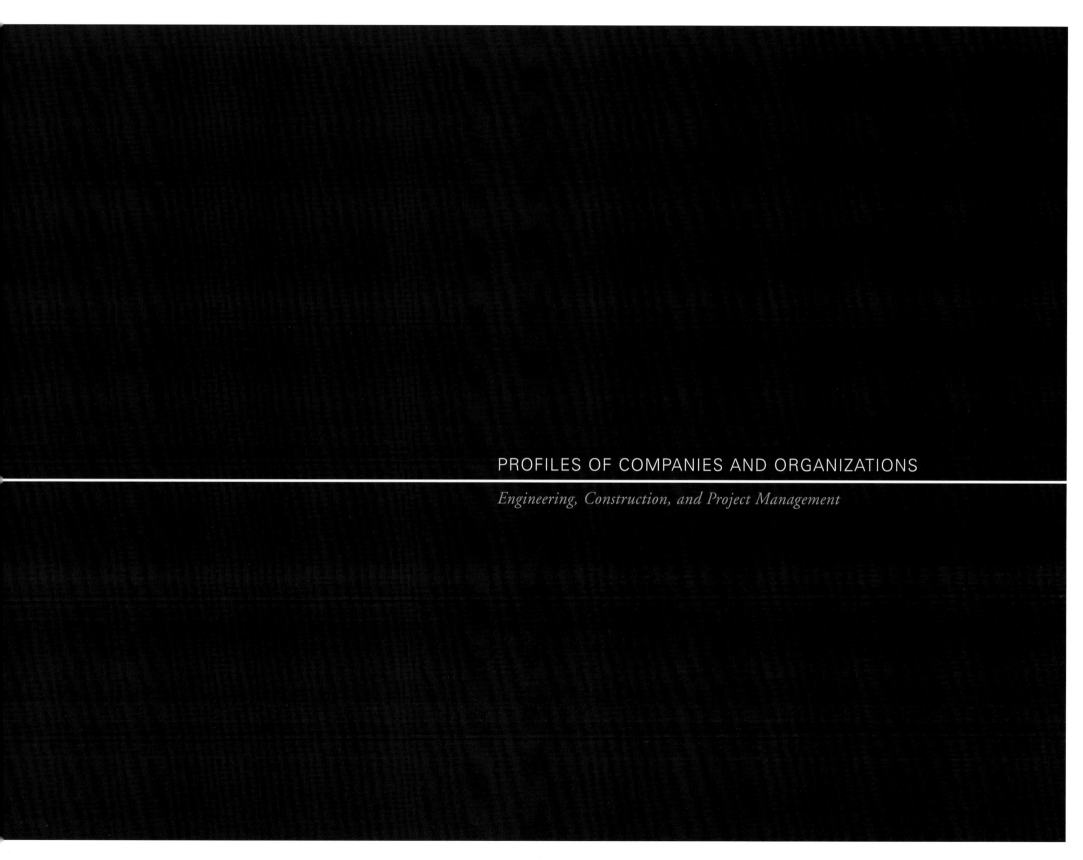

PROFILES OF COMPANIES AND ORGANIZATIONS

Engineering, Construction, and Project Management

Washington Group International, Inc.

From its headquarters in Boise, Idaho, this engineering, construction, and management-solutions firm—one of the largest in the world—addresses some of the biggest challenges facing the globe: improving water and transportation systems, homeland security, environmental cleanup, finding new sources of energy, and more.

Left: Washington Group International, Inc. designed and constructed—and now operates and maintains—the Hudson-Bergen Light Rail line in northern New Jersey, which serves more than 30,000 riders each workday. Center: Washington Group scientists have worked on space programs such as NASA's Mars Rover missions. Right: Washington Group has engineered and/or constructed power plants worldwide that provide a total of nearly 250,000 megawatts of power, equivalent to approximately one-fourth the power-generation capacity in the United States. Top right: As a service company, Washington Group's "product" is its people, and employee development is a top priority. In recognition of its efforts, the company was named one of the 2005 Top U.S. Companies for Leaders by Hewitt Associates (a global human resource consulting firm) and The Human Resource Planning Society (a global association of human resource executives).

A power transmission line across 1,000 miles of African jungle. An enormous hydroelectric irrigation project in a remote part of the Philippines. A 154-mile stretch of the Trans-Alaska Pipeline through the rugged Chugach Mountains. The Hoover Dam and the San Francisco Bay Bridge. Border security systems in the former Soviet Union and the Caspian Sea regions. In Qatar, one of the world's largest sulfur-handling plants for the gas-processing industry.

These and thousands of other projects of all types and sizes are the heritage of a company with deep roots in

Idaho—a leading engineering, construction, and management-solutions company that has left its imprint of progress around the world.

That company, the Boise-based Washington Group International, Inc. (Nasdaq: WGII), today serves markets that include power generation, transmission and distribution, and clean-air solutions; environmental management; heavy civil construction; mining; nuclear services; homeland security and global threat reduction; industrial processes; facilities management; transportation; and water resources.

The company's nearly 25,000 employees work in approximately 30 countries, and its clientele includes the U.S. Department of Energy, the U.S. Department of Defense, NASA, state government agencies, Anheuser-Busch, ExxonMobil, ConocoPhillips, Agrium, Kraft Foods, DuPont, Monsanto, DTE Energy, We Energies, IBM, Caterpillar, Ford, General Motors, and many other leading companies internationally.

Washington Group, through its oil, gas, nuclear power, and mining operations, is at the forefront of the global search for more dependable, cost-effective,

and clean energy sources. Washington Group scientists are developing high-technology solutions to the challenges of homeland security, space exploration, energy production, and environmental cleanup. The company is a national leader in the destruction of chemical weapons and other weapons of mass destruction.

Washington Group gets its name from legendary industrialist (and chairman of the board) Dennis R. Washington, whose vision helped create this global engineering and construction power-house. Washington Group draws on the knowledge, experience, and integrity of

its 20-some "heritage companies," some of which go back more than a century. These include Westinghouse Government Services, Raytheon Engineers & Constructors, the Boise-based Morrison Knudsen Corporation, and other companies.

Washington Group is part of a joint venture managing the Idaho National Laboratory, which develops next-generation nuclear energy technology and serves as a major center for national security development and demonstration. The company also engages in state environmental management and transportation projects.

Washington Group makes a positive impact around the world and in its home state of Idaho. The company shows corporate stewardship in many ways, including charitable contributions that advance education and health-care technology. The company's employees also volunteer in their communities, serve on nonprofit boards, and embrace numerous philanthropic causes.

Eastern Idaho native Stephen G. Hanks, a Washington Group employee since 1978 and company president and CEO since 2001, says making a difference is what the company is all about.

"Washington Group International is making the world a better place," states Hanks. "We are making the world safer through our homeland security and our environmental-management solutions. We are improving the quality of life through clean, dependable power sources and through safe, efficient transportation systems and industrial facilities. We are also giving back to our communities through many company programs and the individual efforts of our employees. The people of Washington Group International are making a difference every day."

Above left: Washington Group designed and constructed the Lost Cabin Gas Processing Plant in central Wyoming as part of its broad-based services to the oil, gas, and chemicals market. Above right: The San Roque Multipurpose Hydroelectric Project in the Philippines shows the company's leadership in creating water-resource facilities for power, irrigation, flood control, and drinking water. Below left: In 2006, Washington Group was recognized as one of Fortune's 10 Most Admired Engineering and Construction Companies and as one of ENR's Top 10 Design-Build Firms.

DeBest Plumbing, Inc.

Through hard work, good people, and strategy, this Boise plumbing and mechanical contractor, in business since 1973, has become one of the largest, most respected companies of its kind in Idaho, with a reputation for delivering quality work and outstanding service to its many clients.

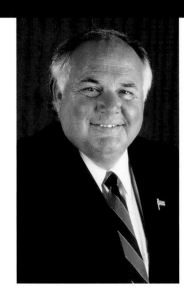

As an orphan, Milford Terrell learned to overcome adversity at a tender age. Moving from one home to another throughout his childhood and being separated from his siblings were hardships that instilled in him a strong work ethic and a will to succeed. In 1973 with a $1,000 loan, a used van, and great desire and determination, Terrell started DeBest Plumbing, Inc. from his garage, with one part-time employee and four contractor clients. Now recognized as an industry leader, the company occupies three acres, employs 125 workers, and serves dozens of clients.

No stranger at turning obstacles into opportunities, Terrell saw Boise's economic downturn in the early 1980s as a chance to diversify from residential work into commercial jobs and government contracts. The new jobs gave the company and its workers opportunities for personal and professional growth and education—excellent preparation for things to come. A few years later, when the economy was on the upswing and Boise experienced a building boom, DeBest was ready. By 1987, after the company completed work on

the Boise Convention Center and Boise Towne Square Mall, it became a well-known fixture in the construction industry and one of the largest plumbing contractors in the state.

Over the years, more business meant more changes for DeBest. Increased government regulations and more competition required more efficient job tracking, so a state-of-the-art computer system was created to help employees track jobs from bidding through completion. Terrell diversified the company again in 1993 to include a fire protection business, which installs sprinkler systems for residential, commercial, and industrial buildings. DeBest Fire Protection, Inc. has won contracts for some of Boise's and Idaho's largest projects. The company's growth also gave way to a service department staffed by capable employees who answer questions and solve problems as they occur.

The DeBest philosophy—to offer the best in service, products, efficiency, and price—is just one way the company maintains its competitive edge. Another is by attracting the best

workers. Terrell strongly believes that "you're only as good as the people who surround you," and credits many dedicated employees as integral to the company's success. DeBest offers an attractive benefits package and apprenticeship training for employees who wish to complete the four-year licensing process required to become a journeyman plumber.

A devoted philanthropist and tireless civic leader, Terrell's passion is

giving back to the community. His financial support of numerous charitable and civic organizations and his leadership in countless business, religious, and cultural committees have made him one of Idaho's most active and admired business owners. If success can be measured by the opportunities given to others as well as by one's own achievements, then Terrell and DeBest are two of Idaho's most enduring success stories.

Above left: From personal experience, DeBest Plumbing, Inc. president and founder Milford Terrell believes that given a chance, anyone can and will succeed. Above right: Based in Boise, DeBest Plumbing is known for its excellent service, quality, and value. DeBest also offers fire protection services.

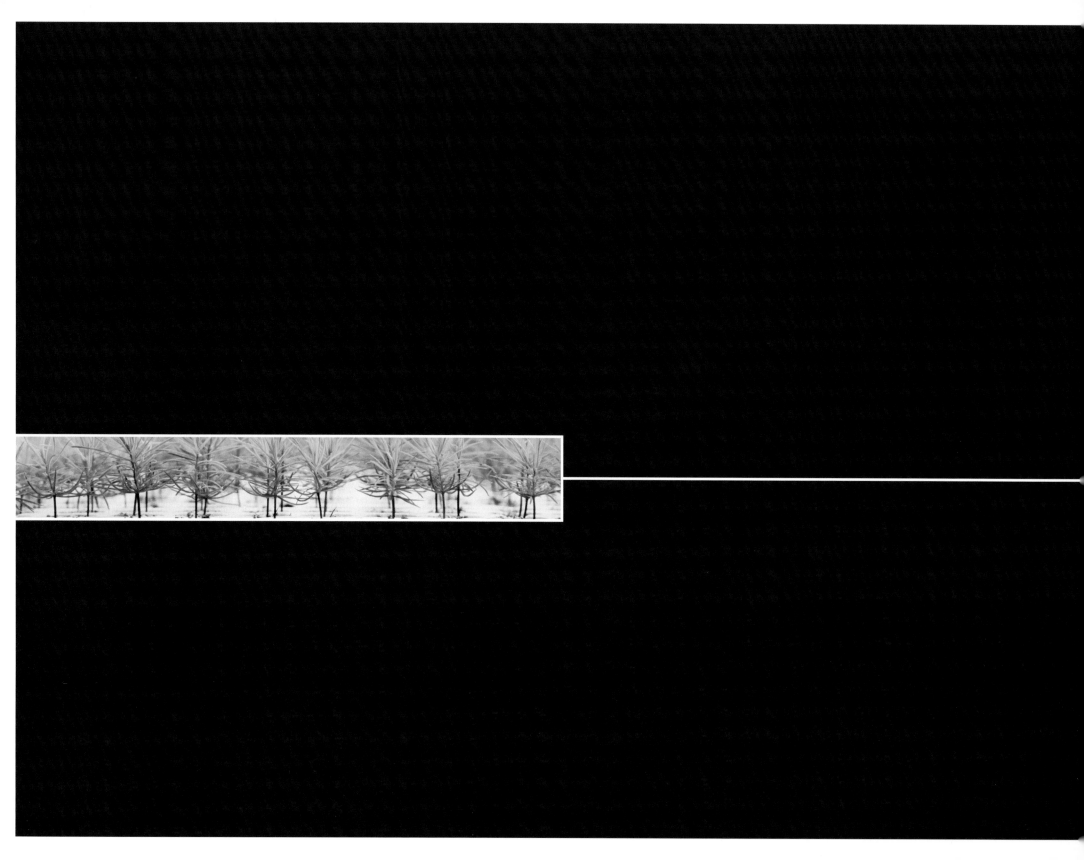

PROFILES OF COMPANIES AND ORGANIZATIONS

Environmental Science and Technology

North Wind, Inc.

This award-winning, woman-owned company—proudly established and headquartered in Idaho Falls, Idaho—serves the state, the nation, and the continent with its groundbreaking environmental consulting services, which are guided by its elite teams of scientists, engineers, and technicians.

Above: Sylvia M. Medina is the founder, president, and CEO of North Wind, Inc., a firm that creates innovative, comprehensive environmental restoration and preservation solutions. Top: North Wind is headquartered in Idaho Falls, Idaho.

Sylvia M. Medina, president and CEO, founded North Wind, Inc. in 1997 with a clear vision: to create a company that would help preserve Idaho's wealth of natural resources. On the strength of her vision and mission, North Wind today is a leading environmental engineering, consulting, and construction firm that works to safeguard the air, land, and water in its home state as well as throughout North America.

Remarkably, in less than a decade, North Wind has grown to employ over 300 professionals dispersed across 19 offices throughout the Intermountain West, the Southeast, and Alaska. In 2005, the company generated more than $39 million in revenue, reflecting its high quality of service and wide-ranging capabilities. North Wind services include:

- environmental restoration;
- waste management;
- decontamination, demolition, and decommissioning;
- construction;
- safety and health;
- natural and cultural resources;
- remediation technology;
- engineering;
- information technology and GIS (geographic information systems);
- public involvement and communications;
- environmental compliance, permitting, and management; and
- antiterrorism research and development.

Among the company's prominent clients are numerous private, public, and governmental entities. A significant portion of North Wind's work is for the U.S. Department of Defense (Army, Army Corps of Engineers, Air Force, Navy), U.S. Department of Energy, and U.S. Department of the Interior.

North Wind's notable projects include the Big Ox Mine Reclamation (for the Montana Department of Environmental Quality) and the Nabob Millsite Groundwater Remediation (for the Idaho Bureau of Land Management). For both of these large-scale projects, a major part of the work involved design-build systems that would ensure environmentally sound practices and restore the surrounding area to its natural state. North Wind's Crystal Mountain Road Obliteration project (for the U.S. Forest Service in Montana), involved obliterating 22 mountainous miles of Forest Service roads and revegetating and restoring the area to its pre-road condition and natural beauty. For the Department of Energy's Idaho National Laboratory, North Wind has performed a host of environment-related activities, from implementation of an innovative groundwater remediation solution at Test Area North to providing meeting and facilitation support for the organization's Citizens' Advisory Board.

An Honored Industry Leader

Since its founding, North Wind has been widely recognized for its outstanding services and quality management. North Wind's numerous awards include the Small Business Administration's 2005 Regional Prime Contractor of the Year award in Region X. North Wind was also selected in both 2004 and 2005 as the Top Diversity Owned Firm in Idaho by DiversityBusiness.com, a primary resource portal for businesses nationwide. In addition, Medina herself has been the recipient of many awards. In 2005 she was honored by the Small Business Administration as one of the nation's top five outstanding women entrepreneurs and by the Boise/Southeast Idaho Chapter of the National Association of Women Business Owners (NAWBO) as Business Woman of the Year.

Overall, key to North Wind's continuing success is Medina's and her teams' commitment to maintaining impeccable customer relations and to positively impacting the environment. The company's top-notch archaeologists, biologists, chemists, engineers, environmental scientists, geologists, industrial hygienists, construction managers, and quality control specialists serve the needs of clients and preserve the natural wealth of Idaho and the nation.

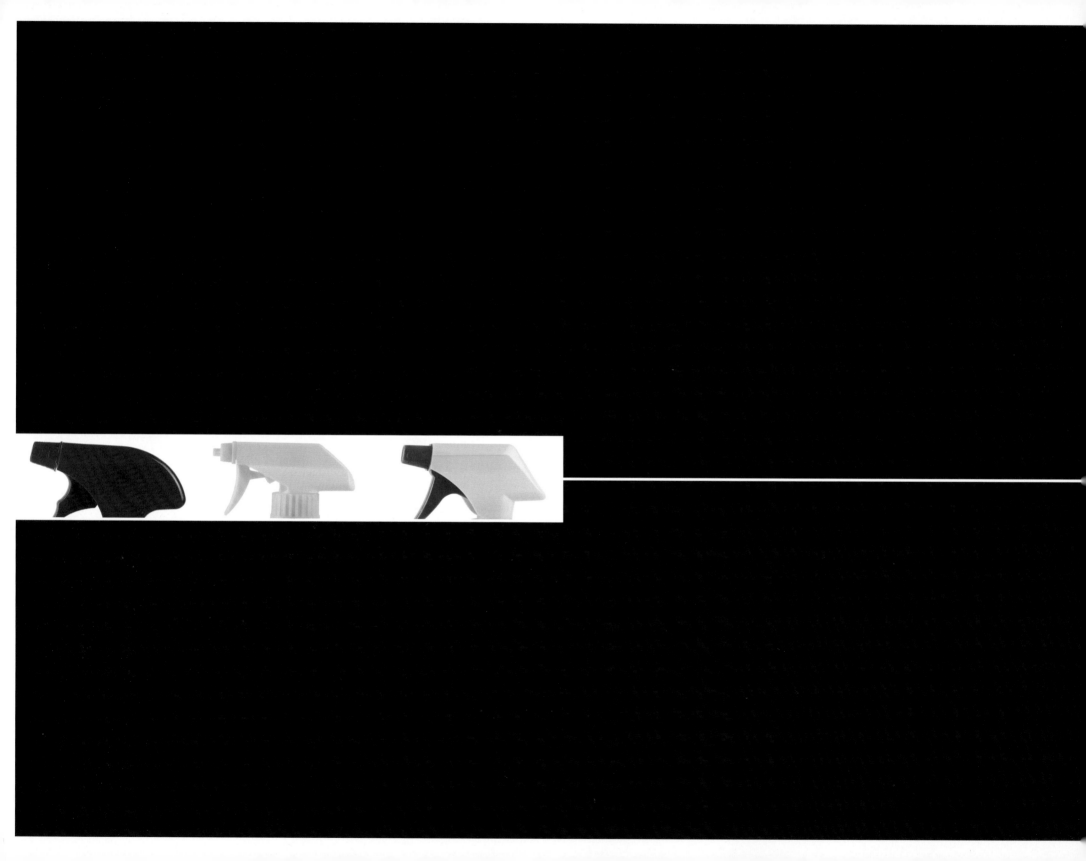

PROFILES OF COMPANIES AND ORGANIZATIONS

Facility Services

Varsity Contractors, Inc.

One of the most trusted names in the facility services industry, Varsity Contractors, Inc. offers a comprehensive line of cost-effective integrated facility services nationwide, from maintenance and construction to plumbing and electrical work, helping its clients' businesses run smoothly.

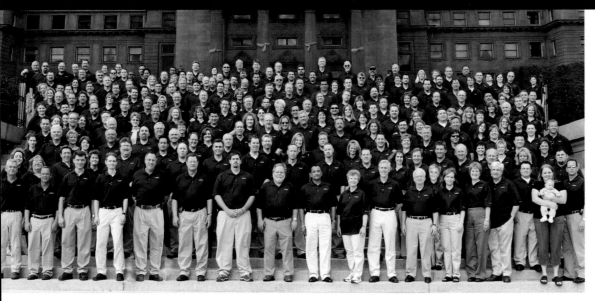

Cleaning Up for a Living

This is the title of the best-selling book by company founder Don Aslett, right, explaining all the ins and outs of running a successful cleaning business. Don's humor—a key ingredient in more than two dozen of his popular books on cleaning and decluttering—is the foundation of Varsity's light-hearted culture. For 25 years his books and media presence (he appears on national television, radio, and at the podium of every imaginable type of gathering) have given Varsity tremendous visibility, making it possibly the best-known cleaning company in the United States.

Spreading the Message of Clean

Through the quarterly *Clean Report* catalog (which has 80,000 subscribers), the Cleaning Center stores, and television's QVC home shopping channel, Don and Varsity continue putting professional-grade tools and cleaners in the home.

Above: The Varsity Contractors, Inc. management team visits Idaho's state capitol building during their annual meeting, hosted in 2005 by Varsity of Boise.

Combining all-American ambition with the need to pay for their own education, a group of college students started "cleaning up for a living" 50 years ago. They developed a professional janitorial company and unique corporate culture that many have copied but few, if any, have equaled.

Today, Varsity Contractors, Inc. is an industry leader with national accounts of all kinds—offices, banks, malls, high-tech and health care facilities, utility companies, schools, and universities across the country. It has expanded beyond total facility service to construction and retail build-outs and even software development for quality assurance. Varsity now directly employs 4,200 people and works with another 3,000 subcontractors.

Based in Pocatello, Idaho, Varsity is dedicated to its goal of "providing customers, employees, and owners a secure, exciting, and satisfying life by being *the* standard of excellence in the entire facility service industry."

The Edge Called Imagination

Cleaning and maintaining things in the most efficient and cost-effective way helped Varsity grow from a tiny college crew to a giant national corporation servicing every state in the country. From the beginning, motivation, competitive spirit, and the habit of always going the extra mile for clients have formed a lively "spirit of service" and a dedication to the ideal of "clean" that can't be matched.

Varsity works at finding ways to spotlight "clean" and raise the morale and visibility of cleaning professionals. Janitor rodeos, janitor fashion shows, carnivals, vacuum race cars, mop art, and dozens of other one-of-a-kind contests keep creative juices flowing at annual meetings, or any time the Varsity team gathers. The company also created the world's largest

Cleaning Museum and Cleaning Library, whose wares are now displayed in the Varsity corporate office in Pocatello. A major expansion of the museum is under way.

Varsity culture also entails volunteerism and community service. Varsity employees are encouraged to be generous with time, talents, money, and other resources.

Arlo Luke, CEO, sets the bar high by donating his time and talents to Pocatello's International Choral Festival, Valley Pride, and the annual citywide performance of Handel's *Messiah*. He has also presided over the industry's trade association, BSCAI (Building Service Contractors Association International).

Every year Varsity performs service projects in neighborhoods where its people live and work, from coast to coast, and it contributes to the Boy Scouts of America. "We take great pride in the success of the company and achieving excellence," says Luke, "but in the end, if we don't use our company and resources to improve our community and the lives of those we associate with, then we don't consider ourselves truly successful. Service is the core ingredient in this."

World-Class Capability

With state-of-the-art marketing, computerized accounting, and its university (see sidebar), Varsity is one of the top-ranked companies in the industry, with a nationwide footprint and strategic partnerships to meet any need. Varsity services major accounts like Simon Property Group, Washington Mutual, Qwest, National City Bank, CB Richard Ellis, Key Bank, Anheuser-Busch, and hundreds more.

Varsity Contractors, Inc. Statistics at a Glance

Services: Comprehensive total facility services include janitorial work, HVAC maintenance, landscaping maintenance, construction, plumbing, parking lot maintenance, and electrical work. The company also offers labor and management services; for example, lighting maintenance and facility asset management.

Locations: Varsity maintains operations in all 50 states and Canada.

Vehicles: Varsity has a fleet of 460 service vehicles.

Staff: Varsity directly employs 4,200 people and works with another 3,000 subcontractors.

Training: With 400 professional development courses and a live instructor–led virtual classroom, Varsity University is the source for online learning and custom training for Varsity employees, customers, and subcontractors.

Sales: Varsity is a closely held corporation with more than $250 million in annual sales.

Above left: CEO Arlo Luke leads a 400-member choir at the 2005 National Boy Scout Jamboree. Left: Varsity comprises a family of diverse businesses and its own university.

Varsity and Related Companies:

| Medical specialists | Hardwood installation & finishing | Educational facilities specialists | Minority-owned subsidiary | Software products & tech services | Publications & personal appearances | Training & professional development | Innovative home products & design | Professional quality supplies |

Net Cash.

PROFILES OF COMPANIES AND ORGANIZATIONS

Financial and Insurance Services

Regence BlueShield of Idaho

A leading health insurer in Idaho since 1946, this company serves 180,000 members, focusing on enabling customers to take control of their health care choices.

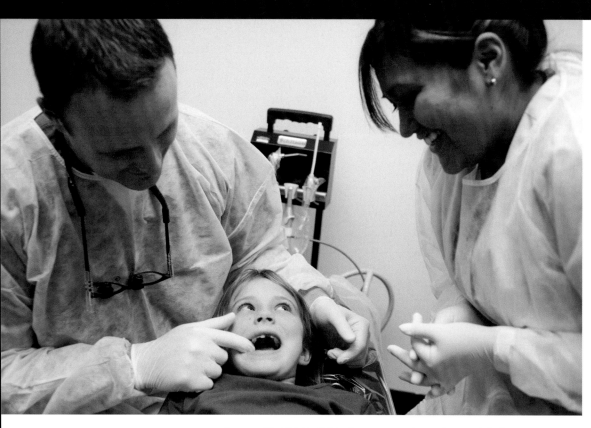

Above: The Regence Caring Foundation for Children provides free dental insurance for children of needy families, contracting with dentists statewide to ensure convenient care.

"By offering wellness and prevention programs and developing new products to keep pace with the accelerated changes in health care, we are able to help hold down costs while delivering maximum service to our members," says John Stellmon, Regence BlueShield of Idaho president.

Health Insurance for Idaho

Regence BlueShield of Idaho is an affiliate of Regence, which comprises four Blue Shield and/or Blue Cross Blue Shield health insurers, located in Idaho, Oregon, Washington, and Utah. Together, these companies provide health coverage for more than three million people and have 6,000 employees.

The company was founded in Lewiston, Idaho, in 1946 as the North Idaho District Medical Service Bureau when 26 physicians contributed $100 each to incorporate as a business that would offer prepaid medical insurance plans.

By 1950 the company was operating in nine of the 19 counties in North Idaho

and soon had 25,000 individual members and 400 companies covered under its varied policies. By the 1960s it had become a member of the national and regional Blue Shield Association of physician-sponsored, prepaid medical-service plans. The company expanded statewide during the1970s, opening an office in Boise and adding "Blue Shield of Idaho" to its name in 1976.

In the mid 1990s, the North Idaho District Medical Service Bureau, Blue Shield of Idaho, along with Blue Cross and Blue Shield of Oregon, King County Medical Blue Shield, Pierce County Medical Bureau, and Blue Cross Blue Shield of Utah came together to form Regence, a regional alliance of health insurers, and North Idaho District Medical Service Bureau, BlueShield of Idaho, became Regence BlueShield of Idaho.

Today, the company's 700 employees staff the company's headquarters in Lewiston and additional locations in Coeur d'Alene, Boise, Twin Falls, and Pocatello, Idaho.

Regence BlueShield of Idaho is a not-for-profit, mutual health insurance company offering medical, dental, vision, and life insurance options for individuals and for employers with companies of all sizes.

Its product portfolio focuses on consumer-driven health insurance options with variety and breadth of coverage in benefits and services, all designed to provide the best care for each member.

Regence Advantages

Regence BlueShield of Idaho, an independent licensee of the Blue Cross and Blue Shield Association, focuses on member access to health care services and long-term wellness through a variety of partnering relationships with employers, health care providers, and local communities. The company offers an online enrollment program; Health Savings Accounts, the latest tool in self-directed health care, which allows members to use their health care money as they see fit; and BlueCard, which is designed to ensure members access to the best in health care while traveling across the United States and abroad. It is committed to providing members with the highest quality health care while still controlling costs. Employee/Individual Assistance, Health Coaching, and Maternity Management programs are designed to offer peace of mind to members choosing care in those areas.

Through the company's award-winning Regence Engine, an interactive environment on its Web site (www.myregence.com), members have direct access to hospital ratings, doctors' profiles, and cost breakdowns, as well as health-related news and details on health-related events in their local communities. It also provides access to weight-loss, hearing, vision, and other fitness programs, information, and discounts.

"We are redefining the health care experience with tools and technology to allow our members to navigate the complex and complicated health care system," Stellmon says. "Our members have told us that they want assistance in navigating the health care maze, but they want to be in the driver's seat. The Regence Engine furthers our goal of transforming access to the health care system by providing a trusted source of information and putting the power back in the hands of the customer."

A Healthy Community

A strong believer in increasing the general public's participation in improving their own health status, Regence BlueShield of Idaho takes pride in its role in the growth of the community's health awareness. Executive staff members participate in the political process, keeping elected officials informed about how their decisions impact the lives of the company's members. The company introduced a "Legislators on the Move" program during the 2005 state legislative session to help raise awareness about the link between individuals' activity levels and good health. In 2006 the program was renamed "Move It!" and was again popular among not only state legislators but also elementary schools in Idaho.

In addition to supporting the activities of its Charitable Giving Committee and its employee volunteers, the company is a sponsor of and administers the Regence Caring Foundation for Children, a charitable organization that provides free dental insurance to children of needy families.

"We are committed to the people of Idaho, Idaho businesses, and Idaho communities to help ensure that our customers receive quality health care services," says Stellmon. "A healthy community—socially, economically, physically, and emotionally—means lower health care costs for everyone and a healthier Idaho." As an instrumental company with a strong leadership role in the community, Regence BlueShield of Idaho will continue to operate as one of the state's leading health insurers by improving care for its members.

Above left: Regence BlueShield of Idaho's Hometown Heroes program rewards people and communities in the company's service area who have taken charge to bring about positive change. Shown here are student body presidents from three high schools in Idaho Joint School District 241 that were recognized in 2006 in the company's program. Above right: The Regence BlueShield of Idaho Web site www.myregence.com—referred to as the "Regence Engine"— is an interactive environment where members can navigate options, obtain advice, and be rewarded regarding their health care decisions.

Blue Cross of Idaho

For more than 60 years, Blue Cross of Idaho has been a vital corporate citizen serving the people of Idaho, and today it is the state's largest health insurer, providing coverage for nearly one in three Idahoans.

In 1945, World War II came to an end. Harry S. Truman succeeded Franklin D. Roosevelt as president. The United Nations charter was signed. And Blue Cross of Idaho first began serving the Gem State as Idaho Hospital Service, a local Blue Cross chapter. Since then, Blue Cross of Idaho has grown from 10,000 members to more than 400,000 today.

Attractive products and services and competitive prices, along with more and more people moving to Idaho, have led to record membership gains. Blue Cross of Idaho achieved a growth rate of 28 percent from 2003 to 2005, making it the fastest-growing of the 38 Blue Cross and Blue Shield plans nationwide during that time period, on a percentage basis. These strong results demonstrate Blue Cross of Idaho's success.

Based in Meridian, just west of Boise, with district offices in Coeur d'Alene, Idaho Falls, Lewiston, Pocatello, and Twin Falls, Blue Cross of Idaho's number one priority is the same today as it was in 1945: serving its members.

Above left: Ray Flachbart serves as the president and CEO of Blue Cross of Idaho. Above right: Blue Cross of Idaho's employees are committed to helping members live healthier lives.

The company's mission also remains unchanged: Provide members with access to cost-effective quality care while providing superior customer service. As Blue Cross of Idaho looks to the future, its focus is firmly on its customers. Focusing on the customer means being there when needed and doing its job well—as an insurer, a health partner, an employer, and a community citizen—so Blue Cross of Idaho members can live healthier lives.

Growing with Idaho

While Blue Cross of Idaho's priority and mission have remained unchanged, what has changed is the portfolio of its products and services to better meet the health insurance needs of its members.

In the beginning, as a not-for-profit insurance company, Blue Cross of Idaho offered only prepaid hospital services for employer groups. Today, Blue Cross of Idaho offers employers, individuals, and families a wide portfolio of health-benefit products, including traditional, preferred provider organization (PPO), managed care, Medicare supplement, and Medicare Advantage products. Blue Cross of Idaho knows that employers

today have the difficult job of balancing their own need to manage costs with their employees' demands for a quality health plan that offers excellent service along with extras that help give them more for their money. This is why Blue Cross of Idaho works as a partner with Idaho employers in meeting their employees' needs.

One to One

As Idaho's largest health insurer, Blue Cross of Idaho believes in being a health care partner for its members and empowering the community to

stay healthy. This is why Blue Cross of Idaho has built a strong team of caring and talented health professionals to work with members' specific needs.

For members with complex medical conditions who might benefit from a closer relationship with a health expert, Blue Cross of Idaho makes available individual case-management nurses. It also offers numerous programs designed around the health needs of members living with specific medical conditions such as asthma, diabetes, and congestive heart failure. As Blue Cross of Idaho

sees it, an important part of its job is to help members be well, stay healthy, and manage their long-term or chronic health conditions.

Blue Cross of Idaho also offers its members the benefit of a comprehensive network of physicians and hospitals across the state. Ninety-seven percent of all Idaho physicians and 100 percent of all hospitals in the state are part of Blue Cross of Idaho's traditional network. Moreover, 92 percent of the state's physicians and 100 percent of its hospitals participate in Blue Cross of Idaho's PPO network. Comprehensive networks, thoughtful benefit designs, and caring customer-service representatives have made Blue Cross of Idaho's health plans a popular and smart choice since 1945.

Committed to Its Community

Blue Cross of Idaho and its employees invest in the community through a variety of charitable donations and volunteer activities. For example, the company and its employees support United Way, donating more than $120,000 in 2005. The company is a United Way Corporate Champion, which ensures that 100 percent of its contributions remain within Idaho to assist those in need. In addition, more than 200 Blue Cross of Idaho employees participate annually in the Treasure Valley Heart Walk—in 2005, these employees helped the American Heart Association raise more than $195,000 toward its fight against heart disease.

Through an ongoing effort to encourage employee and management involvement in volunteer activities and community service, Blue Cross of Idaho's staff donates more than 1,300 volunteer hours each year assisting Special Olympics Idaho, Rake Up Meridian, the Susan G. Komen Breast Cancer Foundation, the Idaho Humane Society, the Idaho Shakespeare Festival, the St. Luke's Women's Fitness Celebration, the Saint Alphonsus Foundation, and other organizations.

Blue Cross of Idaho is locally owned and operated, with a dedicated board of directors, a management team headed by president and CEO Ray Flachbart, and a staff that has grown from 24 associates in 1945 to more than 800 today. Blue Cross of Idaho is an independent licensee of the Blue Cross and Blue Shield Association (BCBSA).

As a partner in Idaho's heroic journey, Blue Cross of Idaho's mission remains to serve as the state's premier health insurer and as a significant contributor to its communities.

Above left: Blue Cross of Idaho's employees participate annually in the Treasure Valley Heart Walk, just one of the many ways in which this company and its employees give back to the community. Above right: Blue Cross of Idaho's headquarters is located in Meridian, Idaho.

United Heritage

Large enough to meet any client's financial and insurance needs, small enough to provide them with friendly, attentive service—this Meridian, Idaho–based group of financial companies now does business in 31 states, helping people reach financial security for themselves and their families.

Above left: The technologically advanced headquarters building of United Heritage is located in Meridian, Idaho, in the heart of the Treasure Valley. Above right: The board of directors of United Heritage Financial Group includes, from left, seated, Dennis L. Johnson, president and CEO; Richard E. Hall, chairman of the board; and Rodney L. Smith, vice chairman of the board; and standing, board members Steven D. Hauschild, James R. Hay, Julie E. Prafke, Ned E. Clark, and Richard C. Waitley.

The United Heritage home office in Meridian, Idaho, employs 111 people, and the Sublimity Oregon office has 20 employees. Altogether, the staff assists 1,200 UHLIC agents, 116 UHFS representatives, 165 UPH&C agency locations, and 142 Sublimity agency locations. This amounts to approximately 1,754 individuals whose primary objective is superior customer service in the financial services industry.

History of Expansion

In 1934 Nampa native W. W. Deal founded Grange Mutual Life Company (GML), which sold affordable life insurance exclusively to grange members in Washington and Idaho. In 1944 GML began selling insurance in Oregon, Montana, and Colorado, and in 1958 it forged ahead by eliminating the membership requirement and selling insurance to the general public. By 1959 the GML coverage territory had stretched to Iowa, Wyoming, and California. Expansion required more office space, and in 1961 GML Nampa moved from an old church to a new building on 12th Avenue Road.

In the early 1970s GML entered Arizona, Nevada, South Dakota, and Utah. In

For much of its history, United Heritage reflected its place in time. Now it surges ahead, outrunning its own strategic plan for progress, accelerating achievement by building upon well-honed philosophies and long-standing relationships. Its finely tuned customer-centered approach, which is based on a personal understanding of its customers coupled with its evolving operations exhibits its unique ability to flex with the times and anticipate trends.

Headquartered in Meridian in the heart of Idaho's most populous valley, United Heritage remains on the leading edge,

concerned about people, and highly visible in its community and far beyond.

United Heritage Financial Group, the holding company for United Heritage, anchors four specialized companies providing a full spectrum of coverage. United Heritage Life Insurance Company (UHLIC), the largest life insurer domiciled in Idaho, offers a wide variety of insurance and annuity products in 31 states. United Heritage Financial Services (UHFS) offers investment products to over 50 mutual fund families, 40 variable annuity carriers, 10 variable universal life insurers, and four limited partnership programs.

UHFS is authorized to conduct general securities business in 31 states and is licensed for insurance business in 22 states. United Heritage Property and Casualty (UHP&C), providing superior service to Idaho customers since 1908, offers homeowners and fire insurance products throughout Idaho, Oregon, and Utah. Sublimity Insurance Company (SIC), an Oregon-based affiliate since 2003, offers a wide selection of homeowners, auto, and fire insurance coverage in Oregon, Idaho, and Utah, retaining the compassion and customer-service orientation that characterized the vision of its founders in 1896.

Richard E. Hall
Chairman of the Board,
United Heritage Financial Group

Dennis L. Johnson
President and CEO, United Heritage
Financial Group and United Heritage
Life Insurance Company

Jack J. Winderl
President and CEO,
United Heritage Financial Services

Brian E. Henman
President and CEO,
United Heritage Property & Casualty

G. Richer Budke
President and CEO,
Sublimity Insurance Company

the next 20 years it brought nine more states into its fold, eventually serving all 22 continental states west of the Mississippi. GML's focus remained life insurance policies, and its growth helped establish the company as a stable, trustworthy fixture in Idaho finance.

In 1991 GML became United Heritage Mutual Life Insurance Company and adopted a landing eagle and mountains as its logo. In the 1990s it was not unusual for banks, financial services firms, and insurance companies to blend their businesses in order to streamline these services for clients. In response to this new era, United Heritage formed United Heritage Financial Services (UHFS) in 1994 as a licensed National Association of Securities Dealers (NASD) broker-dealer marketing equity products such as stocks, bonds, mutual funds, and variable annuities.

Today and Tomorrow

In an effort to remain true to its customer-centered philosophy, in 2000 United Heritage acquired Idaho Mutual Insurance Company, the state's oldest insurer, established in 1908. Renamed United Heritage Property and Casualty (UHP&C), the company's first business in the property and casualty domain was yet another strategic move that United Heritage made in becoming a fully integrated financial services deliverer. In 2001 United Heritage became a mutual holding company with the flexibility to acquire more companies and raise more capital. United Heritage Mutual Holding Company, the top of the organizational pyramid, is the sole shareholder of United Heritage Financial Group, which oversees the four United Heritage divisions. It is owned by the policyholders of United Heritage Life and Sublimity Insurance companies.

Also in 2001, United Heritage moved from Nampa to its modern Meridian headquarters in the Treasure Valley. For a motorist on Interstate 84, the building emerges as an exceptional landmark; unseen are the advanced business features within, such as fiber-optic technology linked to every workstation, electronic whiteboards, plasma displays, and videoconferencing. United Heritage believes that technology is a key building block in the foundation of business efficiency and customer service. And in 2003 United Heritage formed its affiliation with Sublimity Insurance Company.

Helping clients and community members realize their dreams is at the core of the United Heritage family of companies' mission. This includes not only offering the highest quality of service and products but also being active in community events and charities. United Heritage donates funds to various charitable organizations and encourages its employees to volunteer their time and efforts to support numerous causes. In 2002 the company formed a partnership with the Idaho Community Foundation to create the United Heritage Fund, a philanthropic gift fund that is used to distribute monetary donations to IRS-recognized charities, including United Way, Boys & Girls Clubs of Ada County, Boys & Girls Clubs of Canyon County, the Women's and Children's Alliance of Idaho, the Idaho Peace Officers Memorial, the American Red Cross, the Boise Philharmonic, universities in Idaho, and Junior Achievement of Idaho.

In 2005, for the fourth consecutive year, United Heritage Financial Group was named among the Idaho Private 75, which measures the best-performing Idaho-based companies by annual revenue and management excellence. Chosen from 350 candidates, the top 75 companies are determined by *The Idaho Statesman*, Bank of Idaho, and accounting firm KPMG.

United Heritage is large enough to meet the needs of its clients yet small enough to provide a high level of personalized financial services. For a century, United Heritage has successfully positioned itself at the top of its field, translating its strong financial position into protection and security for its policyholders and clients.

Above: The boardroom at United Heritage headquarters makes use of the building's technologically advanced infrastructure, which includes such features as fiber-optic communications lines, electronic whiteboards, plasma displays, and convenient videoconferencing capabilities.

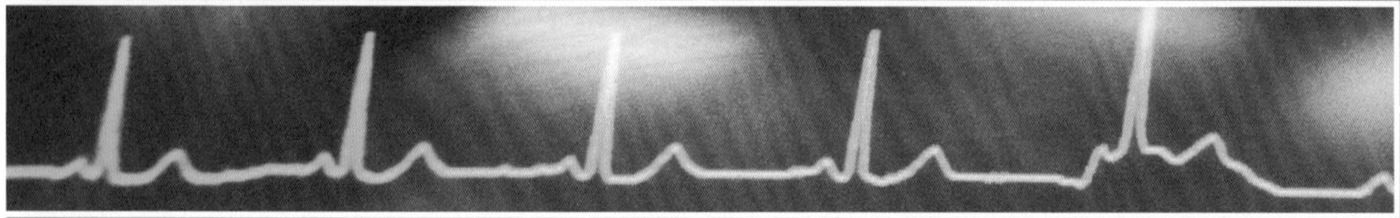

PROFILES OF COMPANIES AND ORGANIZATIONS

Health Care and Medical Technology

Saint Alphonsus Regional Medical Center

Serving southwest Idaho, eastern Oregon, and northern Nevada, this 383-bed regional medical center employs 3,000 people and delivers advanced medical services in a spiritual, healing environment, and it earns high praise for its cutting-edge technology, comprehensive services, and compassionate staff.

Above left: The Center for Advanced Healing is being built on Saint Alphonsus Regional Medical Center's Boise campus. Scheduled for completion in 2007, the center will mainly handle trauma, complex surgery, and intensive care. Above right: Saint Alphonsus has four Life Flight helicopters and one fixed-wing aircraft located at bases in Boise, Twin Falls, and McCall, Idaho.

"Advanced healing begins here." No words could better describe Saint Alphonsus Regional Medical Center and its 100-year-plus legacy in Idaho and the surrounding region.

Founded in 1894 by the Sisters of the Holy Cross, Saint Alphonsus—the first hospital in Boise—offers compassionate health care services to anyone in need. The original facility was located at Fifth and State streets in downtown Boise for more than 80 years. As the demand for health care services in the community and broader region grew, Saint Alphonsus moved west, to 1055 North Curtis Road, in 1972 and built a six-story, 382,000-square-foot facility.

Saint Alphonsus serves people throughout southwestern Idaho, eastern Oregon, and northern Nevada. It continues its legacy of advanced healing, providing residents with comprehensive critical care along with convenient health and wellness services.

Prescription for Technology Innovation

Since 1900, when the hospital installed the first X-ray equipment in Idaho, Saint Alphonsus has been at the forefront of innovative technology and treatment. It was the first facility in Idaho to offer Novalis® Shaped Beam Surgery, a revolutionary noninvasive and highly precise radiation treatment option for cancer, tumors, and vascular disorders. It also has Idaho's only da Vinci® robotic surgical system, and it was the first in the state to perform deep-brain stimulation, to implant drug-eluting stents, and to provide and utilize medical imaging to treat disease.

In addition, Saint Alphonsus is home to Life Flight—the first medical air transport service in the region. Life Flight was among the nation's first medical air transport programs to offer state-of-the-art GPS-guided satellite tracking and night-vision goggles. Since it started at Saint Alphonsus in 1986, Life Flight has flown more than 20,000 missions.

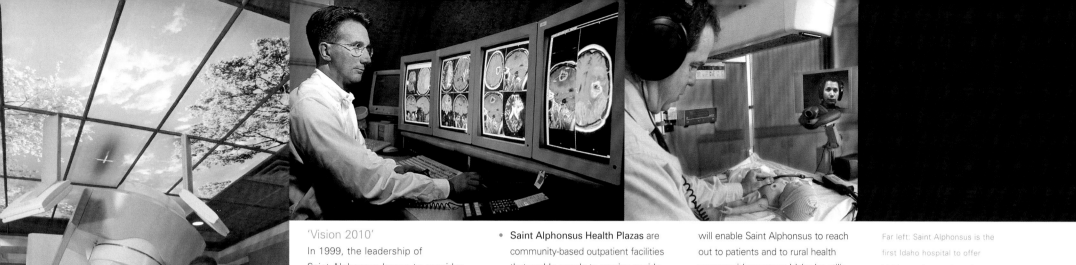

On a national level, Saint Alphonsus has been recognized among the top 100 hospitals in heart, neuroscience, and orthopaedic services. In 2006, Health-Grades, the nation's leading independent health care ratings company, announced that Saint Alphonsus was the only hospital in Idaho to receive the 2006 HealthGrades Distinguished Award for Clinical Excellence. This award places Saint Alphonsus in the top 5 percent of all hospitals in the nation. Moreover, every year since 2000, *Hospitals & Health Networks* magazine has named Saint Alphonsus as one of the nation's 100 Most Wired Hospitals.

'Vision 2010'

In 1999, the leadership of Saint Alphonsus began to consider how to meet the growing needs of the community while keeping pace with the changing health care environment. Based on its research, Saint Alphonsus developed "Vision 2010: The Future of Healing," a robust, comprehensive health care delivery strategy to provide advanced healing through innovative technology, highly skilled staff, a healing environment, a patient-centered culture, and accessible services.

"Vision 2010" is positioned to meet these goals through the following four-point health care delivery strategy:

- **Saint Alphonsus Medical Group** is a primary care network of more than 85 doctors and providers who practice at 18 clinics throughout the Treasure Valley. The group provides a comprehensive range of services to meet individual and family health needs: pediatrics, family medicine, obstetrics and gynecology, internal medicine, occupational medicine, and urgent care.

- **Saint Alphonsus Health Plazas** are community-based outpatient facilities that enable people to receive a wide range of health services closer to their homes. Each facility offers a spectrum of services, including urgent care, lab and diagnostic imaging, rehabilitation services, outpatient surgery, primary care, and specialized physician services. All of the health plazas are digitally linked to the main campus to ensure patient access to information and test results.

- **The Center for Advanced Healing** is being constructed at the Saint Alphonsus main campus, which is located off Curtis Road. This center will double the size of the current campus and specialize in treating acutely ill or injured patients. It will include a nine-story, 400,000-square-foot patient care facility, a 16-room state-of-the-art surgical operating theater, and an expanded family maternity center and neonatal intensive care unit. The center is expected to open in the summer of 2007.

- **Virtual Monitoring and Care,** the fourth component of "Vision 2010,"

will enable Saint Alphonsus to reach out to patients and to rural health care providers across Idaho by utilizing telemedicine for treatment and disease management. This virtual monitoring and care will also help those who lack mobility or access to medically advanced health care centers and services. Health care providers will be able to remotely assess, monitor, instruct, educate, and treat patients through audio-visual means.

Prognosis for the Future

Since its inception, Saint Alphonsus has continued to build a comprehensive system of wellness and health care services that extends beyond its immediate local community into the surrounding regions and neighboring states. Today, its mission remains unchanged from that of its founders— to heal the body, mind, and spirit while creating a link between health care and the church's role as a healing community. Because advanced healing begins at Saint Alphonsus Regional Medical Center, the prognosis for serving the community's future health care needs appears healthy and robust.

Far left: Saint Alphonsus is the first Idaho hospital to offer highly precise, noninvasive radiation therapy treatment with Novalis® Shaped Beam Surgery. Above center: Positron Emission Tomography (PET) scans allow Saint Alphonsus physicians to examine the heart, brain, and other organs by showing the metabolic functioning of the organs and their tissues. The precision of these images helps clinicians monitor patients without having to perform unnecessary tests. Above right: Saint Alphonsus is partnering with Mercy Medical Center in Nampa, Idaho, to allow neonatologists at Saint Alphonsus to use telemedicine to see and hear newborns at Mercy Medical. Telemedicine makes it possible for neonatologists at Saint Alphonsus to give pediatricians at Mercy Medical better advice on how to care for the newborns and, perhaps, permit the newborns to remain in Nampa rather than be transported to Saint Alphonsus in Boise.

St. Luke's Health System

Recognized for excellence in cancer care, cardiology, obstetrics, and children's care, this Idaho-based health system, founded in the spirit of charity more than a century ago, maintains an open door policy, providing superior care to anyone in need—without exception.

Above: Created as a tiny rural hospital in the early 1900s, St. Luke's Boise Regional Medical Center is now the main hospital of St. Luke's Health System, a not-for-profit, Idaho-based health care system that serves patients across a 150,000-square-mile region. Today St. Luke's is recognized as a regional leader in heart, cancer, women's, and children's services.

Founded in 1902 by Episcopal bishop and missionary Reverend James B. Funsten, St. Luke's Boise Regional Medical Center has evolved from a six-bed frontier hospital into St. Luke's Health System, Idaho's largest health care provider, with four full-service hospitals and more than 25 outpatient treatment centers. With more than 6,000 employees and nearly 900 medical staff members, St. Luke's annually serves more than 400,000 patients from throughout Idaho and neighboring states.

St. Luke's meets the medical needs of a diverse region, from its urban to its rural populations and all points in between. In addition to the comprehensive 369-bed St. Luke's Boise Regional Medical Center, the health care system includes the 25-bed St. Luke's Wood River Medical Center, serving rural Wood River Valley; the 104-bed St. Luke's Meridian Medical Center, serving the growing population in the western Treasure Valley; and the 165-bed St. Luke's Magic Valley Regional Medical Center, serving Twin Falls and surrounding communities.

Delivering Excellent Care

St. Luke's Mountain States Tumor Institute, with facilities in Boise, Nampa, Meridian, Ontario, and Fruitland, is one of the Northwest's most respected cancer care centers and offers a complete range of therapies for pediatric and adult patients. Dedicated to the study, prevention, and treatment of cancer, the institute has treated more than 45,000 patients since opening in 1969.

In 1968, St. Luke's surgeons performed the first open-heart surgery in Idaho. Today, physicians at St. Luke's perform more heart procedures than physicians at any other hospital in the state. And because chest pain is one of the most common reasons people visit the emergency room, St. Luke's opened the state's only chest-pain centers at its Boise and Meridian hospitals, where doctors can determine if a patient's chest pain is related to a heart disorder or other condition.

St. Luke's maternity staff and physicians deliver more than 7,000 babies every year. Services for women include general maternity care, the state's only dedicated antepartum unit and maternal fetal medicine specialists, and a dedicated women's unit for postsurgical care. St. Luke's also has five breast cancer detection centers that offer mammography, breast examinations, and education.

St. Luke's operates Idaho's only children's hospital, which has a newborn intensive care unit, a center for complex pediatric conditions, the state's only pediatric oncology program, and, to support children's psychosocial needs during their hospital stay, Child Life services and an inpatient school.

Recognized for Achievement

Over the years, St. Luke's has received many awards and distinctions. The American Nurses Credentialing Center designated St. Luke's a Magnet hospital in 2001 and 2006, a prestigious honor

for demonstrating excellence in nursing, leadership, adherence to national standards for improving patient care, and sensitivity to cultural and ethnic diversity.

For six consecutive years, from 2001 through 2006, St. Luke's was voted Idaho's Consumer Choice hospital for having the best overall quality, doctors, nurses, and reputation. Also in recent years, Avatar International Inc., a leading health care evaluation firm, praised St. Luke's as Overall Top Performer, Exceeding Patient Expectations, and more. Avatar singled out the Wood River hospital for Exemplary Services, Overall Best Performer, and Exceeding Patient Expectations, making St. Luke's one of the top 10 hospitals in Avatar's entire national database.

St. Luke's Health System president and CEO Ed Dahlberg received the

2005 Jerome T. Bieter Leadership Award (established by the University of Minnesota in 1979) for his extraordinary contributions to health care. Also in 2005, the March of Dimes Idaho Chapter honored 10 St. Luke's caregivers as Nurse of the Year.

The Spirit of Charity

In accordance with St. Luke's not-for-profit mission, the organization maintains an open-door policy that translates into caring for all patients, regardless of their ability to pay. This commitment is supported by generous gifts from area benefactors, whose donations help assure the availability and the advancement of health care for the region.

For the future, St. Luke's will further its mission by working in partnership with communities, hospitals, clinics, and providers throughout a

150,000-square-mile service area. Current projects include the development of an outpatient services clinic in Eagle, Idaho; the establishment of Mountain States Urology, offering outpatient diagnosis and treatment; the expansion of St. Luke's Center for Heart and Vascular Health; and the construction of a new hospital to serve the residents of the Magic Valley.

St. Luke's has remained true to the spirit of charity and the mission of

care set forth by its founders more than a century ago. The words of Reverend Funsten, "The great purpose for which this hospital was begun—the helping of suffering humanity back to health and life," have been incorporated into the medical center's present mission statement: "To improve the health of people in our region." St. Luke's has faithfully honored its long-standing commitment to health care with dedication, respect, and compassion.

Above, both photos: Nationally recognized for nursing excellence, St. Luke's provides high quality care with respect and compassion to hundreds of thousands of adult and pediatric patients each year. From maternity services to cancer and heart services, patients and their family members trust St. Luke's nurses, because caring is what they do best.

Mercy Medical Center

Uncompromising, high quality patient care with compassion comes first at this award-winning, full-service health care center, which provides a full range of medical services and offers state-of-the-art diagnostic tools and advanced treatments.

Left: Mercy Medical Center, in Nampa, has provided health care services to the community since 1917. Its parent company, Catholic Health Initiatives, is a nationwide health care provider. Center: The 700-plus employees of Mercy have rated it in the top 1 percent nationally for employee satisfaction. Right: A warm, nurturing environment can be found throughout Mercy; the Mercy Family Birthing Center offers an inviting homelike ambiance.

Mercy Medical Center in Nampa, Idaho, has been serving the Treasure Valley area in southwest Idaho, and excelling in patient satisfaction since the Sisters of Mercy founded the hospital in 1917. Today, this 152-bed, acute care facility continues to fulfill the Catholic Church's mission of healing begun by those pioneering nuns, offering a wide variety of health care services within a culture of reverence, integrity, compassion, and excellence.

A nonprofit, mission-oriented organization, Mercy is part of Catholic Health Initiatives (CHI), one of the largest, most prestigious national nonprofit health care systems in the United States, encompassing more than 60 hospitals and 50 long-term care facilities. Staffed by some of the world's most highly skilled physicians trained at some of the world's finest medical schools, Mercy makes available a full range of medical services. Some of its specialized services are cardiology for heart disease; pediatrics for childhood diseases and illnesses; round-the-clock emergency service; the treatment of respiratory diseases; pathology; nutritional information for diabetes and other diseases; mammography; radiology; orthopedics; rehabilitation; obstetrics; gynecology; and an accredited sleep disorders center—one of the first of its kind in Idaho—where disorders such as sleep apnea, narcolepsy, insomnia, and restless leg syndrome are diagnosed.

Mercy Medical Center also provides a full continuum of patient care beyond the traditional hospital setting with facilities at other locations in Nampa. These include an outpatient surgery center, located on the Mercy North campus, as well as a birthing center, located across from Mercy Medical Center, where childbirth takes place in a homelike setting. Mercy also provides home health and hospice services.

Within the Treasure Valley and beyond, Mercy's reputation is that of a top-notch institution on the leading edge of medical care.

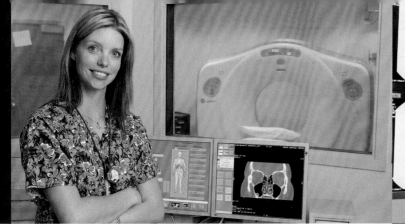

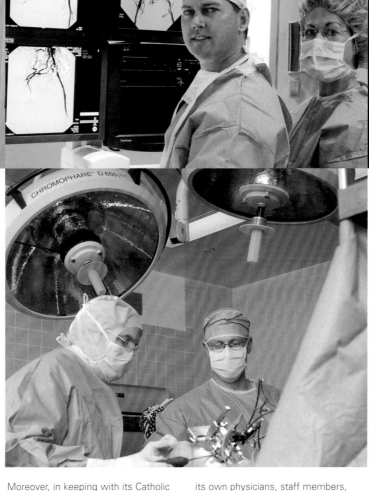

It uses the most advanced computed tomography (CT) scanning and magnetic resonance imaging (MRI), and it was the first hospital in the nation to offer Plus Orthopedics' PiGalileo computer-assisted system for orthopedic surgery. It was also the first hospital in Idaho to offer capsule endoscopy—the "camera pill"—for diagnosing digestive disorders. In addition, it is the only hospital in the Treasure Valley with a nationally certified cardiovascular pulmonary rehabilitation program.

Mercy Medical Center consistently has received some of the highest scores given by the Joint Commission on Accreditation of Healthcare Organizations (JCAHO). In fact, in 1999 it was the only hospital in Idaho to receive accreditation with commendation from the commission, and in 2002 it again received one of the highest scores in the state.

As for employee satisfaction, Mercy's 700-plus staff members rank the hospital in the top 1 percent nationally, making it the "Employer of Choice" in the Treasure Valley, according to

The Jackson Organization, a leading health care industry survey group. What makes Mercy such a good place to work, its employees say, is a work environment that promotes teamwork and a culture dedicated to providing the best of patient care. In fact, dedicated groups of employees meet regularly to focus on ways to increase the hospital's overall quality of patient care and satisfaction. Another reason for the high satisfaction rate of Mercy's employees, they say, is that they have the tools to better diagnose patients, thereby hastening patient recovery.

Mercy's fundamental assets, however, are the values instilled by the Sisters of Mercy since the hospital began, which are put into practice daily by staff members as they carry out their healing ministry. These values include reverence for all God created, compassion especially toward those most vulnerable in contemporary society, integrity, and ongoing dedication to excellence. These values and the hospital's employee code of conduct result in each and every patient at Mercy being treated as an honored guest.

Moreover, in keeping with its Catholic heritage and its commitment to the Gospel of Jesus Christ, Mercy Medical Center is more than a center for treating the diseases and illnesses of the body. It also is a sanctuary for the healing of the mind and spirit. And in keeping with its philosophy of holistic treatment for each person, Mercy has certified chaplains on staff to meet the spiritual needs of its patients and their families and friends, as well as

its own physicians, staff members, and volunteers.

The imprint placed upon Mercy Medical Center by the founding Sisters of Mercy—including their dedication and their faith-based healing ministry, vision, and values—will endure. And the center's commitment to its patients will keep it in the forefront of health care and on the leading edge of diagnostic and therapeutic services.

Left and top right: The most advanced diagnostic and treatment technologies are used by Mercy Medical Center's highly trained staff members. Bottom right: Members of the Mercy Medical staff are ever mindful of the hospital's mission of healing patients and alleviating pain; the core values of respect, integrity, compassion, and excellence are always in evidence.

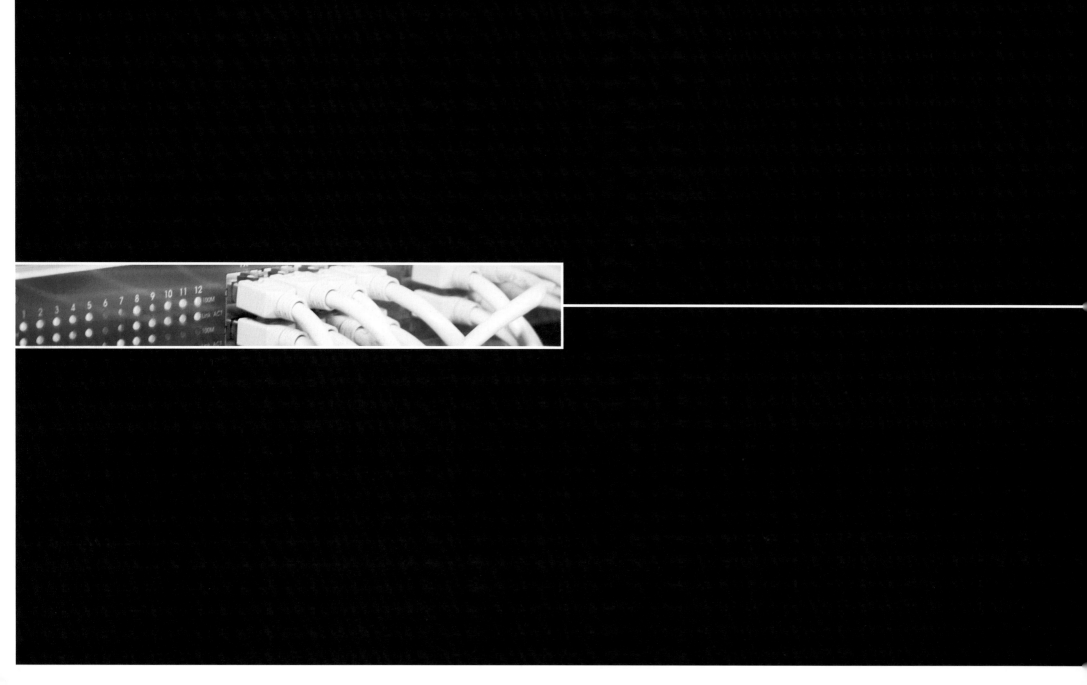

PROFILES OF COMPANIES AND ORGANIZATIONS

Information Technologies

Micron Technology, Inc.

Proudly headquartered in Boise, Idaho, Micron Technology is one of the world's leading providers of advanced semiconductor solutions, an industry model of high quality and cost-efficient production, and an example of dedicated community partnership.

Above: From its headquarters in Boise, Idaho, Micron Technology operates facilities nationwide and worldwide.

Micron Technology and its advanced semiconductor products are an integral part of people's daily lives worldwide. Micron's dynamic random access memory (DRAM) and NAND flash memory are used in today's most advanced computing, networking, and communication products—from computers, workstations, and servers to cell phones, MP3 players, PDAs, GPS devices, and gaming systems. The company also provides complementary metal-oxide semiconductor (CMOS) image sensors for camera phones, digital still cameras, and PC video cameras, as well as for the automotive, medical, and security markets. As one of the semiconductor industry's leading designers, developers, manufacturers, and marketers of memory devices and image sensors, Micron provides unmatched quality, reliability, and sales and technical support for its worldwide customers.

Leading the Industry, Spanning the Globe

This pioneering company—a success story by all measures—was founded and incorporated in October 1978 in Boise, Idaho. By June 1984, Micron had become a publicly held company. Initially listed on the Nasdaq exchange under the "DRAM" symbol, the company moved onto the New York Stock Exchange under its current "MU" symbol in November 1990.

From its headquarters in Boise, Micron operates manufacturing, design, sales, and marketing facilities across the United States and in 18 other countries worldwide. Its U.S. operations are located in California, Illinois, Minnesota, New Hampshire, New York, North Carolina, Oregon, Texas, Utah, Virginia, and Puerto Rico. Its international facilities are located in Canada, Austria, Finland, France, Germany, Hungary, Ireland, Italy, Norway, Sweden, and the United Kingdom, as well as in China, India, Japan, Singapore, South Korea, and Taiwan. The close coordination of research, manufacturing, and support functions among these sites enables Micron to support customers with high quality products and to achieve low-cost production through decreased manufacturing cycle times and increased yields.

Internationally, Micron employs professional and skilled workers, whom the company recognizes and values as integral to its success. The dedication of these Micron employees enables the company to remain consistently in the top 10 percentile of U.S. patent holders.

Delivering Industry Firsts, Innovation, and Excellence

Since its founding, Micron has distinguished itself through its cutting-edge innovations in memory technology. The company has also continued to evolve and succeed through product diversification. "Our strength in computing memory (DRAM) and our expanding success in mobile memory and imaging are creating a powerful combination for the semiconductor industry," states Steven R. Appleton, Micron's chairman, CEO, and president.

Hallmarks of Micron Technology, Inc.

Many characteristics distinguish this high-tech manufacturing company. The following qualities and practices are foundational to Micron's research and development, production, business, environmental, and philanthropic activities.

- Integrity and ethics
- Strategic thinking
- Employee excellence at all levels
- Outstanding innovation
- Ongoing support for research and development
- Extensive quality control and assurance
- Proven success in product engineering
- Unwavering customer focus
- Highest levels of industry and customer recognition
- Dynamic diversification with a low-cost, high quality, broad, and synergistic product portfolio
- Emphasis on overall financial stability
- Strength through momentum and international expansion

"In addition," states Appleton, "as a supplier to many of the world's largest electronics manufacturers, we are always mindful that our continued success depends on making sure our customers have the solutions they need, when and where they need them. We maintain sales and marketing leadership by providing customers with the very finest product lineup and by working collaboratively with them to ensure seamless integration and optimal end-product performance."

Micron's success will continue to grow out of the company's proven ability to take advantage of many new market

opportunities by continually strengthening its core competencies, by accelerating its technological advancements, and by diversifying into new markets.

Earning Accolades and Awards

The common denominator that distinguishes all of Micron's products is quality. As early as February 1994, Micron was one of the first DRAM manufacturers to receive ISO 9001 certification, the most comprehensive level of certification in the internationally recognized ISO family of specifications for quality assurance management systems. Additionally, Micron has long been recognized by

its clients for its excellent product quality and performance.

Over the course of its business history, Micron has also earned industry recognition and numerous annual awards. Some of the company's honors and milestones include:

- In 1980, ground is broken for a 50,000-square-foot wafer fabrication plant on 200 acres in Boise.
- By 1981, this facility—the first of several multimillion-dollar facilities to be built in Boise—is completed, and Micron's first 64K DRAM product is shipped.

- In 1983, the first "shrink" of Micron's 64K DRAM die is completed.
- In 1987 and 1988, Micron introduces the 1-megabit DRAM and the 256K video RAM, respectively.
- In 1991, Micron creates Edge Technology, Inc.—a precursor to Micron Electronics—to manufacture memory-intensive personal computers at competitive prices.

Above left: Such 8 millimeter and 12 millimeter silicon wafers are the foundation upon which Micron builds the circuitry for its semiconductor devices. Above center: Micron uses state-of-the-art equipment to manufacture its leading-edge technology. Above right: Micron values its highly skilled, highly dedicated diverse teams of employees.

- In 1994, Micron is listed in the Fortune 500 for the first time.
- In 1996, Micron creates Crucial Technology, a division to market and sell memory upgrades to end users. Also in 1996, ZEOS International, Micron Computer, and Micron Custom Manufacturing Services merge to become Micron Electronics.
- In 1997, Micron becomes one of the first companies in the United States to attain ISO 14001 certification. Also in 1997, Micron receives the EPA's Evergreen Award for environmental responsibility.
- In 1998, Micron becomes one of the largest memory producers in the world with the purchase of Texas Instruments' worldwide memory operations and business. Also in 1998, Intel invests $500 million in Micron to support the development and supply of next-generation memory products.
- In 1999, Micron's Crucial Technology division launches its direct memory upgrade business in the United Kingdom.
- In 2001, KMT Semiconductor Limited of Nishiwaki City, Japan, becomes a wholly owned subsidiary with Micron's purchase of Kobe Steel's interest in the joint-venture operation.
- Then in 2002, Micron acquires Toshiba's commodity DRAM

operations at Dominion Semiconductor, located in Manassas, Virginia.
- In 2003, Micron delivers the industry's first 4-gigabit DDR SDRAM dual in-line memory module (DIMM) to Intel.
- In 2004, Micron ships its first-production 2-gigabit 90nm NAND flash memory products.
- In 2005, Micron introduces the industry's fastest 1.8V flash memory for mobile applications as well as a family of mobile DRAM devices that provide low standby power and improved stackability. The mobile DRAM product family features Micron's innovative Endur-IC™ technology, which delivers low power consumption, superior bandwidth performance, increased reliability, and an overall robustness that is required for mobile applications. Also in 2005, Micron emerges as the number one

provider of CMOS image sensors for camera phones—capturing more than 30 percent of the market share.

Micron and Intel: A First-Ever Milestone

In 2005, Micron and Intel Corporation—in a first-ever partnership for Intel—announced their agreement to form a new company to manufacture NAND flash memory for use in consumer electronics, removable storage devices, and handheld communication devices. This new company—named IM Flash Technologies—unites Micron's expertise in developing NAND technology and operating highly efficient manufacturing facilities with Intel's multilevel cell technology.

"This strategic relationship positions both Intel and Micron to build on each

other's strengths to become leaders in the fast-growing NAND market segment," states Appleton. And Intel's president and CEO, Paul Otellini, states, "We are looking forward to working with Micron. The creation of this new company supports Intel's intent to maintain its industry-leading position in non-volatile memory and enables us to rapidly enter a fast-growing portion of the flash market segment."

Safeguarding the Environment

Micron's focus on excellence and best-business practices extends to its stewardship of the environment and its partnership with communities.

Above, left and center: Micron's semiconductor products, including the CMOS image sensors shown here, provide real-life solutions for everything from computers and cell phones to consumer electronics and cars. Above right: In 2005, Steven R. Appleton, chairman of the board, CEO, and president of Micron Technology, Inc., announced IM Flash Technologies, a joint venture with Intel to manufacture NAND flash memory.

Photo: Center, © Steve Bly/IdahoStockImages.com

Environmentally, Micron has developed programs worldwide that go beyond legal compliance. These include active programs utilized in its manufacturing process; systems to review chemicals and their effects in the waste stream prior to purchase and use; and systems designed to reduce the impact of emission on air and water over and beyond the limits required by law. Micron also employs many other pollution prevention, reclamation, and recycling programs, and is committed to applying these programs consistently around the globe.

Micron's pioneering work in water recycling at its Boise facility earned this company an award from the Pacific Northwest Section of the American Water Works Association for "Innovation and Commitment to Water Conservation." Moreover, Micron was one of the first companies in the United States to attain certification, for its Boise facility, under the new ISO 14001 Environmental Management Systems Standard, which ensures that

organizations have effective environmental systems.

Partnering with Communities

As a community partner and contributor, Micron has made a positive and wide-ranging impact on Idaho's business life and overall quality of life. According to an economic and fiscal impact study conducted by ECONorthwest (2000–2003), Micron's Idaho operations annually account for 3.7 percent of Idaho's total economic activity. This is considered significant for a single private employer. Also, Micron's operations account for more than 24,000 jobs in Idaho and $1 billion in personal income annually, making it the largest private employer in the state. Fiscally, according to the ECONorthwest study, Micron and its employees contribute a total of $95.7 million in tax revenue to local governments and schools, which is $41.9 million more than the state's cost of providing services to Micron and its employees and their families. The surplus tax revenues are seen as a major benefit to the state's schools and public services.

Micron's total community contributions, however, extend beyond its economic and fiscal impacts. "We realize that dedication to youth, to quality education, and to strong communities is critical to the success of individuals, companies, and society," states Appleton. To these ends, Micron carries out its good works through the Micron Technology Foundation and the Micron Corporate Giving programs.

The Micron Technology Foundation supports the advancement of science and technology worldwide through K–12 and higher education grants and scholarships, as well as through partnerships with civic and charitable institutions in the communities in which Micron has facilities.

Micron Corporate Giving programs encompass community, K–12, and higher education relations and initiatives, including in-kind donations, volunteer outreach, sponsorships, Partners in Research, the Visiting Faculty program, student design projects, and equipment and product donations.

Micron has succeeded in its fundamental mission: "Be the most efficient and innovative global provider of semiconductor solutions." According to Appleton, "We remain focused on our goal of creating an even more profitable company that is universally known as a leading competitor and technology innovator. Overall, we are invigorated by the opportunities for the company today, tomorrow, and well into the future."

Above, far left and center: Micron's environmental team takes a proactive approach to protecting the air, water, and land resources in the communities in which Micron operates. Above, main photo and insets: The Micron Technology Foundation works hand in hand as a community partner to provide innovative science and math educational outreach programs, grants, and scholarships. The Micron Technology Foundation also supports numerous charitable activities.

AMI Semiconductor, Inc.

Drawing on its unique technology portfolio, this company custom designs and manufactures integrated circuits for specific needs, providing optimal value and quickest time-to-market solutions to serve the automotive, medical, and industrial sectors and increasingly, a broad range of fields from aerospace to consumer goods.

Above left: An AMI Semiconductor, Inc. (AMIS) technologist transports silicon wafers in the company's state-of-the-art manufacturing facility in Pocatello, Idaho. Above right: Five-inch and eight-inch silicon wafers are manufactured in two AMIS Pocatello fabrication facilities.

The ability to design and manufacture custom-made microchips and application-specific integrated circuits (ASICs) to the specifications of hundreds of customers worldwide gives Idaho-based AMI Semiconductor, Inc. (AMIS) a competitive edge in the highly charged semiconductor industry. AMIS targets its silicon chips primarily to the automotive, medical, and industrial sectors, and it also is making significant advances in aerospace, defense, communications, computing, and consumer goods.

With world headquarters in Pocatello, Idaho, AMIS is a widely recognized innovator in state-of-the-art integrated, mixed-signal semiconductor products, mixed-signal foundry services, and structured digital products. It is committed to providing customers with semiconductor solutions of optimal value in the quickest possible time to market.

Offering advanced manufacturing flexibility and dedication to customer service, global AMIS operations include the company's European corporate offices in Oudenaarde, Belgium, and a network of sales, design, and technical support centers in key markets of North America, Europe, and the Asia Pacific region. AMIS employs more than 2,500 people throughout the world.

"Idaho's relatively low costs for energy and housing, as well as its low crime rate, enhance our ability to recruit employees from other areas and maintain our talented workforce," says AMIS president and CEO Christine King. "Idaho State University and the area's proximity to national parks and numerous outdoor activities make the quality of life here tough to beat."

Building on Innovation

AMIS celebrated its 40th anniversary as a company in 2006. Founded in Santa Clara, California, in 1966 as American Microsystems Inc. (AMI), it pioneered the MOS ASIC (metal oxide semiconductor ASIC). In spring 1970, officials of the company decided to move its manufacturing operation to Idaho, and by December, its first manufacturing plant in Pocatello was established. Another company milestone was the creation in 1981 of AMI-Philippines, a sort and test facility,

giving the company a presence in Asia that continues today. In 1988, AMIS world headquarters was moved from Santa Clara to Pocatello.

In 1997, AMI completed construction of its Fab 10 fabrication area in Pocatello, where 8-inch silicon wafers are developed and produced. This new facility allowed the company to expand and improve its technological capabilities. In 2000, Francisco Partners and Citicorp Venture Capital acquired majority interest in AMI and changed its name to AMI Semiconductor a year later, when Christine King was named AMIS president and CEO.

Synergistic Expansion

Under King's leadership, AMIS has grown substantially. In 2002, AMIS acquired the mixed-signal business of Alcatel Microelectronics in Belgium, adding more than 800 employees and giving the company tremendous technical resources. That same year, execution of expansion plans continued as AMIS also acquired the Micro Power Products division of Microsemi Corporation in Carlsbad, California, a medical mixed-signal ASIC group.

In 2003, AMIS issued an initial public offering of 30 million shares on the Nasdaq national market [Nasdaq: AMIS].

In 2004, the company acquired Dspfactory Ltd. in Canada and Switzerland, thus becoming a leader in ultralow-power digital signal-processing technology for hearing aids and other medical devices. In 2005, AMIS acquired the semiconductor division of Flextronics (including sites in the Silicon Valley, the Netherlands, and Israel), specializing in custom-made mixed-signal products. In 2006, on its 40th anniversary, AMIS purchased certain assets of Starkey Laboratories' integrated-circuits design center in Colorado Springs, Colorado, specializing in low-power audio technology for hearing aids.

AMIS is Pocatello's largest private employer, with more than 900 employees on its local payroll in 2006, including about 275 engineers. A major anchor for eastern Idaho's high-tech corridor, the company has an estimated annual impact of $100 million on the Bannock County economy.

Eastern Idaho remains strategically important for AMI Semiconductor as the company continues to expand and hone its capabilities in the semiconductor industry's increasingly competitive global market, as it makes "Silicon Solutions for the Real World."

Top right: A fabrication technologist demonstrates AMI Semicondutor's dedication to quality in the company's advanced manufacturing facility. Above, all photos: AMI Semiconductor's application-specific products have important real-world uses and make a direct impact on people's lives. Automobiles perform better. People hear more clearly. Families are safer. Lives are saved.

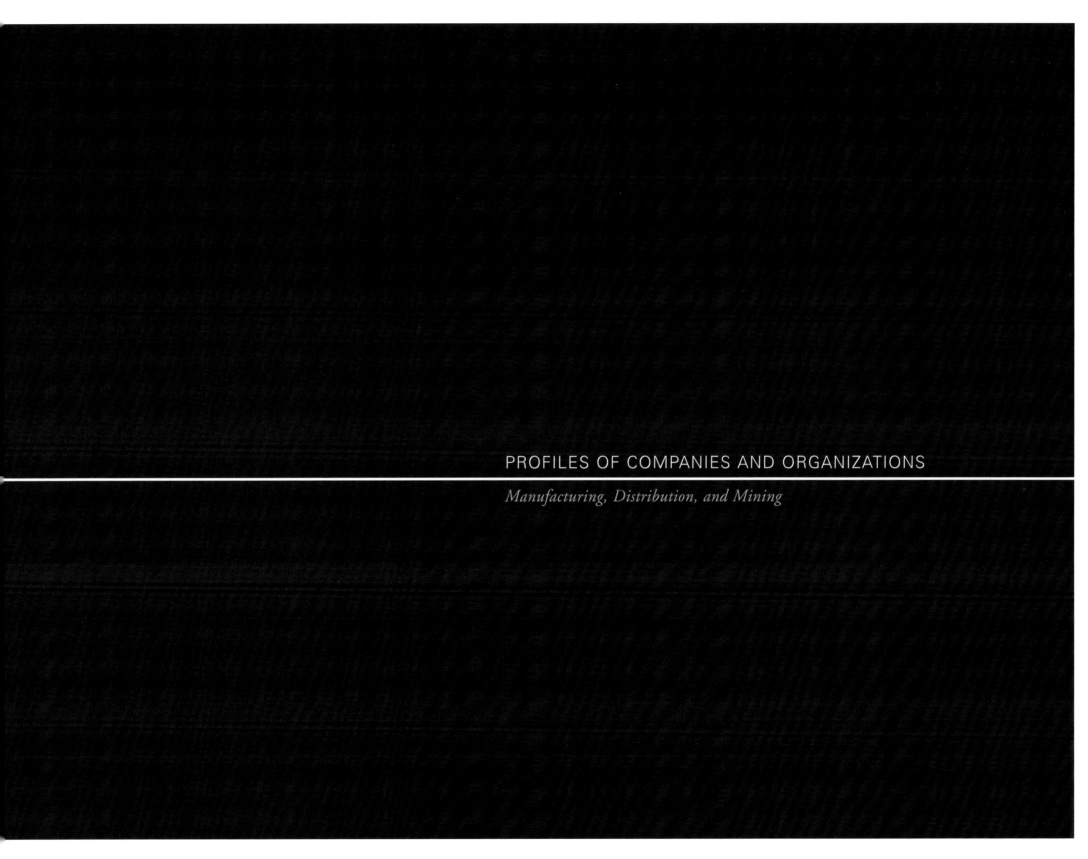

PROFILES OF COMPANIES AND ORGANIZATIONS

Manufacturing, Distribution, and Mining

Woodgrain Millwork, Inc.

This industry-leading manufacturer of mouldings and the world's largest producer of interior pine passage doors was started by one craftsman-entrepreneur and today employs more than 5,500 people, supplies wood building products to international markets, and fosters environmentally friendly practices.

Above left: Woodgrain Millwork, Inc. founder Merrill R. "Bud" Dame (seated) is shown here with his two sons Reed Dame (center), who serves as the company president and CEO, and Kelly Dame, who serves as the executive vice president. Above right: Their family-owned and -operated company is headquartered in Fruitland, Idaho.

Becoming a world leader of manufactured doors, windows, mouldings, and other wood products for the housing industry was not Merrill R. "Bud" Dame's intention back in 1954. At his small plant in Kanab, Utah, he produced delicate wood mouldings—a product he pioneered and continued to develop through the years—often working around the clock to supply the growing mobile home industry. As the designer, manufacturer, and deliveryman for his enterprise—the Dame Lumber & Moulding Company—Bud Dame never compromised his standards of integrity, service, and quality. In time, his products earned a reputation for superior craftsmanship and reliability, and his company prospered, filling an ever-increasing need in the housing industry.

During the 1960s, a lumber shortage in Utah prompted Bud Dame to move his company to Lakeview, Oregon.

The business grew steadily and eventually expanded into Fruitland, Idaho, where it is headquartered today. Increasing demand led to more products, more machinery, and more employees. In the 1970s, Bud Dame's son Reed Dame joined the business and started Woodgrain Mouldings, Inc., a subsidiary of the Dame Lumber & Moulding Company. This new company operated with forward-thinking strategies: branching out with additional plants located close to lumber supplies; initiating sophisticated, high-tech manufacturing processes; and acquiring other wood product companies that rounded out the product line and brought diversification. In 1977, upon graduating with his degree in marketing and finance, Kelly Dame, another son of founder Bud Dame, began his career at Woodgrain Mouldings. Then in 1984, the Dame Lumber & Moulding Company and Woodgrain Mouldings were combined to do business as Woodgrain Millwork, Inc.

Growth and Success Guided by Principles

In 1985 Woodgrain Millwork began selling high quality pine doors in an array of sizes and styles through its acquisition of Meridian Wood Products in Nampa, Idaho. In 1987 wood and vinyl windows were added to the company's product lines when it bought the Windsor Window Company of West Des Moines, Iowa, and Heritage Window of Monroe, North Carolina. Woodgrain Millwork's additional acquisitions included Jessup Doors of Dowagiac, Michigan; Atrium Patio Doors of Greenville, Texas;

and DecraMold of Oklahoma City, Oklahoma. Reed and Kelly Dame also invested in the Chicago-based CraftMaster Manufacturing company, thereby enabling Woodgrain Millwork to supply new markets. Today Woodgrain Millwork's products include mouldings of all types and shapes, prefinished mouldings, a wide variety of interior doors, and wood and vinyl windows.

Woodgrain Millwork is now led by the founder's sons Reed Dame, who serves as president and CEO, and Kelly Dame, who serves as the executive vice president. They both carry on their father's dedication to the company and its workers. In North and South America, Woodgrain Millwork has 13 manufacturing facilities that provide extensive product offerings and exemplary service. In South America, the company harvests from plantation forests and practices the highest degree of forest stewardship possible.

Woodgrain Millwork's commitment to the environment extends to its use of raw materials, which is one of the most complete and efficient in the

industry. A variety of manufacturing methods are in place to make use of virtually 100 percent of wood fiber: an optimizer machine minimizes waste by determining cuts to produce the highest yield for each board; sawdust is collected and recycled into bedding for animals; and scrap material is used for making particleboard and fiberboard. Woodgrain Millwork is certified by the Forest Stewardship Council, with whom it shares a mission to promote environmentally appropriate, socially beneficial, and economically viable management of the world's forests.

Recognizing People as 'Our Most-Valued Resource'
Woodgrain Millwork considers its employees to be the company's greatest asset and at the heart of the company's success. As such, Woodgrain Millwork hires only the best and provides an environment in which these

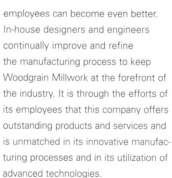

employees can become even better. In-house designers and engineers continually improve and refine the manufacturing process to keep Woodgrain Millwork at the forefront of the industry. It is through the efforts of its employees that this company offers outstanding products and services and is unmatched in its innovative manufacturing processes and in its utilization of advanced technologies.

Woodgrain Millwork has created an atmosphere of working in partnership with its employees, providing them with educational and advancement opportunities along with many other

benefits. It considers its investment in people to be the most effective way to build the kind of products that lead to more satisfied customers. The principles of Bud Dame and his sons have become part of the corporate philosophy: encouraging the input of employees at all levels; operating the business in the best interests of customers, employees, and stockholders; taking pride in delivering the finest quality products and services; maintaining high ethical standards; striving for excellence in every phase of the business; and working toward the greatest common benefit for all of Woodgrain Millwork's associates and communities.

Above left: Bud Dame crafted small wood mouldings of superior quality and formed the company that would become today's Woodgrain Millwork. Above: Woodgrain Millwork's Nampa, Idaho, pine door manufacturing facility incorporates numerous technologically advanced operations, making it possible for 345 employees to efficiently build and ship thousands of pine doors per week.

Norco, Inc.

Efficiently serving the Northwest with 45 locations in six states and a fleet of over 100 trucks, this longtime Boise-based company distributes welding, safety, and medical supplies—more than 23,000 items—with an emphasis on 'outstanding service to our customers, employees, vendors, and community.'

Above: Norco, Inc.'s first store, shown here, was located in Boise, Idaho. Today, Norco operates 45 stores across the Northwest.

Norco, Inc. began in Boise, Idaho, in 1948 as the welding supply division of the Nordling Auto Parts Company. In 1968, the division was purchased by Larry Kissler, formerly of Union Carbide's Linde division (now Praxair). Kissler, who had served as regional manager of 11 eastern states at Linde's New England facility in Sudbury, Massachusetts, headed west with his wife, Fran, and their four children to purchase Norco, which at the time had annual sales of $600,000, 15 employees, and two locations, in Boise and Twin Falls, Idaho.

Kissler teamed up with Dan Steele, who became Norco's general manager and eventually company president, and they began acquiring other welding supply distributorships in the Intermountain West region. They expanded the business into Montana in 1974, eastern Oregon in 1981, and central Oregon in 1983. Kissler and Steele put providing excellent customer service at the top of their list and led a highly dedicated team of employees through three decades of growth and profitability. As a symbol of their commitment to service, they placed the customer at the head of the organizational chart. Kissler often told his employees and vendors, "The customer provides our paychecks."

Building the Business

In 1985 Kissler's son Jim bought the company. Since that time, Jim has led his management team to expand the business at a remarkable rate of nearly 15 percent annually. In 1987 Norco bought locations in northern Nevada. It acquired locations in eastern Washington in 1988 and again in 1996, while infilling its existing footprint with numerous other business acquisitions. In 1990 it started NorLab as a specialty gas division. NorLab produces calibration mixtures and pure specialty gases. In 2001 Norco acquired locations in Utah, and in 2002 it took a major step in the U.S. gas business by building its own air-separation plant, in Nampa, Idaho.

Today, Norco's day-to-day management is led by Ned Pontious as president, and Jim Kissler is CEO and chairman of the board. Norco has revenues of over $130 million annually and 650 employees. The company is headquartered in Boise and operates 45 branches across Idaho, Oregon, Washington, Montana, Nevada, and Utah—all within a radius of 500 miles from its Boise base.

In addition to its retail locations, Norco operates two acetylene facilities and is building a new plant near its headquarters, projected for completion in 2006. This plant will be located at a new, specially designed fuel gas facility that will also handle the rapidly increasing demand for

Norco's hydrogen filling service and its propylene fuel gas business. The plant will offer the most advanced palletized, automated cylinder-filling equipment, as well as cylinder maintenance and repair.

Quality and Efficiency
Norco is focused on quality operations and management and continually seeks new ways of improving. New products and markets are added to the mix, and internal processes are fine tuned to produce optimal results. One Norco innovation for increased efficiency is its ingenious, centrally located hard-goods inventory system that is based on a multitiered,

automated carousel system used for order fulfillment, which enables increased efficiency and accuracy.

Growth Platforms
Norco has two primary operations and growth platforms—industrial and medical. According to Pontious, "Norco's two businesses have recognizable differences in marketing, sales, service, and certain operations, but whenever possible they share facilities, operations, staff resources, and overhead." He also states, "Norco is focused on its retail locations, and the walk-in aspect is important. Convenience and location, plus an attractive store appearance, are key to our success."

Norco's medical business serves both the hospital and home care segments of this steadily growing market. Several Norco branch locations deal primarily in medical products, and virtually all branches have a focus on this line, which serves a significant share of the region's hospitals, nursing homes, and other institutions, and a large number of home care patients. According to Pontious, "The strategy for Norco's medical business is three-pronged—respiratory, obstructive sleep apnea, and rehabilitation technologies." Norco's medical slogan "Hey . . . Life Just Got Started!" supports this three-part mission:

to provide patients with improved respiratory health, comfort, and mobility with oxygen therapy in institutions and at home; increased healthy, comfortable sleep with a variety of special products; and greater mobility and physical comfort with wheelchairs and scooters.

Today, Jim Kissler, Ned Pontious, and the Norco team continue to fulfill the company's original motto, "Serving You Better," by delivering welding, safety, and medical products to thousands of customers each day, in the same way that Larry Kissler and Dan Steele did when the company began, more than 50 years ago.

Above left: This Norco showroom is one of several Norco retail locations that focus on medical products for use in hospitals and home care, such as oxygen therapy; comfortable adjustable seating, wheelchairs, and scooters; and many more.
Above right: Norco's air-separation plant in Nampa, Idaho, is one of four plants.

Hess Pumice Products, Inc.

The 'largest producer of finely ground, processed pumice on Earth!'—this southeastern Idaho company mines and refines superior quality pumice, and also perlite, for a great variety of industries, from dental supplies and horticulture to electronics, plastics, and construction.

Above left: Hess Pumice Products, Inc. (HPP) operates processing and manufacturing facilities in the Malad City, Idaho, area. The complex shown here includes its Malad Milling plant, which processes finely ground and precisely graded pumice, and the HPP Stone Products division, which manufactures stone veneer.

Above right: At the HPP Wright Creek Mine in northern Oneida County, approximately 250,000 tons of pumice is extracted annually.

Hess Pumice Products, Inc. (HPP), located in Malad City, Idaho, is a mining and manufacturing operation specializing in the extraction and refining of high quality pumice and perlite, as well as derivative, value-added products.

HPP has been in continuous operation since 1958. Equipped with the most advanced technology available, HPP has a stable source of supply and a commitment to produce and distribute the highest quality products in every sector it serves. This focus and determination has made HPP the leading supplier of refined pumice in the United States, Canada, Brazil, Germany, the United Kingdom, Japan, and most of southeast Asia.

In fact, HPP is the world's largest supplier of refined, high-grade pumice, shipping nearly 60 percent of the pumice powder it produces to customers abroad. Key markets for its finely ground pumice include television glassmakers, for grinding and polishing; printed circuit board (PCB) copper treatment plants; the dental-supplies industry; the soap industry; manufacturers of high quality paint and coating products; and many others.

Hess Pumice Products (HPP) is composed of five divisions: Hess Pumice Products, US Grout, Hess Stone, Hess Perlite and Idaho Minerals, Inc., and Hess Ready Mix, with plants located in and around Malad City.

HPP's US Grout plant in Malad produces an extremely fine grade of cementitious grout, which is used to seal water seepage in mines, tunnels, and dams. This grout is also used in the construction industry as a soil stabilizer.

The Hess Stone plant, new in 2005, manufactures stone veneer in an exclusive contract with Owens Corning. The main ingredient in the cultured stone is a high quality pumice aggregate, which is produced at the HPP pumice mine at Wright's Creek, about 24 miles northwest of Malad City.

Hess Perlite and HPP-owned Idaho Minerals, Inc. process crude perlite ore from a perlite mine that is just a few miles east of the Wright's Creek pumice mine. This ore is crushed and sized for shipment to HPP's two expander plants in Malad. Under high heat, the ore expands, similar to the way popcorn expands when heated. This expanded product is sold to horticulture markets in the western United States and Canada. Additional markets for expanded perlite include makers of cryogenic insulation, masonry-grade insulation products, and concrete, in which it is used as a lightweight filler.

Hess Ready Mix in Malad City serves the local community's concrete needs with products such as lightweight pumice concrete for foundations and other applications.

Hess Pumice is a family-owned company that was established by Marion Hess in 1958. He was joined by his son Marvin Hess in 1970, and Marvin's son Michael Hess, COO, is now the principal shareholder in the company and its future CEO.

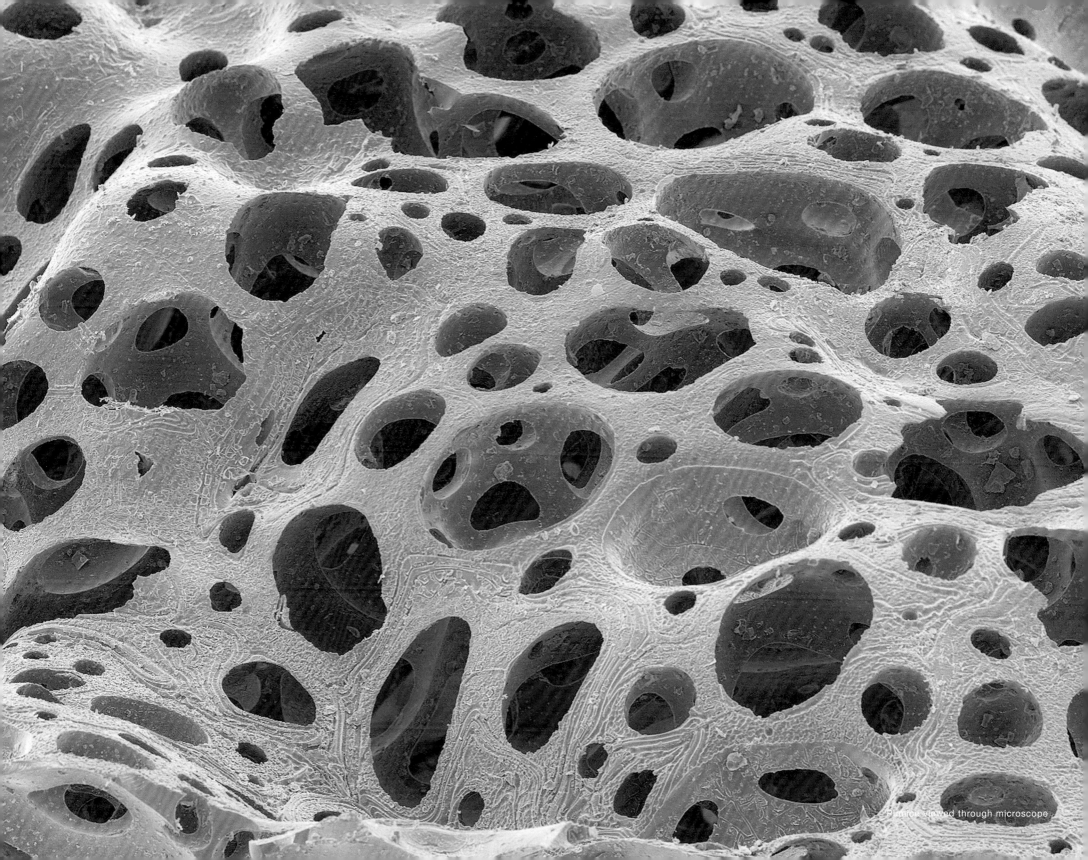

Pumice viewed through microscope

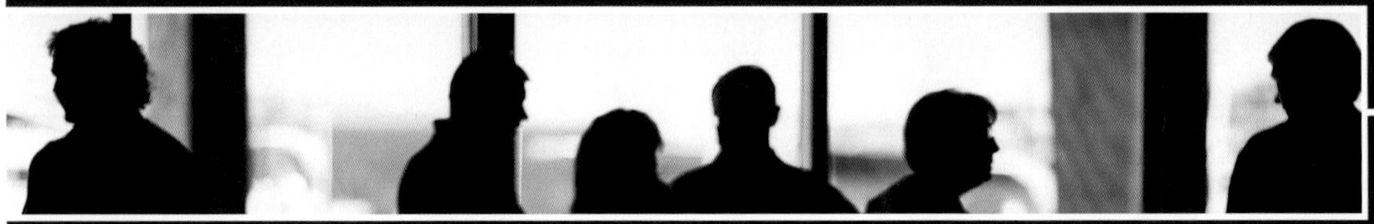

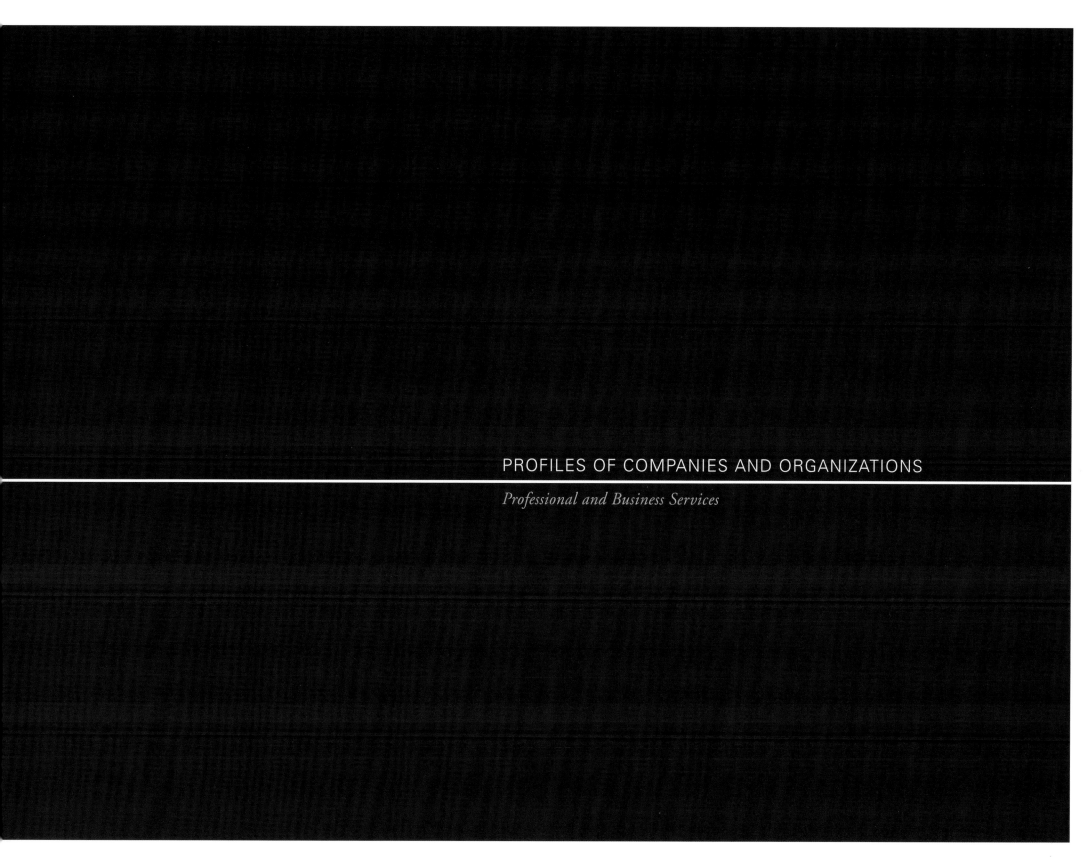

PROFILES OF COMPANIES AND ORGANIZATIONS

Professional and Business Services

Idaho Commerce & Labor

This partner in progress with the state of Idaho promotes tourism, encourages business, and supports trade and commerce by providing employer services and programs for expansion, information for local communities, and access to employment services for all citizens.

Right: The unique and award-winning floating green of the Coeur d'Alene Resort's golf course (top photo) and the magnificent Sawtooth National Forest (bottom photo) are just two examples of Idaho's natural and man-made wonders. Idaho Commerce & Labor is proud to support and promote the natural beauty, the dynamic economy, and the great people of its home state of Idaho.

In 1805 when Meriwether Lewis, William Clark, and the Corps of Discovery crossed into an area now known as Idaho, they were challenged by rugged terrain and what lay beyond the Beaverhead Mountains—vast natural resources that two centuries later remain fundamental to the Idaho way of life.

Within 30 years of Lewis and Clark's arrival, the first covered wagons rolled into the central Idaho mountains, and in another decade the Oregon Trail opened the expansive Snake River Plain to settlers.

Miners cashing in on rich deposits of gold and silver followed the mountain men and fur trappers, making mining the state's first industry in the mid 1800s. The Panhandle's Sunshine Mine may be better known for the 1972 fire that killed 91 miners, but it was also America's richest silver mine, producing more than 300 million ounces of silver, more than the entire output of Nevada's famous Comstock Lode.

Idaho's miners were quickly followed by pioneer settlers, who were the first to bring a tract of southern Idaho desert under irrigation, setting the stage for agriculture to become one of the state's cornerstone industries.

The state's forests, rich with white pine and other conifers, attracted large timber companies, and scores of towns sprung up around the mills.

In 1890, Idaho became a state, and by the turn of the century, timber, mining, and agriculture made up the state's economic foundation in boom and bust cycles. Strikes, vigilante justice, hard winters, and some extremely dry summers marked the period.

The National Reclamation Act of 1902 provided financing for the canal systems that opened vast desert areas to settlement under the Carey Act and turned those tracts into productive farm land—land that made the potato king and produced a third of the nation's potatoes for generations.

Two-thirds of Idaho's geography consists of public land managed by the federal government, and in the 1970s, the advent of environmentalism challenged the status quo while regulations to prevent degradation increasingly restricted timber, mining, and livestock operators.

For many, the 1970s symbolized a transition away from the economic reign of Idaho's resource-based industries. For example, whether Asarco could mine molybdenum in the White Cloud Mountains of central Idaho was a focal point. Those defending the mine's development were overruled by those who maintained there was no need to destroy a pristine area for a mineral that was in surplus worldwide. The belief that the only way Idaho could grow was to expand agriculture and exploit natural resources was waning.

Hewlett-Packard located a manufacturing plant in Boise in the 1970s,

Idaho entrepreneurs—Joe Albertson, whose lone grocery store in Boise in 1939 evolved into the nation's number two grocery and drug chain in the 1990s, and Harry Morrison, who founded the Morrison Knudsen Corp. in 1912 and later engineered the Hoover Dam and the Trans-Alaska Pipeline. All of these companies struggled through a near depression that gripped Idaho in the mid 1980s to emerge with the rest of the state on the threshold of a new era.

Idaho's natural beauty and its international destinations such as Sun Valley, the Sawtooth Mountains, Hells Canyon, and Coeur d'Alene turned tourism into a multibillion-dollar industry, and economic development based on these natural assets became an imperative for state and local policy makers. Idaho companies expanded, and business

owners in other states started eyeing Idaho for its progressive business climate and top-notch quality of life, easy access to nature's attractions, and a skilled and dedicated workforce.

From just 1 million residents in 1990 (after suffering a population decline in the mid 1980s), today Idaho has nearly 1.5 million residents and is one of the fastest growing states in the nation. More than 25,000 new jobs were created in 2005, driving the unemployment rate to a record low. Agriculture remains strong, and the state's economy is growing with a wave of high-tech companies, health care providers, tourism industries, and a cadre of manufacturers.

Today, through a network of 24 offices located throughout the state, Idaho Commerce & Labor—a state agency —delivers a variety of programs

designed to keep Idaho's economy strong. Idaho citizens can access information on employment services, including career counseling and job referrals. Businesses are introduced to a menu of tax incentives and other services designed to increase a company's bottom line, including tax credits for job creation and broadband connectivity as well as employment services such as workforce training and employee recruitment. Travelers receive information on Idaho's vacation and convention destinations, and for Idaho communities, the agency administers multimillion-dollar state and federally funded programs designed to help construct public facilities and senior and emergency centers throughout the state.

For additional information on Idaho's economy and the many services provided by Idaho Commerce & Labor, visit the agency's Web site (cl.idaho.gov).

and in 1978 Joe and Ward Parkinson founded a computer chip manufacturing company in the basement of a professional building in Boise. The Parkinsons received significant financial help from cattle and potato baron J. R. Simplot to create Micron Technology, Inc., which is today one of the leading computer chip makers in the world. The Parkinsons followed in the footsteps of two other major

All photos, clockwise from far left, bottom photo: Additional snapshots of contributors to Idaho's vibrant economy as well as the state's natural assets include the high-tech Idaho National Laboratory, the beautiful Coeur d'Alene Resort, the snow-capped Sawtooth Mountains, world-famous Sun Valley, and the awe-inspiring Shoshone Falls.

Greater Pocatello Chamber of Commerce and Bannock Development Corporation

A great place to live, work, and operate a business, the greater Pocatello area offers an exceptional quality of life, a diverse economy, ample space for personal and business growth, economic incentive programs, a highly supportive infrastructure, and some of the nation's lowest business costs.

Nestled in the Rocky Mountain foothills in southeast Idaho's Bannock County, the city of Pocatello offers small-town warmth with big-city advantages. With a diverse economy of emerging industries, such as high technology and renewable energy, and thriving mature industries, such as manufacturing and agriculture, Pocatello is a business powerhouse. It's easy to see why doing business in Pocatello simply makes good business sense.

Greater Pocatello Chamber of Commerce

Within an idyllic environment that includes snowy mountains, verdant hillsides, and whitewater rivers, the Greater Pocatello Chamber of Commerce is a champion of Pocatello and the larger Bannock County. Its mission is to foster a favorable business climate to benefit the local community as well as chamber members. In effect, the chamber is the "front door to the community," providing information on area business, health care, education, population, and even lifestyle.

In short, the chamber is a tireless advocate for business in the city, the county, and the state. It works with the city and other economic development partners to improve the economy of the greater Pocatello area.

Beyond business, the Greater Pocatello Chamber of Commerce plays an integral part in community development for the area. It actively enriches the quality of life through a variety of programs, including Leadership Pocatello, the Proud to Be Pocatello Campaign, Spring Clean-Up, and various other beautification programs.

Following a tradition that dates back to its beginning in 1901, the Greater Pocatello Chamber of Commerce will continue to create a thriving business environment.

Additional information may be found on the chamber's Web site at www.pocatelloidaho.com.

Bannock Development Corporation

In 1987, the Greater Pocatello Chamber of Commerce, along with other civic leaders, began a concerted effort to diversify and strengthen the area's economy as well as shape its future by creating jobs. One result of that effort was the formation of Bannock Development Corporation (BDC).

Today, this nonprofit professional economic development organization continues to work for growth and diversity in Bannock County. BDC offers a comprehensive menu of services to assist businesses in starting up, expanding, or relocating in southeastern Idaho. A seasoned and professional development team is available to assist in accessing economic and demographic data, researching and securing financing, locating and securing affordable real estate, and facilitating permits. BDC can also assist in recruiting and training employees, utilizing local public improvement programs, assessing and minimizing operating costs, and coordinating site visits to the area.

The favorable business environment in southeastern Idaho is the direct result of an aggressive approach to diversify and develop the economic base of the Pocatello area. Bannock Development Corporation is at the forefront of this effort, offering direction, expert assistance, and a vast resource to the many advantages of doing business in the greater Pocatello area.

For more information, visit BDC's Web site at www.bannockdevelopment.org.

Fountain at Simplot Square in Old Town Pocatello

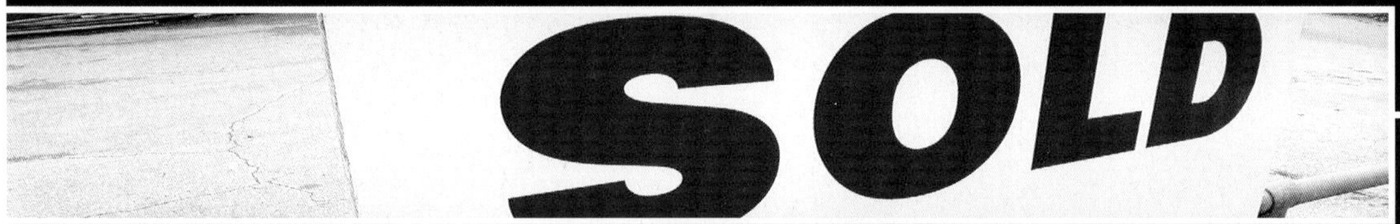
SOLD

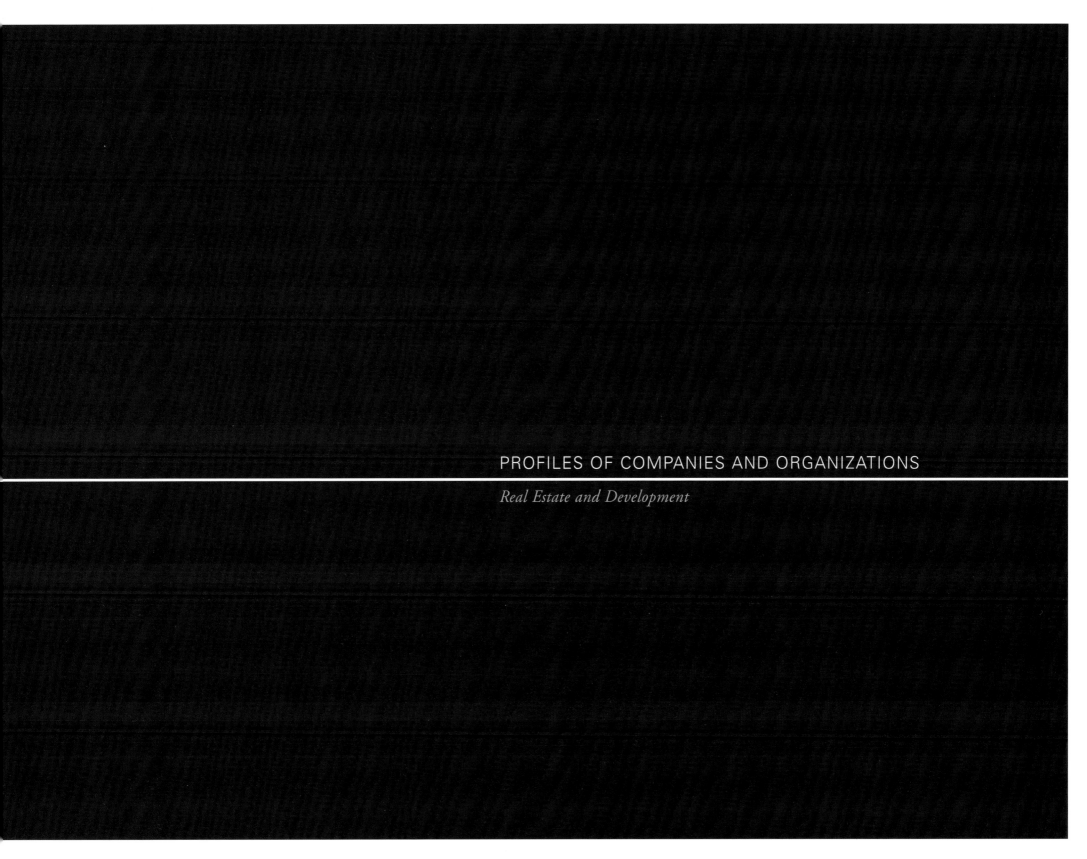

PROFILES OF COMPANIES AND ORGANIZATIONS

Real Estate and Development

Group One Real Estate

With decades of service and growth, this leading real estate company attributes its success and commanding market share not only to the remarkable location of Treasure Valley but also to its own commitment to deliver premium, full-service real estate representation, marketing, and sales.

Above: Group One Real Estate represents premier homes like this throughout the Boise area.

Boise, Idaho, which has several Fortune 500 corporations headquartered downtown and a surplus of natural beauty, is one of the most desirable places in which to live and work. It is not surprising that the Boise housing market continues to be in high demand as it steadily appreciates and grows. With a population of more than 400,000, the Boise metropolitan area is home to one in every three residents in Idaho.

The area also has the distinction of being one of the biggest and best "playgrounds" in the continental United States. The Treasure Valley is ideally situated for a myriad of outdoor activities, ranging from skiing, hiking, and biking in the local mountains to white-water rafting and fishing in numerous surrounding rivers. Equally appealing to those who live in or are relocating to the area, the average commute time in Boise is remarkably only 18 minutes.

Given these attractive qualities, it is not surprising that the Boise housing market continues to appreciate at a brisk pace. In 2005 single-family homes appreciated 27 percent. Lawrence Yun, a senior economist with the National Association of Realtors, characterizes Boise as a small city with great potential, noting that there is "still more room to grow in Idaho than in any West Coast city, from San Diego to Seattle."

A Commitment to Service and Community

Group One Real Estate, a premier real estate firm in Idaho's Treasure Valley, attributes its success to its unwavering commitment to excellence. With decades of experience in the Treasure Valley, Group One offers superior real estate expertise and first-hand knowledge of the community that is invaluable to the influx of newcomers, builders, and developers alike. It understands and knows the intricacies and trends of the local market —from century-old farms and ranches to starter homes and mansions in established neighborhoods, to new homes in the Treasure Valley's first master-planned community, Hidden Springs (Web site: www.hiddensprings.com) in northwest Boise.

Today, more than a dozen planned communities are on the drawing board for Treasure Valley. Group One not only leads the market in selling new homes in planned communities, it also has a proactive leadership role in working with developers to plan, create, and market livable, sustainable communities in Treasure Valley.

Combining Experience with Technology

Since its founding in 1982, Group One has fulfilled its commitment to real estate excellence by delivering consistently exceptional service to thousands of clients, ranging from individual homebuyers and sellers to builders of custom-designed homes to large-scale developers and production builders.

Group One delivers premium, full-service real estate representation and property sales and marketing services. The company's success is evident: a commanding market share, annual sales totaling more than $100 million dollars, and a highly seasoned team of Realtors who average 15 years of experience.

The company is able to attract and retain top Realtors in the Treasure Valley by providing state-of-the-art tools and world-class support services. Whether searching for a new home or an investment property, seeking to sell a home, or marketing new construction or a planned community, Group One is dedicated to achieving positive results.

Recognizing that superior service does not simply happen, Group One has created a number of automated tools to assist its agents and clients in quickly accessing information they need. Proprietary Group One technology leverages use of the Internet and access to the Treasure Valley's largest database of real estate data for obtaining accurate property pricing and a detailed view of the market, as well as customer identification, acquisition, and retention.

Group One University

Attracting and retaining the area's best new agents is a top priority at Group One—and so is providing the best post-licensing and continuing education programs. Through its own Group One University, the company sponsors numerous seminars and workshops focusing on industry best practices to keep its agents on top of market news and information.

Group One University provides post-licensing education with a comprehensive interactive curriculum. Long-term case studies provide close simulations of actual real estate situations, while role playing helps to demonstrate techniques for obtaining accurate market pricing, handling objections, making presentations, and negotiating transactions through all phases of the closing cycle. Experienced agents lead roundtable discussions, sharing their views on prospecting, housing inspections, open houses, and other aspects of the real estate profession, as part of the company's own Real Estate and Life Masters (REALM) program.

Group One also encourages its full-time professionals to pursue special designations such as Council of Residential Specialists (CRS), Certified New Home Sales Professional (CSP), or Member, Institute of Residential Marketing (MIRM).

Throughout its history, Group One has maintained and expanded its position by keeping its finger on the pulse of change in the Treasure Valley community while continuing to provide a superior level of service to its clients.

Above left: Dynamic adults and families move to Idaho to live active lifestyles and to enjoy the exceptional quality of life made possible by the immediate access to nearby foothills and rivers. Above right: Among the properties represented by Group One Real Estate are master-planned communities such as Hidden Springs, in northwest Boise, which provide an increasing percentage of the housing stock in the Treasure Valley.

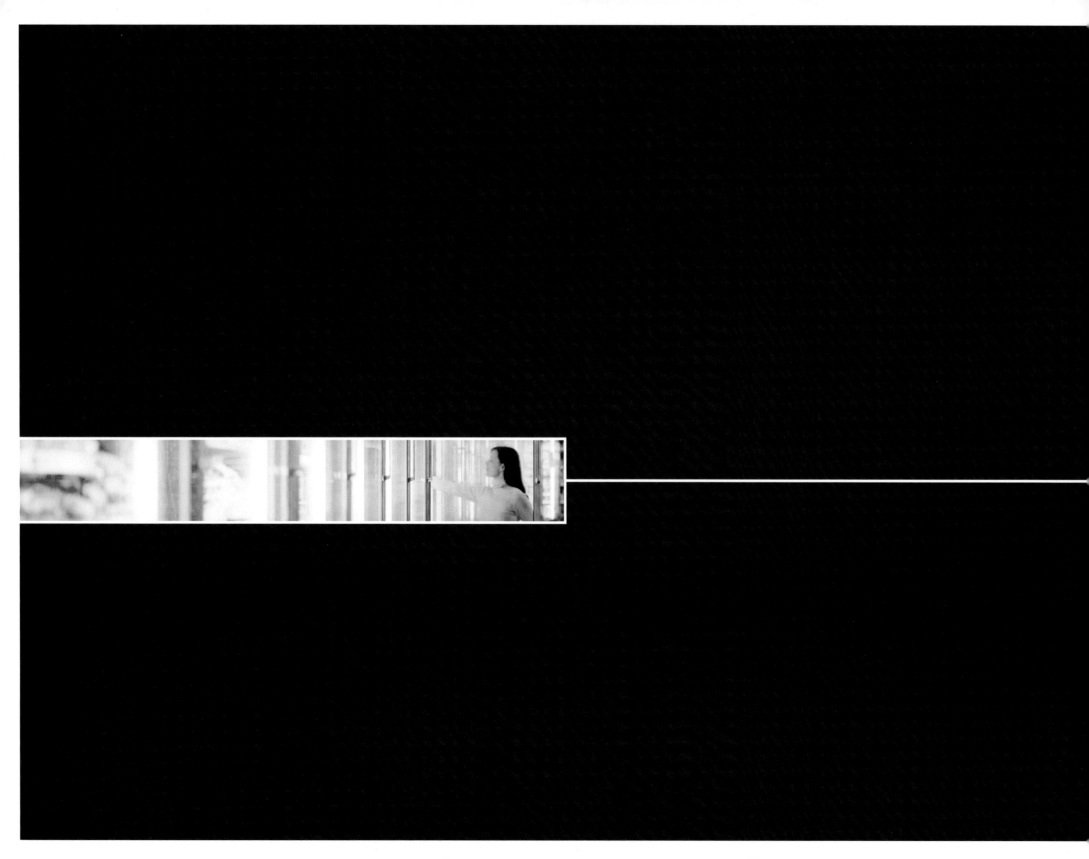

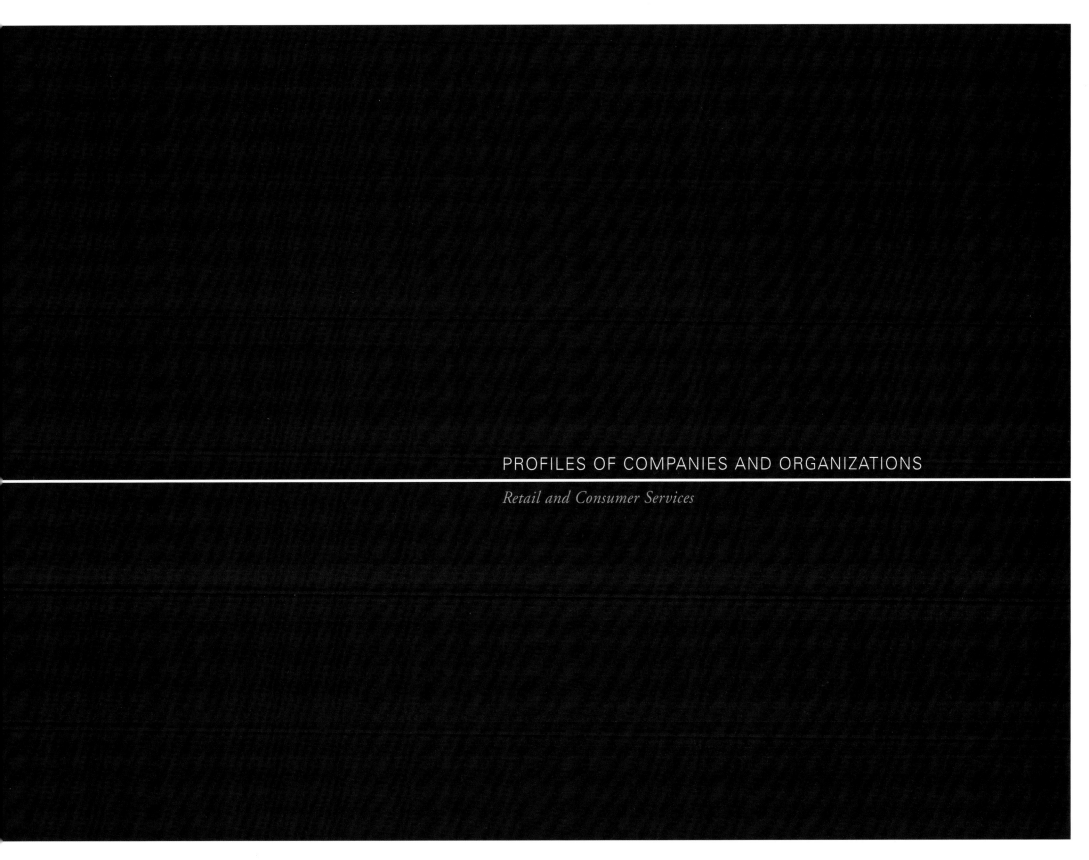

PROFILES OF COMPANIES AND ORGANIZATIONS

Retail and Consumer Services

Albertsons

Proudly established in Boise, Idaho, in 1939, as 'Idaho's largest and finest food store,' this pioneering grocery retailer delivered unprecedented customer benefits and services that have been its standard ever since. Today, Albertsons is part of SUPERVALU Inc., one of the largest companies in the United States grocery channel.

Above: Albertsons was founded by Joe Albertson in 1939. The first Albertsons store, located at 16th and State streets in downtown Boise, was referred to in an *Idaho Statesman* ad as "Idaho's largest and finest food store." The store attracted multitudes of people with its wide variety of products, exceptional service, and innovative perks such as free parking, a money-back guarantee, and an in-store ice cream shop.

For more than six decades, Albertsons has succeeded on the strength of its dedication to its customers, its employees, its shareholders, and its communities. This leading grocery retailer focuses on continual improvements to better serve customers, on steady growth through intelligent acquisitions, and on always giving back to the community. Then as now, innovation, service, and good works are the hallmarks that distinguish Albertsons.

The philosophy of founder Joe Albertson, "to give customers the merchandise they want, at a price they can afford, complete with lots of tender, loving care," was ahead of its time. And over the years, his store introduced many services, including some that revolutionized retail food stores—Albertsons scratch bakeries, homemade ice cream, fresh popcorn, roasted nuts, automatic doughnut machines, and magazine racks set the standard.

Today, in keeping with Joe Albertson's business philosophy and practices, Albertsons stores are designed to match the needs of the community in which they are located. In addition, specialty departments called "stores within a store" are created and stocked with the needs of today's shopper in mind. Albertsons' informed, often busy customers who look for the best and freshest products—including healthy produce, homemade breads, and meal solutions—find everything they need in Albertsons' clean, streamlined stores, with the assistance of friendly, knowledgeable associates.

Albertsons also employs modern research tools, such as questionnaires, focus groups, and face-to-face interactions, to acquire the direct feedback it uses in determining the products and services that are offered. All of these ingredients have provided the recipe for Albertsons' success.

With Roots in Idaho and Branches Nationwide

When the first Albertsons was opened in Boise in 1939, it became an immediate local favorite, due in large part to the pride and affection that Joe and his wife, Kathryn, expressed for their community and its people. Joe and Kathryn's new business flourished. In the early 1940s, sales hovered at about $1.5 million per year; by 1945, the Albertsons Corporation consisted of six premium supermarkets and sales of $3 million per year.

By the mid-1950s, Albertsons was well established in Idaho, Oregon, Utah, and Washington. New stores were continually added and to ensure good service across the board, Albertsons established an extensive employee-training program at its headquarters in Boise.

In 1957, Albertsons purchased a small drugstore, marking the beginning of its pharmacy service and enhancing the one-stop shopping concept. Albertsons made its first public stock offering in 1959, providing more capital for its operations and facilitating rapid expansion throughout the 1960s. By the end of the decade, Albertsons was the 38th-largest merchandising firm in the country with 200 stores, 8,500 employees, and 7,200 stockholders.

Part of the phenomenal growth and success of Albertsons can be attributed to its uncompromising standards. Every store is modern, efficient, and customer friendly, incorporating the same values set forth during the company's infancy. In 1972, Albertsons purchased a wholesale company in Boise, the first step in its development of a distribution system. The seventies were also a time of increased consumer-oriented programs for shoppers, several management changes, and continuing growth in size and scope.

During the eighties and nineties, advanced technology made product distribution, store operations, and customer service more efficient for Albertsons. The number of specialty

departments was increased, pharmacy computers filled orders faster, and new product categories were added that catered to customers from Kosher, Hispanic, and Asian communities.

In 1998, Albertsons acquired several food and drugstore chains across the United States, and in 1999, the company merged with American Stores, bringing the Jewel-Osco and Acme Markets retail banners and Sav-on and Osco pharmacy brands on board—making Albertsons the second-largest food-and-drug retailer in the country.

Reaching Out Locally, Nationally, and Internationally

As it has grown and succeeded, Albertsons has also given back to its communities in ways that go far beyond an excellent in-store shopping experience. Through its philanthropic contributions and activities, this company has added greatly to the quality of life in the many diverse communities where it operates.

In 2004 alone, for example, Albertsons provided nearly $82 million in cash and in-kind donations to organizations focused on hunger relief, health and nutrition, education and youth development, and the arts, as well as to its own environmental affairs. These contributions included $100,000 donated to the Red Cross Disaster Relief Fund; a canister campaign that raised $400,000 to help hurricane victims in Florida; and $1.2 million donated by customers for families affected by the 2004 tsunami in Southeast Asia. Through these and many other gifts, Albertsons demonstrates its ongoing commitment to being a good corporate citizen.

Building on Albertsons' Legacy

In 2006, Albertsons became a part of the SUPERVALU family of companies. SUPERVALU, grounded in its own 135-year history of fresh thinking, shares Albertsons' vision and mission to innovate the supermarket industry. As the third-largest food-retailing company in the United States, SUPERVALU holds leadership positions in major U.S. markets, including Boston, Massachusetts; Philadelphia, Pennsylvania; Washington, D.C.; Chicago, Illinois; Minneapolis and St. Paul, Minnesota; St. Louis, Missouri; Las Vegas, Nevada; and Los Angeles, San Diego, and Orange County, California.

As Albertsons begins its new era as part of the SUPERVALU family, its mission remains unchanged—to serve customers better than anyone else could serve them. Albertsons will continue to provide customers with value through its products and services, committing itself to providing the quality, variety, and convenience they expect, while also providing increasing value to shareholders.

The responsibility of Albertsons to investors—namely, to ensure continuous present and future profit growth—has also been a guiding factor for SUPERVALU. Albertsons, as a major part of SUPERVALU's powerhouse of grocery retail banners, will continue to prosper through a balance of innovation and good business decisions that enhance its operations and create superior value for customers. Through these actions, Albertsons will help SUPERVALU deliver on its goal of being one of the best places to invest in the industry.

Above, both photos: By joining the SUPERVALU family, Albertsons has become part of a retail powerhouse that shares Albertsons' goal of providing exceptional customer service. Through diverse and unique product offerings and innovative services, Albertsons will continue to provide the quality, variety, and convenience its customers expect.

Franklin Building Supply

This construction materials supplier, one of the top 75 private companies in Idaho, takes pride in providing not only the highest quality products but also the highest level of customer service from its knowledgeable, friendly, and always accessible staff.

Since opening its first retail lumberyard in 1976, Boise, Idaho–based Franklin Building Supply (FBS) has been striving to be the best building products supplier in the state. The company offers a full inventory of quality building materials, from lumber, trusses, and pre-hung doors to vinyl siding, insulation, and lighting fixtures—not to mention its wide range of power tools and hardware.

Dick Lierz and Bud Fisher founded the company on the idea that anyone could sell boards and nails; to set their company apart, they knew they had to understand and meet customer needs. They hired employees carefully and then trained Franklin people to innovate, experiment, and reach for new ways to help customers succeed. As a result, FBS is widely known for its extraordinary customer service.

"We not only go the extra mile for our customers—we go 20 extra miles. We jump through hoops, and we sometimes perform outright miracles. We say 'Yes!' to our customers and very, very rarely tell them 'No,'" says Rhonda Millick, co-owner and chief financial officer.

Above: From lumber to lighting fixtures, Franklin Building Supply offers a full selection of quality building materials.

The company founders strongly believed that customers should be able to access the people who run the company. Early on, FBS implemented its own "open door" policy that put everyone, from the owners to the file clerks, out in front of customers. In fact, it is rare to find an actual office with a door in any of Franklin's stores—they just do not exist. Any customer who wants to talk finds an empty chair to sit in and a pair of ears to listen. Many builders have learned about the latest ups and downs in the lumber market or price changes in Sheetrock while sipping coffee or munching popcorn with owners and staff at any of FBS's 12 locations.

FBS maintains that same accessibility to vendors and its more than 900 employees. The company strives to provide a work environment both challenging and rewarding. Not only does

FBS reward its employees with year-end bonuses and generous profit sharing, the company also provides job opportunities to help employees grow in the business and find lifelong careers in the construction and distribution industries.

Today, a second generation of FBS owners upholds the company's commitment to outstanding service, top quality products, accessibility, and integrity. FBS has emerged as the largest professional dealer of building products in Idaho. It provides more residential building supplies and services to professional builders in the state than any other company. FBS appears annually among the "Idaho Private 75," a list compiled by the accounting firm

KPMG of the top 75 private companies headquartered in Idaho. In 2000, FBS also won the Better Business Bureau's Integrity Counts! award. This prestigious award is given to companies that demonstrate the highest ethics when conducting business.

Building strong business relationships to help home builders manage risk and build better homes, FBS will "bend over backwards helping home builders so their jobs run smoothly and without delays," says co-owner Mike Hyer. "If their framers need 10 more two-by-fours, we have the drive, the people, and the equipment to get it there quickly, to keep the job going without interruption." Like its people and can-do attitude, FBS's reach and capabilities

are unmatched. FBS has the largest and most diverse delivery fleet of any building materials supplier in the state.

FBS also supports its local communities. In addition to sponsoring local charity events, youth groups, performing arts, and sports teams, the company regularly supports the Boy Scouts of America and Habitat for Humanity. In 2005, FBS sponsored a complete Habitat for Humanity house, with the company providing all of the building materials, and employees donating their own time to build the home.

Over the years, FBS has expanded to better serve commercial and residential builders statewide. The company operates 12 Franklin Building Supply

stores as well as specialty suppliers Boise Supply Company (in Boise) and Sawtooth Door Company (in Twin Falls). Service—ingrained in FBS like fibers through wood—draws new builders to the company and earns their loyalty. "For over 29 years, we have been striving to get better," says co-owner Rick Lierz. "And in the face of inevitable company growth, we continually seek to live up to the reputation we have earned."

Top left: Franklin Building Supply (FBS) continually strives to help home builders manage their risk and build better homes. Top right: With Idaho's biggest building-materials delivery fleet, FBS can reach customers quickly and dependably, minimizing construction delays. Above right: FBS builds strong business bonds with its customers, willingly jumping through hoops to see them succeed.

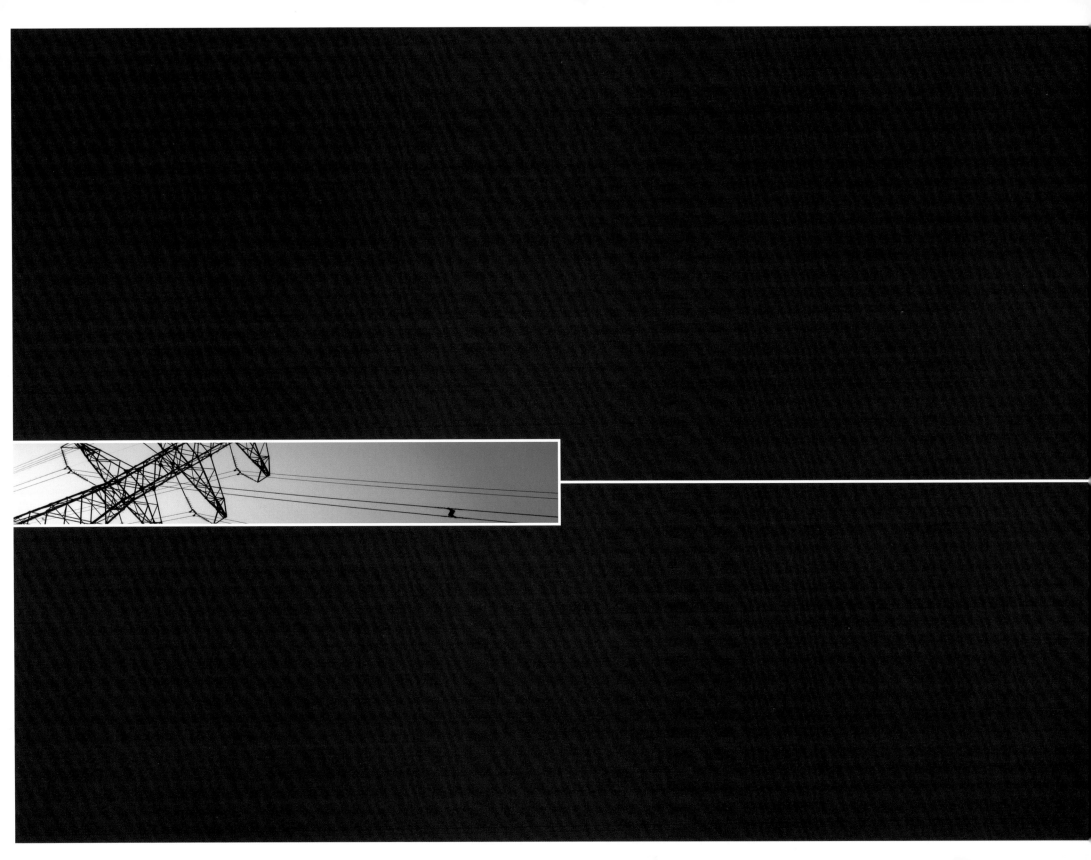

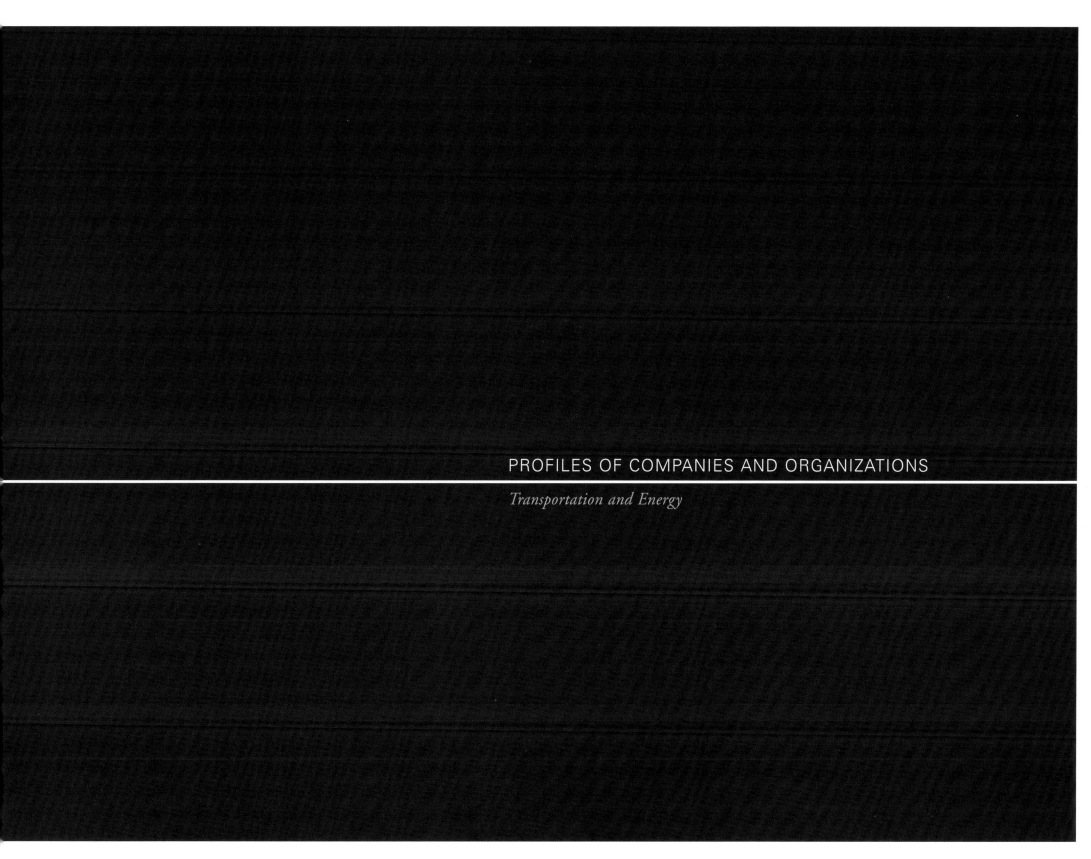

PROFILES OF COMPANIES AND ORGANIZATIONS

Transportation and Energy

Idaho Power

Harnessing the power of falling water, this utility has supplied clean, low-cost energy to southern Idaho and eastern Oregon for almost a century, keeping homes cool and farmland green; today it combines hydro and thermal power to generate over 3,000 megawatts of electricity.

Right: Hells Canyon Dam—the last part of the Hells Canyon Complex built by Idaho Power—began generating power in 1967 and has a total nameplate capacity of 391.5 megawatts (MW). Right, center: Shoshone Falls Power Plant, the first hydroelectric plant in southern Idaho's Magic Valley, began operating in 1907 and today can generate 12.5 MW; Idaho Power plans to raise its capacity. Shoshone Falls, the "Niagara of the West," is 35 feet higher than Niagara Falls and spans 1,000 feet. Far right: Swan Falls, the first hydroelectric dam and power plant on the Snake River, was built between 1899 and 1901 by a mining company. In 1916 Idaho Power acquired the plant, whose 10 units could generate 10.4 MW. In 1994 two generating units called "pit turbines" were installed, increasing capacity to 25 MW. That year the old generating units and powerhouse were decommissioned, stabilized for safety, and converted into a hydropower museum.

Idaho Power was born during the boom and bust days of the early 1900s. Price wars and technology gaps caused many small utilities to sell their businesses to larger companies. In 1916, the five largest of these companies combined assets, including water rights and hydroelectric facilities on the Snake River, and formed Idaho Power.

Much has occurred since 1916. In the 1920s the company convinced skeptical farmers that electricity could improve life and productivity. In the 1930s the company promoted electrical appliances; every lightbulb, electric stove, and refrigerator consumed the company's sole product—electricity.

The company built more hydroelectric facilities in the 1940s, 1950s, and 1960s, culminating in the three-dam Hells Canyon Complex in 1968. Today these dams—Brownlee, Oxbow, and Hells Canyon—provide nearly two-thirds of the company's hydroelectricity. The company runs 14 other hydro plants upstream on the Snake River and its tributaries. Altogether, hydroelectric resources account for 1,707 megawatts (MW) of the company's native generation. This source of low-cost, emission-free energy has ensured that Idaho Power's electricity rates compete with the nation's lowest.

In the 1970s and 1980s, the company added portions of three coal-fired (thermal) power plants to complement its hydroelectric facilities. (Until then, Idaho Power was entirely hydro-based.)

From 1974 to 1985, the company partnered with other utilities to build plants at Rock Springs, Wyoming; Boardman, Oregon; and Valmy, Nevada. Today thermal plants provide about 1,369 MW of the company's native generation.

Since 2000, the company has added two gas-fired facilities largely to meet summer demand, when customers need electricity most. Unlike most of its counterparts in the Northwest, Idaho Power sees peak demand in summer instead of winter due to residential air-conditioning and irrigation pumping. More than 2.2 million acres of cropland in Idaho Power's service area—covering 24,000 square miles in southern Idaho and part of eastern Oregon—are pump-irrigated.

The Idaho Power of 1916 could generate 22.3 MW and had 17,789 customers. Today the company's nameplate generating capacity is 3,077 MW, and its customer count is more than 460,000.

Swan Falls Dam on the Snake River, southern Idaho

Western Aircraft, Inc.

Covering the Northwest, this Boise, Idaho–based premier aircraft services company provides aircraft parts sales, line service/fixed-base operations, maintenance/avionics, aircraft sales, and charter/management services for corporate, private, government, and commercial aircraft operators.

Above: Shown here is an artist's rendering of Western Aircraft's private terminal at Gowen Field in Boise, Idaho. This expansion at Gowen Field was necessary to suit the growth of Western Aircraft and the surrounding region. Above right: Western Aircraft sells, charters, and services the Swiss-built Pilatus PC-12 (foreground) and performs heavy maintenance on other business jets such as the Raytheon Hawker and the Dassault Falcon Jet (background).

Created in the 1930s as the corporate flight department of the Morrison-Knudsen Company, Western Aircraft is recognized as Boise, Idaho's oldest aviation company. In response to increased demand for business aviation, the company's aircraft maintenance facility became certified by the Federal Aviation Administration (FAA) in 1957 and was offering services to both the public and private sectors by 1970. Incorporated in the 1980s, Western Aircraft was purchased in 1995 by Al Hilde Jr., Allen G. Hoyt, and Tim Hilde, who continue as its owners today.

In the years since transitioning ownership, Western Aircraft has become the largest independent business-aircraft services company in the Northwest. Its facilities have grown to include five hangars, totaling more than 100,000 square feet, and its workforce has doubled in size to nearly 150 aviation professionals.

Western Aircraft offers services to corporate, private, government, and commercial aircraft operators. Its diverse offerings include aircraft parts sales, line service/FBO services, maintenance/avionics sales and installation, aircraft sales, airline fueling, and aircraft charters and management services. Western Aircraft provides more information on its Web site (www.westair.com).

All departments have played a role in earning Western Aircraft the reputation of being a leader in its industry. The parts sales department, with offices in Boise and also in Binghamton, New York, has developed a worldwide parts business. Western Aircraft's full-service fixed-base operation (FBO) pumps more than 18 million gallons of fuel annually, and its hangars can accommodate the largest corporate aircraft. The company's maintenance and avionics capabilities are factory authorized by many of the world's top aviation manufacturers.

The company's aircraft sales division specializes in the sale of both the Swiss-built Pilatus PC-12 and the U.S.-built Aviation Technology Group (ATG) Javelin. Western Aircraft is the leading PC-12 dealer worldwide. In 2005 it became the first dealership to sell more than 100 new PC-12s.

Western Aircraft's commercial charter, WestAir Charter, began service in 2002. WestAir Charter's specialty is its fleet of Pilatus PC-12s, which offer first-class seating for up to eight passengers. WestAir Charter's aircraft are based in Boise and Seattle, and many companies and individuals are now experiencing the convenience of flying on their own schedule to hundreds of destinations that may not be served by scheduled airlines.

Raytheon Hawker in flight

Cherbo Publishing Group

Cherbo Publishing Group's business-focused, art book–quality publications, which celebrate the vital spirit of enterprise, are custom books that are used as high-impact economic development tools to enhance reputations, increase profits, and provide global exposure for businesses and organizations.

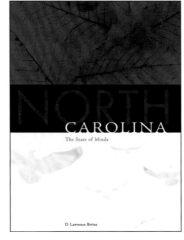

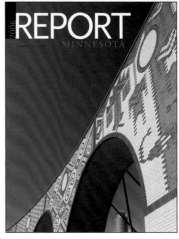

Both pages, all: Cherbo Publishing Group produces custom books for historical, professional, and government organizations. These fine publications promote the economic development of America's cities, regions, and states by chronicling their history—the people, enterprises, industries, and organizations that have made them great.

The Story Behind Cherbo Publishing Group (CPG)

Jack Cherbo, Cherbo Publishing Group president and CEO, has been breaking new ground in the sponsored publishing business for more than 40 years.

"Previously, the cost of creating a handsome book for business developments or commemorative occasions fell directly on the sponsoring organization," Cherbo says. "My company pioneered an entirely new concept—funding these books through the sale of corporate profiles."

Cherbo honed his leading edge in Chicago, where he owned a top advertising agency before moving into publishing. Armed with a degree in business administration from Northwestern University, a mind that never stopped, and a keen sense of humor, Cherbo set out to succeed—and continues to do just that.

CPG, formerly a wholly owned subsidiary of Jostens, Inc., a Fortune 500 company, has been a privately held corporation since 1993. CPG is North America's leading publisher of quality custom books for commercial, civic, historical, and trade associations. Publications range from hardcover state, regional, and commemorative books to softcover state and regional business reports. The company is headquartered in Encino, California, and operates regional offices in Philadelphia, Minneapolis, and Houston.

Who Uses CPG's Services?

CPG has created books for some of America's leading organizations, including the U.S. Chamber of Commerce, Empire State Development, California Sesquicentennial Foundation, Chicago O'Hare International Airport, and the Indiana Manufacturers Association. Participants have included ConAgra, Dow Chemical Company, Lucent Technologies, Merck & Company, and BlueCross/BlueShield.

About CPG Publications

CPG series range from history books to economic development/relocation books and from business reports to publications of special interest.

The economic development series spotlights the outstanding economic and quality-of-life advantages of fast-growing cities, counties, regions, or states. The annual business reports provide an economic snapshot of individual cities, regions, or states. The commemorative series marks milestones for corporations, organizations, and professional and trade associations.

To find out how CPG can help you celebrate a special occasion, or for information on how to showcase your company or organization, contact Jack Cherbo at 818-783-0040, extension 26, or visit www.cherbopub.com.

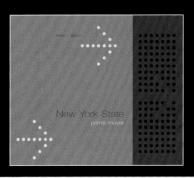

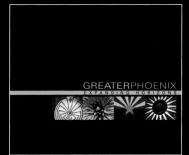

Select CPG Publications

VISIONS OF OPPORTUNITY
City, Regional, and State Series

**AMERICA & THE SPIRIT
OF ENTERPRISE**
Century of Progress, Future of Promise

CALIFORNIA *Golden Past, Shining Future*

CONNECTICUT *Chartered for Progress*

DELAWARE
Incorporating Vision in Industry

DUPAGE COUNTY, ILLINOIS
Economic Powerhouse

EVANSVILLE
At the Heart of Success

GREATER PHOENIX
Expanding Horizons

INDIANA
Crossroads of Industry and Innovation

LUBBOCK, TEXAS
Gem of the South Plains

MICHIGAN *America's Pacesetter*

MILWAUKEE *Midwestern Metropolis*

MISSOURI *Gateway to Enterprise*

NEW YORK STATE *Prime Mover*

NORTH CAROLINA *The State of Minds*

OKLAHOMA *The Center of It All*

SOUTH DAKOTA *Pioneering the Future*

TOLEDO *Access. Opportunity. Edge.*

UPSTATE NEW YORK
Corridor to Progress

**WESTCHESTER COUNTY,
NEW YORK**
Headquarters to the World

WEST VIRGINIA *Reaching New Heights*

LEGACY
Commemorative Series

ALBERTA AT 100
Celebrating the Legacy

**BUILD IT & THE CROWDS
WILL COME**
Seventy-Five Years of Public Assembly

CELEBRATE SAINT PAUL
150 Years of History

DAYTON *On the Wings of Progress*

THE EXHIBITION INDUSTRY
The Power of Commerce

MINNEAPOLIS *Currents of Change*

**NEW YORK STATE ASSOCIATION
OF FIRE CHIEFS**
Sizing Up a Century of Service

VISIONS TAKING SHAPE
*Celebrating 50 Years of the Precast/
Prestressed Concrete Industry*

ANNUAL BUSINESS REPORTS
MINNESOTA REPORT *2006*

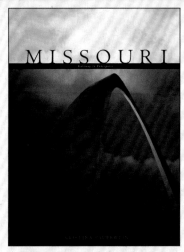
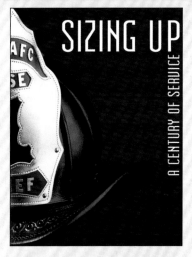
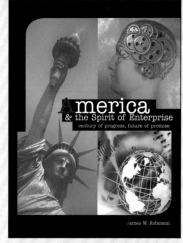
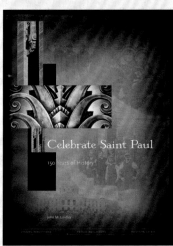
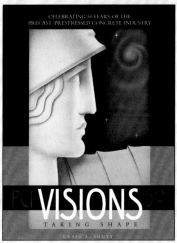
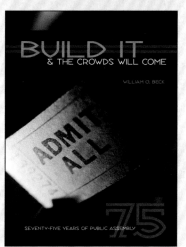

SELECTED BIBLIOGRAPHY

Aiken, Katherine G. "Gender and the Congressional Career of Idaho's Gracie Pfost." *Journal of the West* 42, no. 3 (Summer 2003): 44–51.

———. *Idaho's Bunker Hill: The Rise and Fall of a Great Mining Company, 1885–1991.* Norman, OK: University of Oklahoma Press, 2005.

Allen, Anne Wallace. "EPA Comes to the Rescue of Town Overrun by Growth." *The [Portland] Oregonian,* December 25, 2005.

Andrus, Cecil, and Joel Connelly. *Cecil Andrus: Politics Western Style.* Seattle: Sasquatch Books, 1998.

Arrington, Leonard J. *History of Idaho.* 2 vols. Moscow: University of Idaho Press; Boise: Idaho State Historical Society, 1994.

———. "Idaho and the Great Depression," *Idaho Yesterdays* 13 (Summer 1969): 2–8.

———, and Davis Bitton. *The Mormon Experience: A History of the Latter-day Saints.* New York: Knopf, 1979.

Ashby, LeRoy. *The Spearless Leader: Senator Borah and the Progressive Movement of the 1920s.* Urbana: University of Illinois Press, 1972.

———, and Rod Gramer. *Fighting the Odds: The Life of Senator Frank Church.* Pullman: Washington State University Press, 1994.

Attebery, Jennifer Eastman. *Building Idaho: An Architectural History.* Moscow: University of Idaho Press, 1991.

Austin, Judith. "The CCC in Idaho." *Idaho Yesterdays* 27 (Fall 1983): 13–17.

Baird, Dennis, Diane Mallickan, and W.R. Swagerty, eds. *The Nez Perce Nation Divided: Firsthand Accounts of Events Leading to the 1863 Treaty.* Moscow: University of Idaho Press, 2002.

Beal, Merrill D. *"I Will Fight No More Forever": Chief Joseph and the Nez Perce War.* Seattle: University of Washington Press, 1963.

———, and Merle W. Wells. *History of Idaho.* 3 vols. New York: Lewis Historical Publishing Company, 1959.

Bigler, David L. *Fort Limhi: The Mormon Adventure in Oregon Territory, 1855–1858.* Logan: Utah State University Press, 2004.

Boise's Natatorium. *Imaging Boise.* Boise State University. http://www.boisestate.edu/hemingway/imagingboise/natatorium.html.

Cawley, R. McGreggor. *Federal Land, Western Anger: The Sagebrush Rebellion and Environmental Politics.* Lawrence: University Press of Kansas, 1993.

Chapman, Sherl L. "Irrigated Agriculture: Idaho's Economic Lifeblood." Idaho Water Users Association. http://www.iwua.org/history/idhistory.html.

Chittenden, Hiram Martin. *The American Fur Trade in the Far West.* 2 vols. 1935. Reprint. Lincoln: University of Nebraska Press, 1986.

Colson, Dennis C. *Idaho's Constitution: The Tie that Binds.* Moscow: University of Idaho Press, 1991.

Conley, Cort. *Idaho for the Curious: A Guide.* Cambridge, ID: Backeddy Books, 1982.

Dahlgren, Dorothy, and Simone Carbonneau Kincaid. *In All the West No Place Like This: A Pictorial History of the Coeur d'Alene Region.* Coeur d'Alene: Museum of North Idaho, 1991.

Daniels, Roger. *Concentration Camps USA: Japanese Americans and World War II.* New York: Holt, Rinehart and Winston, 1972.

Digital Atlas of Idaho: Idaho's Natural History Online. Idaho State University. http://imnh.isu.edu/digitalatlas/.

Duniway, Abigail Scott. *Edna and John: A Romance of Idaho Flat.* Pullman: Washington State University Press, 2000.

Ewert, Sara E. Dant. "Evolution of an Environmentalist: Senator Frank Church and the Hells Canyon Controversy." *Montana: The Magazine of Western History* 51, no. 1 (Spring 2001): 36–51.

Fahey, John. *Saving the Reservation: Joe Garry and the Battle to Be Indian.* Seattle: University of Washington Press, 2001.

Fiege, Mark. *Irrigated Eden: The Making of an Agricultural Landscape in the American West.* Seattle: University of Washington Press, 1999.

Fisher, Vardis. *Idaho: A Guide in Word and Picture.* Caldwell, ID: Caxton Printers, 1937.

Foner, Eric, and John A. Garraty, eds. *The Reader's Companion to American History.* Boston: Houghton Mifflin, 1991.

Forstall, Richard, comp. "Idaho Population of Counties by Decennial Census: 1900 to 1990." http://www.census.gov/population/cencounts/id190090.txt (accessed January 18, 2006).

Fruits, Eric, and Alec Josephson. *Economic Impacts of Micron's Idaho Operations.* Prepared by ECONorthwest. Boise: Micron Technology, Inc., February 18, 2005.

Gaboury, William J. "From Statehouse to Bull Pen: Idaho Populism and the Coeur d'Alene Troubles of the l890s." *Pacific Northwest Quarterly* LVIII (January 1967): 14–22.

Gamboa, Erasmo. *Mexican Labor and World War II: Braceros in the Pacific Northwest, 1941–1947.* Seattle: University of Washington Press, 2000.

Greenwood, Annie Pike. Foreword by Jo Ann Ruckman. *We Sagebrush Folks.* Moscow: University of Idaho, 1988.

SELECTED BIBLIOGRAPHY

Grote, Tom. "Brundage Mountain History." *[McCall] Star News*, November 1986. Reprinted in Brundage Mountain Resort. http://www.brundage.com/Aboutus/history.asp (accessed December 12, 2005).

Gunter, Bob. "Schweitzer Mountain History." Sandpoint.com, n.d. http://www.sandpoint.com/Community/schweitzermountain.asp (accessed December 12, 2005).

Holl, Jack M. "The National Reactor Testing Station: The Atomic Energy Commission in Idaho, 1949–1962." *Pacific Northwest Quarterly* 85, no. 1 (January 1994): 15–24.

Idaho Department of Commerce and Development. *Idaho Almanac: Territorial Centennial Edition, 1863–1963*. Boise: Syms-York Company, 1963.

Idaho Department of Commerce and Labor. "Idaho Community Profiles." February 22, 2005. http://community.idaho.gov/Profiles/tabid/440/Default.aspx (accessed February 6, 2006).

Idaho Department of Water Resources. "Snake River Basin Adjudication History." http://www.idwr.state.id.us/water/srba/history.htm (accessed January 19, 2006).

Idaho State Historical Society. "The Idaho Nonpartisan League." *Idaho State Historical Society Reference Series*, no. 224. Boise: Idaho State Historical Society, 1969.

Idaho Transportation Department. "Idaho's Motor Vehicle History." http://itd.idaho.gov/dmv/dmvhistory.htm.

Johansen, Dorothy O., and Charles M. Gates. *Empire of the Columbia: A History of the Pacific Northwest*. New York: Harper & Brothers, Publishers, 1957.

Jones, Errol. "The Shooting of Pedro Rodriguez." *Idaho Yesterdays* 46, no. 2 (Spring/Summer 2005): 41–55.

Josephy, Alvin M., Jr. *The Nez Perce Indians and the Opening of the Northwest*. New Haven, CT: Yale University Press, 1965.

Libecap, Gary D., and Zeynep Kocabiyik Hansen. "'Rain Follows the Plow' and Dryfarming Doctrine: The Climate Information Problem and Homestead Failure in the Upper Great Plains, 1890–1925." *Journal of Economic History* 62 (March 2002): 86–120.

Linenberger, Toni Rae. *Dams, Dynamos, and Development: The Bureau of Reclamation's Power Program and Electrification of the West*. Washington, D.C.: U.S. Government Printing Office for the Bureau of Reclamation, 2002.

Link, Paul Karl, and E. Chilton Phoenix. *Rocks, Rails, and Trails*. Pocatello: Idaho State University Press, 1994.

Lukas, J. Anthony. *Big Trouble: A Murder in a Small Western Town Sets Off a Struggle for the Soul of America*. New York: Simon and Schuster, 1997.

Malone, Michael P. C. *Ben Ross and the New Deal in Idaho.* Seattle: University of Washington Press, 1970.

————, and Richard W. Etulain. *The American West: A Twentieth-Century History.* Lincoln: University of Nebraska Press, 1989.

Mann, John W. W. *Sacajawea's People: The Lemhi Shoshones and the Salmon River Country.* Lincoln: University of Nebraska Press, 2004.

McArthur, Aaron. "Building Zion." *Idaho Yesterdays* 47 (Fall/Winter 2006): 46–59.

McKeown, William. *Idaho Falls: The Untold Story of America's First Nuclear Accident.* Toronto: ECW Press, 2003.

McWhorter, Lucullus Virgil. *Yellow Wolf: His Own Story.* Caldwell, ID: Caxton Printers, 1940.

Mouton, Gary E., ed. *The Journals of the Lewis and Clark Expedition.* Lincoln: University of Nebraska Press, 1983–2001.

Nash, Gerald D. *A Brief History of the American West since 1945.* Fort Worth: Harcourt, Inc., 2001.

————. *The American West in the Twentieth Century: A Short History of an Urban Oasis.* Englewood Cliffs, NJ: Prentice-Hall, Inc., 1973.

National Park Service. "Historic Context Statements: Craters of the Moon." August 27, 1999. http://www.nps.gov/crmo/hcs2a.htm.

————. "Robert W. Limbert: Explorer, Author, Visionary." March 28, 2000. http://www.nps.gov/crmo/limbert.htm.

Neil, J. M. "Boise Gets Julia Davis Park, 1890–1917." *Idaho Yesterdays* 46 (Winter 2005): 44–57.

————. *To the White Clouds: Idaho's Conservation Saga, 1900–1970.* Pullman: Washington State University Press, 2005.

Nokkentved, Niels Sparre. *Desert Wings: Controversy in the Idaho Desert.* Pullman: Washington State University Press, 2001.

O'Connell, John. "American Falls: The City Beneath the Dam." *Idaho State Journal,* September 30, 2003.

Pence, Julie. "More Rights than Water, Agency Head Says." *The [Twin Falls] Times News,* October 21, 2004.

Petersen, Keith. *Company Town: Potlatch, Idaho, and the Potlatch Lumber Company.* Pullman: Washington State University Press; Moscow: Latah County Historical Society, 1987.

Peterson, F. Ross. *Idaho: A Bicentennial History.* New York: Norton, 1976.

SELECTED BIBLIOGRAPHY

Peterson, Jim. "The West is Burning Up! Stories of the 1910 Fire." Idaho Forest Products Commission. http://www.idahoforests.org.

Potlatch Historical Society. "A Company Town." http://www.potlatchidaho.org/historicalsociety.

Pyne, Stephen J. *Year of the Fires: The Story of the Great Fires of 1910*. New York: Penguin Books, 2001. Quotation on page 40.

Schwantes, Carlos A. *In Mountain Shadows: A History of Idaho*. Lincoln: University of Nebraska Press, 1991. Quotation on page 197.

Shallat, Todd, ed. *The Secrets of the Magic Valley and Hagerman's Remarkable Horse*. Boise: Black Canyon Communications, 2002.

Sims, Robert C. "'A Fearless, Patriotic, Clean-Cut Stand': Idaho's Governor Clark and Japanese-American Relocation in World War II." *Pacific Northwest Quarterly* 70 (April 1979): 76–81.

———, and Hope A. Benedict, eds. *Idaho's Governors: Historical Essays on Their Administrations*. Boise: Boise State University College of Social Sciences and Public Affairs, 1992.

Spence, Clark C. *For Wood River or Bust: Idaho's Silver Boom of the 1880s*. Moscow: University of Idaho Press, 1999.

Stacy, Susan M. *Proving the Principle: A History of the Idaho National Engineering and Environmental Laboratory, 1949–1999*. Idaho Falls: Idaho Operations Office, U.S. Department of Energy, 2000.

Stapilus, Randy, ed. *The Snake River Basin Adjudication Reference: Water for Idaho's Next Century*. Boise: Ridenbaugh Press, 1999.

Stene, Eric. "The Minidoka Project." *Dams, Projects, and Powerplants*. Denver: Bureau of Reclamation History Program, 1997. http://www.usbr.gov/dataweb/projects/idaho/minidoka/history.html.

Studebaker, William, and Rick Ardinger, eds. *Where the Morning Light's Still Blue: Personal Essays about Idaho*. Moscow: University of Idaho Press, 1994.

Svingen, Orlan, ed. *The History of the Idaho National Guard*. Boise: Idaho National Guard, 1995.

Swanson, Merwin R. "The New Deal in Pocatello." *Idaho Yesterdays* 23 (Summer 1979): 53–7.

U.S. Army Corps of Engineers. Walla Walla District. "Dworshak Dam and Reservoir." Digital Project Notebook, n.d. http://www.nww.usace.army.mil/dpn/dpn_project.asp?project_id=43 (accessed December 12, 2005).

U.S. Census Bureau. Population Division. "Table 1: Annual Estimates of the Population for the United States and States, and for Puerto Rico: April 1, 2000 to July 1, 2005." http://www.census.gov/popest/states/tables/NST-EST2005-01.xls (accessed January 18, 2006).

———. "Table 2: Cumulative Estimates of Population Change for the United States and States, and for Puerto Rico and State Rankings: April 1, 2000 to July 1, 2005." http://www.census.gov/popest/states/tables/NST-EST2005-02.xls (accessed January 18, 2006).

U.S. Department of the Interior. Bureau of Reclamation. "Idaho Dams." Dams, Projects, and Powerplants, n.d. http://www.usbr.gov/dataweb/html/iddams.html (accessed December 12, 2005).

Vogt, Andrea. *Common Courage: Bill Wassmuth, Human Rights, and Small-Town Activism*. Moscow: University of Idaho Press, 2003.

Walker, Edward E., Jr. *Indians of Idaho*. Moscow: University of Idaho Press, 1978.

Weatherby, James B., and Randy Stapilus. *Governing Idaho: Politics, People, and Power.* Caldwell, ID: Caxton Press, 2005.

Wegers, Priscilla. "World War II Kooskia Internment Camp." *Idaho Yesterdays* 46 (Winter 2005): 15–30.

Wells, Merle W. "The Creation of the Territory of Idaho." *Pacific Northwest Quarterly* 40 (April 1940): 106–123.

———, and Arthur A. Hart. *Idaho: Gem of the Mountains*. Northridge, CA: Windsor Publications, 1985.

White, Richard. *"It's Your Misfortune and None of My Own": A New History of the American West.* Norman, OK: University of Oklahoma Press, 1991.

Woodworth-Ney, Laura. "Elizabeth Layton DeMary and the Culture Club: True Womanhood in a Reclamation Settlement Community." *Portraits of Western Women*. Edited by Dee Garceau-Hagen. New York: Routledge, 2005.

———. *Mapping Identity: The Creation of the Coeur d'Alene Indian Reservation, 1805–1902*. Boulder: University of Colorado Press, 2004.

INDEX

INDEX

INDEX

INDEX

INDEX

INDEX

PHOTO CREDITS

Unless otherwise noted, all images that appear on the same page are listed from left to right.

Pages ii–iii: © Richard Sisk/
Panoramic Images

Page v: © Danita Delimont/Alamy

Pages vi–vii: © Monserrate J.
Schwartz/Alamy

Page viii–ix: © Steve Bly/Alamy

Page ix: © Visual&Written SL/Alamy

Page x: © David Stoecklein/Corbis

Page xii: © Andre Jenny/Alamy

Pages xii–xiii: © Ron Stroud/Masterfile

Page xv: © Lise Gagne

Page xvii: © Masterfile

Pages xviii–xix: © Steve Bly/Alamy

Page xix: © Vitit Kantabutra

Page xx: © Patrick Bennett/Corbis

Page 2, top: © Bettmann/Corbis

Page 2, bottom: © Stock Montage/
Getty Images

Page 3, bottom left: Historic
Photograph Collection, University
of Idaho Library, #2-110-1

Page 3, top: Courtesy, Idaho State
Historical Society, 42

Page 3, bottom right: Courtesy,
Idaho State Historical Society,
1114-A

Page 4, top: © Bettmann/Corbis

Page 4, bottom: © Louie Psihoyos/
Science Faction Images

Page 5, top left: © Sunset
Boulevard/Corbis Sygma

Page 5, top right: © Bettmann/Corbis

Page 5, bottom: © Bettmann/Corbis

Page 6, top: © Bettmann/Corbis

Page 6, bottom: © Aurora/
Getty Images

Page 7, top left: Courtesy, Parker
Portraits, Inc., Boise, Idaho

Page 7, top right: © TempSport/
Corbis

Page 7, bottom: Courtesy, the View
Systems in partnership with the
Idaho National Laboratory

Page 11: © Corbis

Pages 12–13: © Neil Gilchrist/
Panoramic Images

Pages 14–15: © Bettmann/Corbis

Page 16: Courtesy, Idaho State
Historical Society, 74-5.59

Page 17: Courtesy, Idaho State
Historical Society, 78-129.11

Page 18: Courtesy, the Gertrude
Maxwell Collection, Idaho
Goldfield Historical Society, Elk
City, Idaho

Page 19: Courtesy, Idaho State
Historical Society, 60-181.1

Page 20: Courtesy, Idaho State
Historical Society, 80-37.76

Page 21, top: Courtesy, Idaho State
Historical Society, 71-204.0

Page 21, bottom: Courtesy, Library
of Congress

Page 22, top: © Corbis

Page 22, bottom: Courtesy, Idaho
State Historical Society, 2741

Page 23, top: © Stock Montage/
Getty Images

Page 23, bottom: Courtesy, Library
of Congress

Page 24, top: Courtesy, Special
Collections and Archives,

University of Idaho Library

Page 24, bottom: Courtesy of
Murray Hudson Antiquarian Books
and Maps

Page 25: Courtesy, Idaho State
Historical Society, 73-29.3

Page 26: Courtesy, Idaho State
Historical Society, 2710

Page 27: © Bettmann/Corbis

Pages 28–29: © Corbis

Page 30, top: Courtesy, Idaho State
Historical Society, 66-16.1

Page 30, bottom: Courtesy, Idaho
State Historical Society, 79-92.34

Page 31: Courtesy, Idaho State
Historical Society, 60-1.1.255

Page 32, top left: Courtesy, Idaho
State Historical Society, 72-189.4

Page 32, top right: Courtesy, Idaho
State Historical Society, 78-39.3

Page 32, bottom: © Lake County
Museum/Corbis

Page 33: Courtesy, Library of
Congress

Page 34: Courtesy, Idaho State
Historical Society, 213-I

Page 35: Courtesy, Library of
Congress, Eastern Washington
State Historical Society

Pages 36–37: Courtesy, Idaho State
Historical Society, 78-130.59

Page 37, top: © Corbis

Page 37, bottom: © Corbis

Page 38, top: Courtesy, Idaho
State Historical Society,
Postcard Collection

Page 38, bottom: © Bettmann/
Corbis

Page 39: Courtesy, Idaho State
Historical Society, 63-311.232

Pages 40–41: Courtesy, Idaho State
Historical Society, 69-4.98h

Page 41: Courtesy, Idaho State
Historical Society, 73-2.52

Page 42: © Corbis

Page 43: Courtesy, Idaho State
Historical Society, 3023

Page 44, top: Courtesy, Idaho State
Historical Society, 78-94.100

Page 44, bottom: © Corbis

Page 45, top: Courtesy, Idaho State
Historical Society, P1997-6-24

Page 45, bottom left: © Underwood
& Underwood/Corbis

Page 45, bottom right: Courtesy,
Bureau of Reclamation

Page 46, top: Courtesy, Idaho State
Historical Society, 3219

Page 46, bottom: © Corbis

Page 47, left: Courtesy, Idaho State
Historical Society, 70-98.1

Page 47, right: Courtesy, Library of
Congress

Page 48–49: Courtesy, Idaho State
Historical Society, 73-221.533

Page 50: © Bettmann/Corbis

Page 51: © Bettmann/Corbis

Page 52: Courtesy, Idaho State
Historical Society, 3201

Page 54, top: © Bettmann/Corbis

Page 54, bottom: © Bettmann/
Corbis

PHOTO CREDITS

Page 55: Courtesy, Bureau of
Reclamation
Page 56: Courtesy, Pocatello Historic
Preservation Commission
Page 57, left: © Bettmann/
Corbis
Page 57, right: Courtesy, National
Park Service
Page 58, top: © Bettmann/Corbis
Page 58, bottom: Courtesy, Chicago
Daily News negatives collection,
Chicago Historical Society,
DN-0058814
Page 59, spot: Courtesy, Idaho State
Historical Society, 78-2.81
Page 59: © Corbis
Pages 60–61: © Corbis
Page 62: © Corbis
Page 63, top: © Corbis
Page 63, bottom: Courtesy,
Idaho State Historical Society,
75-189.2/B
Page 64: © Bettmann/Corbis
Page 65, top: Courtesy, Library of
Congress
Page 65, bottom: © Corbis
Page 66, top: Courtesy, Library of
Congress
Page 66, bottom: Courtesy, Library
of Congress
Page 67: Courtesy, Library of
Congress
Page 68, top: Courtesy, Idaho State
Historical Society, 76-28.1A
Page 68, bottom: Courtesy, Latah
County Historical Society

Page 69: Courtesy, Idaho State
Historical Society, 79-124.32
Pages 70–71: Courtesy, Idaho State
Historical Society, 77-103.1/B
Page 71: © Lake County
Museum/Corbis
Page 72: Courtesy, Idaho State
Historical Society, P1991-8-6
Page 73: Courtesy, J. R. Simplot
Company
Page 74: Courtesy, Idaho State
Historical Society, 73-184.1
Page 75: © Corbis
Pages 76–77: Courtesy, Idaho State
Historical Society, 78-2.23/a
Page 78: © Jon Arnold Images/
Alamy
Page 79: © George D. Lepp/Corbis
Page 80: Courtesy, Idaho State
Historical Society, 61-168.3
Page 81: Courtesy, Idaho State
Historical Society, 2209
Page 82: Courtesy, Idaho State
Historical Society, 2647
Page 83, top: Courtesy, Idaho State
Historical Society, P1996-26.352 2d
Page 83, bottom: © Bettmann/
Corbis
Page 84: © Corbis
Page 85: Courtesy, Idaho State
Historical Society, 63-35.26
Page 86: Courtesy, Idaho State
Historical Society, 65-22.13
Page 87, top: © Bettmann/Corbis
Page 87, bottom: Courtesy, Idaho
State Historical Society, 62-203.1

Page 88: © Bettmann/Corbis

Page 89: Courtesy, Idaho State Historical Society, 80-151.1

Pages 90–91: © Roger Ressmeyer/Corbis

Page 92: © Bettmann/Corbis

Page 93, top: © Robert Maass/ Corbis

Page 93, bottom: © Dan Lamont/ Corbis

Page 94: Photo courtesy of AMI Semiconductor

Page 95: Courtesy, Micron Technology, Inc.

Page 96, top left: © David Butow/Corbis

Page 96, top right: © Kevin R. Morris/Corbis

Page 96, bottom: © Dean Conger/Corbis

Page 97: © Kevin R. Morris/Corbis

Pages 98–99: © Michael DeYoung/Corbis

Page 99, top: © Andrew Lichtenstein/Corbis

Page 99, bottom; © Jeff T. Green/Getty Images

Page 100, top: © Jim & Jamie Dutcher/National Geographic/ Getty Images

Page 100, bottom: © Jim Richardson/Corbis

Page 101: Public domain. Photo by Aldis Garsvo

Page 102, top: © Charlie Munsey/Corbis

Page 102, bottom: © David Butow/Corbis

Page 103, top: © Greene Jeff/Corbis Sygma

Page 103, spot: Courtesy, The Spokesman-Review/Spokane, WA

Page 105: © Masterfile

Page 106: © geotrac

Page 109: © Andriy Doriy

Page 110: © Stefan Klein

Page 121: © Frédéric Cirou/ agefotostock

Page 123: © Amanda Rohde

Page 124: © Todd Pearson/ Getty Images

Page 129: © Steve Bly/Alamy

Page 130: © James McQuillan

Page 143: © Corbis

Page 144: photodisc

Page 149: © José Carlos Pires

Page 150: © Lloyd Sutton/ Masterfile

Page 153: © Tomislav Stajduhar

Page 154: © Ryan Klos

Page 158: © Christine Balderas

Page 166: © Corbis

Page 174: © Bernd Klumpp

Page 182: © Alvaro Heinzen

Page 189: © phototake Inc./Alamy

Page 190: © Steve Lovegrove

Page 195: © Edwin Guerra

Page 196: © Andrea Gingerich

Page 200: © Getty Images

Page 206: © Joseph Jean

Page 209: Courtesy, Idaho Power

Page 211: © George Hall/Corbis

cherbo publishing group, inc.

TYPOGRAPHY

Principal faces used: Adobe Garamond, designed by Robert Slimbach in 1989,
which was derived from previous designs by Claude Garamond, Jean Jannon, and
Robert Granjon; Univers, designed by Adrian Frutiger in 1957; Helvetica, designed
by Matthew Carter, Edouard Hoffmann, and Max Miedinger in 1959.

HARDWARE

Macintosh G5 desktops, digital color laser printing with Xerox Docucolor 12, digital
imaging with Creo EverSmart Supreme

SOFTWARE

QuarkXPress, Adobe Illustrator, Adobe Photoshop CS2, Adobe Acrobat,
Microsoft Word, Eye-One Pro by Gretagmacbeth, Creo Oxygen, FlightCheck

PAPER

Text Paper: #80 Luna Matte

Bound in Rainbow® recycled content papers from
Ecological Fibers, Inc.

Dust Jacket: #100 Sterling-Litho Gloss